Silent Looms

Women and Production

in a Guatemalan Town

Revised Edition

TRACY BACHRACH EHLERS

Foreword by June Nash

University of Texas Press, Austin

First University of Texas Press edition, 2000

Requests for permission to reproduce material from this work should be sent to Permissions, University of Texas Press, Box 7819, Austin, TX 78713-7819.

♾ The paper used in this book meets the minimum requirements of ANSI/NISO Z39.48-1992 (R1997) (Permanence of Paper).

LIBRARY OF CONGRESS CATALOGING-IN-PUBLICATION DATA

Ehlers, Tracy Bachrach.
    Silent looms : women and production in a Guatemalan town / Tracy Bachrach Ehlers. — Rev. ed.
        p.   cm.
    Includes bibliographical references and index.
    ISBN 0-292-72103-x (pbk. : alk. paper)
        1. Women in development—Guatemala Case studies.
    2. Women—Guatemala—Social conditions Case studies.
    3. Matriarchy—Guatemala Case studies.   I. Title.
    II. Title: Women and production in a Guatemalan town.
    HQ1240.5.G9E34   2000
    305.42'097281—dc21   99-38484

Silent Looms

In memory of Jerry M. Goldstein
(1947–1998)

Contents

Foreword

IN HER BOOK, *Silent Looms: Women and Production in a Guatemalan Town,* Tracy Bachrach Ehlers captures the paradox of gender relations in a society that accords power and authority to men yet leaves the major burden of child care and economic maintenance of the family to women. Most monographs on Maya populations have either ignored women's contributions to the indigenous economy or, when they have included women's work, have ignored the contradiction between patriarchal ideology and observed behavior that is increasingly sharpened by the political and economic transformations taking place.

Ehlers makes these the focus of her study of the household production system. She raises the questions, What roles had *Sampedranas* played in the developing economy of the town? How did the entry into a modern consumer economy affect female interaction with men? And to what extent did women take advantage of increased economic and social power? During the decade that Ehlers has studied the town of San Pedro Sacatepéquez, from the mid-seventies to the present, there has been an extraordinary expansion of commercial activity accompanied by regional transformation and national-level political violence. Within a climate of rapid economic expansion, the differential opportunities for men and women have had unpredictable consequences on the traditional economy and social relations of a peasantry that turned from small plot cultivation and handicrafts to trade and trucking. Although men have greater access to commercial pursuits, some women have overcome obstacles to their participating in development, diversifying their market trade and learning new skills to adapt to the new economy. Yet the majority of the women in the traditional economy have lost the autonomy they had as weavers and traders selling to a local market, and, as a result, marital relations have moved from the balanced equality characteristic of traditional peasantry to the *machismo* of *ladino* families.

Ehlers tells this story with style and verve. She begins her book with the saga of Gloria Fuentes, a young woman who, rejecting marriage with the lover who impregnated her, went on to a successful career as an educator. We learn why Gloria made the choice and how the case illustrates the profound contradictions women experience as some move into the modern economy. Whether they choose the anomalous position of Gloria or put up with the philandering and abuse of a *macho* husband in order to acquire children, they are constantly strategizing to survive amidst dramatic social transformations.

The author absorbs the attention of the reader to such an extent that s/he may not perceive the powerful ethnographic style and methods that Ehlers is developing. I would like to call it an ethnography of engagement. In the first place, Ehlers enters her ethnographic study not only as a participant observer but thoroughly engaged in the lives of the people. Using this method, she is able to show the links between personal biography and structural context. Through intimate examination of women's lives, she makes penetrating observations that show the personal impact development may have. Ehlers writes, for example, that when Gloria's illegitimate baby died she was able to take advantage of the educational opportunities newly available for rural women in the seventies and start her own career. Ehlers narrates the story of passionate teenagers whose premature marriage resulted in a mature relationship as the at-first miscast parents became a commercial success story in the burgeoning regional economy. We learn of women living in scattered hamlets who were able to make a successful transition to the commercial sale of homemade soap by taking advantage of new roads, while others who once wove traditional *huipiles* sank into deeper impoverishment when the demand diminished. The distinct patterns of adaptation are forcefully drawn, overcoming both structural determinism and fácile generalization.

The potential and the contradictions of female-managed family businesses in trade, shops, services, and cottage industries is clearly developed in Ehlers' study. Daughters are the main link intergenerationally, yet sons, who are not socialized to help as much as daughters, are the benefittors of surpluses gained by women since they are more likely to go on to higher education. Paradoxically, the more successful these women entrepreneurs are, the more likely they are to turn over the control of money to men. Men, whose enterprises are better capitalized, more mobile, and less occupationally segregated, more often usurp family labor power for their businesses that command higher returns in the market.

The impact of the changing economic relations in San Pedro Sacatepéquez is traced in the sexual relations of marital and consensual unions. Ehlers departs from the model of male *machismo* and female *marianismo* as a static and symbiotic balance "popularized as a patriarchal fantasy." Rather, she shows how it sanctions more abuse, irresponsibility, and brutalization. Class relations that set distinct patterns for gender roles are explored, both in courtship practices as well as marital life, where the ideal of segregated, privatized domestic life can only be ensured by wealth. Here Ehlers' technique of engaged ethnology gives one an intimate picture of how people proceed to act out the game of sexual power in a time of changing rules. Transient conquests have become parallel marriages characteristic of the dominant *ladino* population, yet marriage as an institution prevails despite male transgressions.

Ehlers concludes that modernization and development bring with other changes inequality and dependency of women on men. At the same time that some women benefit, because the majority are economically marginalized in the process of expanding market relations, most *Sampedranas* are deprived of their productive control. We learn all this—the heavy burden women bear and the strategies they employ to survive—through intimate portraits of the women of San Pedro. These are prevalent patterns throughout the world and warrant the careful attention of social scientists and development agents.

June Nash
City University of New York

Acknowledgments

IN TWELVE YEARS OF TRAVELING to Guatemala, thinking about Guatemala, worrying about Guatemala, and writing about Guatemala, I have had support and encouragement from many people. Waldemar (Richard) R. Smith introduced me to the town of San Pedro Sacatepéquez, San Marcos, leading me by the hand to the house where I lived, to the family that became my family. Over the years we have shared an attachment to San Pedro and to the Sampedranos whose lives we each chronicled. It saddens me that Richard Smith is no longer a working anthropologist, but for a premature retiree, he has been an extremely astute and helpful critic. Jerry Goldstein, the best volunteer the Peace Corps will ever see, was my best friend in San Pedro. We shared the woes and wonders of living in a Latin culture. We protected each other from the ravages of desperate loneliness. We got drunk with our Sampedrano friends on their saints' days and our birthdays. We gossiped right along with the rest of the town, although much of the gossip was about the two crazy gringos. I probably would have made it on my own, but had Jerry not lent me his fabulous style and cynical sense of humor, fieldwork certainly would have been less exciting. I am deeply indebted to my friend and colleague, Paul Shankman, who provided intellectual inspiration, made me conceptualize my argument, and forced clarity from murkiness. Deepest thanks go to my Westview editor, Barbara Ellington, who first proposed this book to me. She babied and coddled me through rewrites, made me change the title twelve times, and generally applied her anthropological knowledge and fluid sense of the music of language to the chapters. My appreciation also goes to June Nash, Duncan Earle, and Fran Rothstein for their patience in reading the many versions of the manuscript and their astute and lucid comments and suggestions. Robert Carlsen has shared his extensive understanding of Guatemalan textiles and dyes to help me understand the history of weaving in San Pedro. Linda Fuller lent me an expert opinion on international monetary matters when I could not figure out my dollars and *quetzales*. My colleagues gave me their help and wisdom, but of course, any mistakes in the book are my own.

My most important acknowledgment goes to Michael C. Ehlers, without whom this research would never have taken place. My husband has supported me—in every way—through all my work in Guatemala. He steadfastly believed that I could go to San Pedro by myself and get the job done professionally and well. He never expressed his concern for me when the military situation intensified in the 1980s, allowing my mother to carry that burden for both of them. He read and re-read every word of the book and never complained when I locked out the rest of the world while I finished.

In San Pedro, members of the Orozco Arriola family—all nineteen of them—have made more than a decade of research possible by including me in their warm, secure, and bustling entrepreneurial home. When I return to my solitary academic existence in Colorado, I miss the noise of children, the three shifts at dinner, and the non-stop conversation. When my goddaughter, Eliza Maria, was baptized in 1987, I knew I was tied to them forever.

Elcira Fuentes Im has for years been my companion and confidant in San Pedro. When I returned to her store after eight years away, we immediately fell into our old comfortable routine. Elcira lustily handled the constant stream of customers, and in between told me the story of her life and the choicest gossip about everyone else. It was she who convinced me that one could live in Guatemala without television or trashy novels because just being a woman was so unendingly melodramatic.

I also wish to extend my thanks to Dr. Roberto Fuentes and his wife, Angela, Rubén and Anabela Pérez, Julieta Velásquez, Rene Velásquez, Lic. Rosalinda Cabrera, and Dr. Roberto Pedroza, each of whom spent long hours trying to set me straight about what was going on in San Pedro.

The Orozco Miranda family were especially helpful in guiding me into the history and spirit of the town where they were born. Don Marcos Orozco Miranda regaled me for many days recounting his mother's life in San Pedro. His brother, Don Bonifacio Orozco Miranda, gave me his sense of humor, his knowledge of the agricultural problems of the region, and the assurance that his house was my house, his family, my family. Their sister, Doña Emelia Orozco Miranda de Mérida, allowed me to go back and forth with her to markets in Quezaltenango and Palestina and gave me my first textile history lessons. Sadly, these three members of a remarkable family have died since 1978. An especially warm feeling exists for Emelia's daughters, Toni, Silvia, and Anita Mérida Orozco, with whom I have spent countless afternoons gossiping and eating enchiladas. Their father, Don Alcalde Jorge Mérida, kindly allowed me to rifle through civic chronicles and census material. Maryknoll nuns Sister Terry and Sister Julia took me along on their trips to give *la palabra de Dios* to rural folk. It was an association that stuck, so that people from those *aldeas* still think me a nun as well. The sisters were not only an invaluable source of analysis and about the state of things in San Pedro, they also buoyed me up through bouts of frustration, depression, loneliness and *angst*. Their endlessly unselfish commitment to helping the poor, and their sage advice about my own inconsequential problems, gave me a profound sense of gratitude that they were there and a tremendous respect for their calling.

In San José Caben, I always went first to the home of Doña Eve Orozco and her husband, Don César. I watched their eight children grow up, and three of their daughters, Cori, Eli, and Sheldy have become good friends and informants. In Chamac, I am indebted to the family of Don Raimundo Velásquez, his wife Doña Petronilia, and in particular their son and daughter-in-law, Reyna and Claudio. And, in La Grandeza, I have to express my gratitude to Doña Turivia de Leon, who has been a constant friend over these many years. Finally, to all the *Sampedranos* who invited me into their homes, fed me, and took time away from their work to talk to me, thank you. You permitted me to be there for your families' births, deaths, and celebrations, as well as the ordinary days. Without your kindness and honesty this book would never have been written.

T.B.E.

Acknowledgments for the Revised Edition

IN THE INTRODUCTION TO THIS NEW EDITION of *Silent Looms,* I wanted to show that while many elements of life in San Pedro Sacatepéquez had changed, overall, the town was much the same. In that spirit, I am delighted to say that most of the people I thanked in 1980 are those to whom I owe my gratitude now. The hospitality of the entire Orozco family buoyed me through a potentially lonely field visit. My "co-compadres," Tono and Luci Orozco, housed me, fed me, and indulged my endless questions. Reyna and Claudio Gonzalez, who had thought me dead after so many years away, rallied from their shock to be faithful guides to the new San Pedro economies. The family of Doña Eve Orozco swooped me up in San José Caben, giving me many enjoyable hours chatting about the post-weaving revolution in their town. In my investigation of Pacas, Doña Melvy Fuentes welcomed me into her store and talked freely about the business. The family of Don Gumercindo Fuentes volunteered to do a survey of Pacas for me. Chata Orozco was my guide through the smuggling business. There are many others who made this visit such a pleasure: Dr. Julio Roberto Fuentes, Doña Turivia de Leon, Profesora Tony Merida, Alcalde Edwin Honero Bravo Soto, Don Saul Navarro, and many other *Sampedranos.*

In the States, I must thank Paul Shankman for his continued support and honest criticism. Robert Carlsen provided encouragement and a Guatemalanist's perspective in his careful reading of the new introduction. Helayne Jones gave me thoughtful comments on the last draft. During a visit to San Pedro in late 1998, Linda Kelly sent me helpful corrections to a manuscript I had left behind with the Orozcos. As always, my husband, Michael C. Ehlers, supported my being away (again). I am indebted to him for adding a businessman's head and an editor's eye to the new writing. The University of Denver sponsored my 1997 research with a Faculty Internationalization Grant. At the University of Texas Press, Theresa J. May has been a caring, sensitive editor. I am especially grateful to her for believing that *Silent Looms* merited a new edition.

My dear friend and adopted brother, Jerry Goldstein, who had so enhanced my original research in San Pedro in the 1970s, completed the circle in 1997 by driving me to San Pedro from his home in Panajachel. It was Jerry who, in 1985, encouraged me to work in San Antonio Palopó, which then became my second highland field site. In countless field visits, we talked and laughed together, sharing stories about the two towns and all the people we knew. We were so fascinated by local life that we rarely paid attention to anything else, even when cable TV came to Panajachel in the early 1990s. Sadly, this visit to Guatemala was to be the last one I shared with Jerry. In July 1998 he succumbed to AIDS after a twelve-year battle.

Introduction to the Revised Edition

WHEN I FIRST WENT TO San Pedro Sacatepéquez, I wasn't planning to write about Mayan women. I arrived in the town with my advisor, Waldemar (Richard) Smith. During the 1960s Smith had spent three years in San Pedro with his wife, Linda, researching the impact of development on this commercially viable community (W. R. Smith 1975, 1977). My dissertation proposal, assiduously prepared for months before leaving for fieldwork in Guatemala, was titled "The Value of Children in the Family Productive System." It was December 1976. Richard introduced me to his informants, found me a place to live, and, with our spouses in tow, we celebrated the new year with his *Sampedrano* friends. During that first overwhelming week in Guatemala, Richard turned to me and, in an offhand way, said, "You seem to be getting along so well with the women. Why don't you change your topic to the impact development has had on them?" In a trice, I did exactly that.

The vigorous jump start Richard Smith gave to my work on gender is doubly ironic when considered against the backdrop of Smith's own conclusions on modernization in San Pedro. Smith's reputation as an anthropologist emerges from his assessment of San Pedro Sacatepéquez as one of the most productive and entrepreneurial "boom" economies in all of Guatemala. Before other ethnographers (e.g., C. Smith 1977, Goldin 1986) described the rich markets and economic potential of a number of highland productive systems like Almolonga or Totonicapán, San Pedro seemed almost anomalous in the ability of this Indian town to take advantage of rapidly expanding market opportunities. In light of this groundbreaking research on development, it is dismaying to see how much Smith had overlooked by never

1. The author and Waldemar (Richard) Smith with San Pedro friends.

considering women in his enthusiastic embrace of this "pattern of economic progress."

In the first edition of *Silent Looms,* I demonstrated that an expanding, modernizing base of production destroyed women's traditional work, transforming them into a dependent and exploitable rural proletariat competing for scarce economic opportunities. In fact, where development had been effective, it hadn't benefited women as much as it had benefited men, as benefits were often at the expense of their wives, daughters, and mothers. Richard Smith never realized that while development may have been an overall boon in San Pedro, it was a major socioeconomic catastrophe where women's production and independence were concerned. For example, in his book, Smith celebrates the "completely new machine-knitting industry" that had sprung up since the 1950s as yet another example of "real economic advance." Clearly, he did not appreciate that what drove the knitting machine industry and afforded its owners considerable wealth was its exploitation of women knitting piecework at home or being paid sweatshop salaries in urban factories. Although he visited factories, he never realized that the apprenticeship system he applauded fooled workers into believing they needed a year without pay to learn to knit.

Smith's case study of "Anselmo Orozco" further illustrates my point.[1] He describes Anselmo as running a soap business with his wife. But Anselmo realized the handmade soap business was a dead end given the stiff competition of industrially produced soaps like Fab, so he took his savings (from the business that he had shared with his wife), bought a truck, and got rich in transport. We never learn from Smith what happened to Anselmo's wife. Did she go on to become "wealthy and modern" too? When I tracked her down, I found that her life had changed, but not in the same way that Anselmo's had. She continued in the marginally profitable soap business in order to generate whatever small earnings she could to support her children. While they had a new house and educated sons symbolizing their father's newfound status, wife and children lived a precarious existence. Anselmo's trucking profits went into his own pocket and into the *huipil* of any one of a string of girlfriends he now supported. Household budgetary responsibilities fell to the wife who found herself dependent and abused in the house of this newly rich and modern San Pedro entrepreneur. In short, what Richard Smith painted as an optimistically entrepreneurial town looked very different to me when I included women.[2]

Two Decades of San Pedro Fieldwork

After my initial year of fieldwork in San Pedro, I, like most other Guatemalanists, stayed away from the region. As members of a solidarity group called the Guatemalan Scholars Network, most ethnographers agreed that our presence could endanger the lives of our friends and informants during the terror and violence of the early 1980s. Accordingly, my work came to a halt until the election of Vinicio Cerezo as President of Guatemala in 1985. Cerezo's victory signaled (falsely, as it turned out) a return to democracy and thus the reopening of ethnographic research in the highlands.

In those years, I turned my attention to San Antonio Palopó, a more traditional Mayan community on the shores of Lake Atitlán. I again examined gender as a critical variable in the move toward an expanded economy and the search for a less impoverished way of life (Ehlers 1991, 1993). But in almost every field season, I would make the all-day bus trip from the lake to visit the *Sampedrano* families I now considered my friends.

And so it went until 1997, when I decided that San Pedro merited a second, more serious ethnographic look. I could not see *Sampedranas* encased like bugs in amber within a cultural explanation that might no longer fit. They were not static, inert case studies, but real people in a dynamic reality that might defy many of the predictions that emerged from *Silent Looms.* Intimate knowledge of two very different Indian communities has caused me to re-think many of my early assumptions.

METHODS

Aided by a travel grant from the University of Denver, where I teach, I spent much of my 1997 summer in San Pedro Sacatepéquez. I lived with the same people I had stayed with in the 1970s, the Fuentes family. I made the same morning treks to San José Caben to visit weavers and did my rounds in the marketplace where many old friends still sold on Thursdays and Sundays. Although I had been back for briefer visits, there were many people I had not seen again. Happily, grown women I had only known as little girls welcomed me as a long-lost relative. Old friends had my photo with their families on their mantles, and stories were told about me that I, of course, had long forgotten. I brought photos of them in their youth and an album of my family in Boulder. Fortunately, almost no one among my informants or friends had died or disappeared or left town. Only Juana (my original guide to Guatemalan love and marriage) had gone to live on the coast, forced out of town after one too many ventures involving stolen car parts.

In my first San Pedro fieldwork, I ate *almuerzo,* the main meal of the day, with the Fuentes family, but I was adamant about having my evenings alone in my little apartment where I made a sandwich and read novels to escape. To a certain extent, I felt more like a boarder than a guest or member of the family. The Fuentes daughters had their boyfriends, their parents were busy, and their brothers were off limits. Only the elderly maiden aunt, Violeta, was around enough for serious heart-to-heart chats, and they were mostly about her. Twenty years later, beyond the few minutes I needed every day for organizing my field notes, I couldn't imagine being by myself. I allowed and encouraged the Fuentes family to take care of me. We were all older and wiser now. They had become my best friends and most trusted associates. I found myself making the rounds of their offices and shops just to check in every day. While previously they devoted hours and hours to watching the newfangled TV they had bought, now we were all too involved with our nighttime discussions and gossip to even turn it on.

Where the Fuentes family was concerned, I confess to no longer maintaining the orthodox anthropological distance, or hiding my routines and habits so as to fit in better. I introduced my *comadre,* Liliana, to power walking, for example. Every morning at six, we were off for an hour's brisk hike. Then we'd linger over breakfast while she filled me in on the family's stories and the town's developments. Although I had always believed an anthropologist should eat everything and anything so as not to offend, after twenty years, I was over seeking entry.[3] And I have to watch my fat intake! So my breakfast was cereal and skim milk yogurt (one of the blessings of development), while Liliana ate her daily scrambled egg and white buttered toast. At lunch I was inserted into the family of what was now twenty-five adults and children. Everyone knew I was a vegetarian of sorts, so they made sure I had enough of the squash and corn when everyone else was eating pork. Basically, the 1997 field trip was like going home. We laughed a lot. We made up jokes that we still giggle about on the phone. We worried together about a friend's health, compared notes on our own bodily functions, and went out drinking, dancing, and visiting. In short, I stopped being outside the culture. I had found a comfortable vantage point, and I nestled in for a good look.

SAN PEDRO TWENTY YEARS LATER

After my original research, the people of San Pedro lived through the extremely difficult and frightening *violencia* of the 1980s. Everyone has a story of a friend, neighbor, local official, or teacher who was assassinated or kidnapped by death squads, the paramilitary, or hired thugs. The army had established itself at a military base in neighboring San Marcos, a fact which occasioned considerable numbers of rapes, drunken brawls, and beatings in both towns.[4] Highway robberies at gunpoint were common fare, as was the presence of the Organization of the People in Arms (ORPA) guerrillas who lived in the surrounding mountains or in the lowland region, and who made trips to town for supplies and propaganda purposes.

While the implementation of peace accords has brought an end to much of the institutionalized violence, the community, the highlands, and the country continue to confront lawlessness, corruption, and civil mayhem almost on a daily basis.[5] This social anarchy seriously undermines the progressive image being carefully developed by the national administration. Television ads show runners—one male and one female—traversing the country while the voice-over says "Guatemala—We Are Changing." Billboards announcing new roads proclaim, "Work. Not just words." New road safety laws bespeak this modern orientation of the country, e.g., they forbid cell phones or headsets while driving and seatbelts are now mandatory. At the same time, however, Guatemala ranks fourth in the world in kidnappings, usually the kind where ransoms are paid (twice in some cases) and the victims killed anyway. Analysts look at kidnapping almost as an entrepreneurial opportunity for an increasingly desperate tide of unemployed people.

Rising social inequality means more Guatemalans continue to live wretched, impoverished lives. In a recent essay, ex-president de León Carpio pointed out that during 36 years of war 150,000 people died due to war and repression. At the same time, 450,000 children under five years old died from malnutrition, poor health care, and social injustice. As support he notes that in an analysis of human development indicators among its 185 member nations, the UN now puts Guatemala as a lowly number 117, down from number 112 the year before (de León Carpio 1997).

Today, the town has recovered from the fear and paranoia that separated neighbor from neighbor but remains divided, in part, by growing class distinctions made even more complicated by religious factions begun in the 1970s and crystallized during the 1980s. In 20 years, the number of evangelical churches in the town center of San Pedro grew from only two to twenty-five, and at least one such temple exists in each of the seventeen *aldeas*.[6] Although these new churches are distinct in their origins and orthodoxy, they tend to share a sense of cultural separateness and a suspicion of nonbelievers that is unsettling and seriously off-putting to the majority Catholics.[7] The Catholic Church, seriously dispirited by the political assaults of the 1980s, has been further demoralized by this new competition. At the same time, robberies and attacks at various neighborhood chapels have given Catholic parishioners a strange sense of being besieged. Who, they wonder, would steal the statue of the Niño de Atocha, the patron saint of my own San Pedro parish?

This sense of vulnerability seems to be occasioned by the new atmosphere of rootlessness, alienation, and uncertainty in the town. Partly, this is a result of population growth, but due as well to a huge spurt in immigration. In my original fieldwork, I often took walks with Violeta Miranda and she could greet by name (or identify and avoid) nearly everyone we passed. That does not happen anymore. People complain that the strong *Sampedrano* identity and shared sense of community described by W. R. Smith (1977) is being undermined by the number and diversity of newcomers who now live and work in the town.

Indeed, it is true that population has grown far beyond what normal reproductive patterns would have suggested. Immigrants from all over the country now compete with locals in hundreds of easily capitalized plaza businesses. Not only have they brought in businesses previously unheard of in the plaza (e.g., ice cream cones, fresh-killed chickens, Pepsi in cans, etc.), but they compete side-by-side with longtime traders selling the same products for the standard, and invariably higher, price. Who are these strangers? They are the thousands of people attracted by the opportunities for entrepreneurship, investment, a quick buck, or a route through Mexico to the United States, who have flooded the town in the last few years. Some come only for the market, but many have relocated for a longer stay. They are from all over Guatemala, Central America, and even places as far away as South America.

I took a walk through one rather tawdry example of this commercial influx, the red-light district that has evolved near the old bus station behind the church. In *Silent Looms,* I wrote about the one whorehouse in town, a dingy cantina with a jukebox out in the cornfields. Then, the working girls were bored *ladinas* (non-Indians) who shared a table and their conversation with the three local women (teachers, it turned out) who had recently inherited the business. Now, the prostitutes are indigenous teenagers as young as thirteen, brought in from the *altiplano* still in their *huipiles* and speaking Quiché. They behave like preteenagers, giggling and doing each other's hair while waiting for clients. Their pimps are unsavory, secretive men who direct their charges and their clients to the many open storefronts with only a flimsy screen to hide the bed.

Seemingly without exception, locals blame deviance and delinquency not on their own children, but on the aforementioned immigrant population. I was repeatedly told that these were the people, especially those from the coast, who were stealing money from plaza merchants, hanging out at the disco, dealing drugs, getting pregnant, and generally debasing the traditional values of the town. One variation on this theme of "the other" is to blame teens from the neighboring *ladino* town of San Marcos for all these problems. This was more common among teenagers themselves who found an easy target in their rivals and enemies from across the tracks.

I knew that immigrant influx only explained a small part of the 1990s version of San Pedro Sacatepéquez. One Sunday, eager to have another look at the changing local scene, I decided to stand outside the Catholic church after mass. Among the usual *Sampedranos* in *traje* (indigenous costumes) or worn dresses and pants, I saw men in expensive leather jackets sporting ponytails and earrings, and women with French-braided hair and high heels. Their sons looked like suburban skateboarders with baggy clothes and swoosh caps worn backwards, while their gum-snapping, heavily made-up daughters might have just wandered over from the nearest shopping mall.

Who were these people exhibiting such affluence? I knew they were locals, because I actually remembered some or recognized family members of others. When I asked around, people told me that locals or not, they were, without any doubt, drug dealers. While this suspicious finger-pointing may be true for a few of these people, it cannot explain what is indeed a marked trend to a pervasively upscale, Westernized affect in San Pedro. I believe that influenced by television, by travel, by visits to relatives in the United States, and by their college-educated children, many middle-class *Sampedranos* have adopted a "look" that expresses their desire for social mobility. To some people, such conspicuous consumption is grounds for suspicion—thus the drug-dealer analysis. To others, it is easy to understand. Their mothers and grandmothers eschewed the traditional clothes that they believed would mark them as backwards, rural *"inditos."* They opted for the clothes local *ladinos* wore as a sign of their being modern. Today, they and their more sophisticated offspring have selected a novel identity, one found in Miami or even Guatemala City, but until recently, not in San Pedro Sacatepéquez. I couldn't help wondering if what I was witnessing was the simple conscious adoption of Western styles, or a more serious choice, i.e., the abandonment of the entire indigenous culture package.

In short, I think it is fair to say that although drug dealers or invaders from elsewhere are partially responsible for the kinds of changes associated with rapid urbanization, it is development that has destroyed the very heart of the town. Money and affluence have caused the collapse of the nuclear family and to some extent have reshaped the values that have sustained the community for centuries. Disposable income accumulated since the 1970s has meant that family members are free to do things other than work night and day. Fathers no longer insist that their children carry on the family business. Instead, they demonstrate their own success and newfound status by investing in the education of their offspring. This movement has been so pervasive that this newly modernized Indian town has more professionals than its state capitol neighbor, San Marcos.

Since parents may no longer expect children to be working by the side of their mother or father, television, video games, and roughhousing on the streets take up the free time many young *Sampedranos* have after school or in the evenings. Teenage girls are conspicuous shoppers and media addicts who have adopted the *ladino* custom of greeting each other (and every adult they encounter) with a cheek kiss. Elaborate parties are held for children's birthdays with expensive gifts, piñatas, cake, Cokes, and specially made favors for guests. Bikinis have replaced *huipiles* in local beauty pageants, and several youth-oriented radio stations have opened, sponsored by national brands of junk food, clothing, and cosmetics.

Looking at these teenagers wandering around the town in packs, I was reminded of a story I often tell from my first fieldwork in San Pedro. Arriving in San José Caben after a 30-minute uphill trek, I realized that I had forgotten my notebook. "No trouble," said Don Carlos Fuentes, whom I had come to visit. "Manuelito will run to your house to fetch it." And before I could say a word, off went his nine-year-old son, eager to do his father's bidding. There, I thought, is a well-adjusted boy, confident of his value to his family, even if that day it consisted of running a silly errand. Here is a lesson about the value of work. When I tell this story, I always contrast this poor, rural family with that of the wealthy Velasquezes, Norma and Juan Carlos, the owners of the town's hotel and movie theater. Their son, Vinicio, was a bored, pampered, diffident little boy who always seemed to be rattling around his big house with nothing to do. In spite of having every comfort, a life of affluence did not provide him with more than disquiet about who he was, where he fit in, or what his purpose was in life.

This bit of amateur psychology has long been my guide to understanding middle-class angst and the value of work, Guatemalan or otherwise. And now it seems an apt model for explaining the seemingly pointless existence of a growing group of *Sampedrano* teenagers. Like Vinicio, they seemed to have a lot of spare time to hang out, party, and get into trouble.[8] Sadly, one of the costs of this modernizing economy has been that young *Sampedranos* were now being schooled beyond their usefulness to family businesses, and, to a certain extent, to themselves.

Work Today to Eat Tomorrow: Stasis and Change in San Pedro

I learned several basic lessons about San Pedro during that summer field-work. First, things had stayed the same in terms of the "all business, all the time" nature of the community. As I had anticipated, people of all ages and financial situations worked as obsessively as ever. *Sampedranos* seem to have internalized their own reputation as hardworking, clever businesspeople. They know they are energetic and skilled, and many of them, especially those with educations, are constantly coming up with new ideas and new businesses. Thus, the commercial sector was, at least to look at it, booming with activity. The streets were clogged with cars, buses, and trucks moving goods and people into the market from all over the region. There seemed to be a photocopy store on every corner, and even the corner drugstore used a computer to keep track of bills and inventory. Fast, modern self-service bakeries had been introduced by educated children of traditional bakers who had patronized such places in Guatemala City. Film could be developed in an hour across the street from where I lived. There were more doctors than I could count, and more than a dozen development agencies had offices employing local college graduates to implement projects targeting the rural poor.

Most people, especially women, still worked several jobs, or combined commerce with a job or perhaps two jobs. My friend Ana Miranda taught first grade, managed a clothing store, oversaw her husband's auto parts store, and, in her spare time, made decorated Styrofoam crosses for funerals. If I could convince Ana to put down her work for a coffee and a chat on a Sunday afternoon, I considered myself lucky.

THOSE WHO MADE GOOD

As one would expect, over a twenty-year period, the lives of individuals had evolved in both predictable and surprising directions. Gloria, the young woman whose baby had died in 1977, never did marry and now has a Ph.D. in education. I had imagined that César and Ana Gabriela, the teenagers who were forced to get married when her pregnancy was discovered, would be miserable together quite soon after they were wed. As it turned out, however, they went on to become successful and happy with three daughters and

2. Inside a new supermarket.

more than a dozen profitable businesses and investments. Mari, a seemingly poor soap maker from Chamac, had built, with her husband, a large, comfortable house and had two children in college. Doña Angélica was still doing a little weaving two decades after we met, but her investment in the education of her eldest son had paid off. He had become a highly placed executive with Aviateca, the Guatemalan airline, and made a sizeable salary. He provided his family with the economic security they had never had, as well as five TVs, two stereo systems, and a pickup truck.

The children of my closest informants and friends had been educated as professionals. After high school some of them found jobs as teachers, usually with the help of a considerable bribe to the right officials. The pay is poor and the commute to distant *aldeas* or rural communities long, but it is a job. Few of the growing hordes of high school graduates actually work in their chosen fields. Doña Yolanda's parents, for instance, wanted to provide their children with the means to better themselves. Accordingly, Yolanda and her siblings acquired degrees in teaching, nursing, accountancy, and technology. Their current jobs are as a sweater maker, shoemaker, tailor, candy seller, and shopkeeper.

Those who had been able to afford the time and money for college returned to San Pedro as dentists, architects, doctors, lawyers, and engineers. Like their *compañeros* with lesser degrees, however, very few of them have work in their professions. If they do practice, they make little money as their clients are usually too poor to pay more than a pittance for the service. Thus, young professionals are often obligated to open shops or work in their family businesses to make ends meet. Eve, for example, is a doctor's daughter and has a dental degree from the University of San Carlos. But local *técnicos* with minimal training can do much of the routine dental work for far less money than she would charge just to maintain her office. Thus, she has opted for a more traditional female role. She works in her clinic two days a week, but she helps out in her husband's store much of the rest of the week. In addition, all the nurturing of their two children falls to her.

As the discussion of *Pacas* will illustrate, educated *Sampedranos* have been able to infuse the economy with dynamic organizational models, innovative products and services, and confident business leadership, bringing a new, sophisticated emphasis to San Pedro commerce. It seems that young adults prefer doing business in their hometown to practicing their professions in Guatemala City, where they might have a better chance to succeed. I found this to be true for both college-educated men and women. For example, Manuela Miranda was wooed back from her job as an educational administrator in Totonicapán by the offer of a partnership and leadership role in her family's chicken business. Instead of having her weekends free for excursions and parties with her colleagues, Angélica now lives at home where she works seven days a week managing the business and considering what improvements she might introduce.

In short, many *Sampedranos* have made good. Deeply embedded in a growth mode in their town, the middle class has ridden the economic wave toward affluence and has arrived there with financial security, educated children, and a sense of accomplishment. For most, the secret to their success has been the loyalty to their families and to their town. While the promise of more money lured other Guatemalans to Texas or California or Miami, very few *Sampedranos* have moved away. Always there is the potential of the marketplace, the promise of an income from the vibrant San Pedro economy, and the ability to apply oneself to making a living.

THOSE WHO DIDN'T MAKE GOOD

At the same time that the town's growing middle class can look back proudly on its accomplishments, the majority of *Sampedranos* still struggle to survive. There simply isn't enough profit to go around. Crowded out of the market by competition, comparatively weak business skills and networks, or a simple lack of opportunity, many people's pocketbooks are empty. These people fall into two camps.

First, there are those for whom the town's abundant opportunities have been irrelevant, i.e., they had never had the resources to take advantage of the market or the schools or the jobs in any real sense. Doña Tomisina, for instance, has never been able to afford her own house. Twenty years ago she cooked at a makeshift fire on the fringes of her in-laws' home, and today she lives with her son's family. Still landless and desperately malnourished, Tomisina and her husband are barely subsisting on the Q15 ($2.50) a day each makes, he as a day worker and she washing clothes for the Fuentes family. Strategizing around poverty has not changed either. Doña Tomisina's son, Chepe, allows his sons to study, but has pulled his daughters from school after three years (in spite of their good grades and eagerness to learn) so that they might produce some kind of income.

Clearly, Chepe learned this strategy from his father, who similarly denied education to his daughters. In *Silent Looms,* I talked about Doña Tomisina's granddaughter María Dolores, who as a five-year-old was considered valuable to the female family business because she could already wash dishes. Obviously, helping her mother with domestic tasks was the only skill she was ever encouraged to develop. Today, she describes her life in these words: "I have always suffered." Pregnant at eighteen, now with four children, her husband beats her and rarely gives her enough money. She only has the *gasto* (minimal household budget or allowance) from selling the vegetables her husband grows on their little piece of ground. On the day I sat with her in the market, María Dolores had brought only a few lettuces and bunches of cilantro, and in the first two hours had only sold about Q20 ($3.33) worth.

This picture of a battered, struggling young woman is all too normal in bustling downtown San Pedro. Everywhere I saw women scraping together meager profits from the sale of marginal products. I counted several hundred young women like María Dolores entering the commercial arena with just a few bunches of flowers or radishes in the plaza but with no means for investing in a more sizeable inventory. Most established plaza businesses had not changed at all since my first visit years ago. Women were running the same stalls, selling the same products their mothers and grandmothers had, without any expansion into more profitable items or capital improvements. When queried about their futures given rapidly diminishing sales, they shrugged and suggested it was all in God's hands. This part of the story of women's production has remained remarkably constant.

MANY SILENT LOOMS

The second group of hard-pressed *Sampedranos* are those who had done well during the 1970s and 1980s, but who have been caught in the maelstrom of the economic transformation confronting the town and Guatemala in the 1990s. Hard times are erasing their progress. Previously, I wrote that Rosario and Edulina Ramirez had built a fine house in town with the profits from ten years of plaza business in soap and comestibles. They had been able to afford to educate all three of their daughters, whose labor was only minimally integral to the running of the store, the plaza stall, or any of a half dozen other moneymaking activities. In the last year, however, serious competition, both locally and from Mexico, means their business has dropped more than seventy percent. They've had to rent out rooms, and Rosario, desperately searching for income, quizzed me about the possibility of work in the States. This was not an unusual request. On this trip I had daily inquiries about jobs and salaries and routes to the United States, something that had never happened to me before in San Pedro.

The *Típica* Weaving Business

In *Silent Looms,* I wrote about the male-driven *tipica* business taking over looms from women when their traditional weaving businesses collapsed in the move toward modernization. During the 1960s and 1970s, many people from town and the near *aldeas* made their fortunes by selling yard goods of Maya-based textiles to wholesalers and exporters in Guatemala City and Xela. For instance, Gumercindo Miranda, one of the dozen or so weavers who founded what seemed at the time a rather modest textile cooperative in San José Caben, now owns a house in Guatemala City and a square block of real estate in downtown San Pedro.

Today, these wildly successful *típica* operations are no more. U.S. interest in importing Guatemalan textiles has waned. Of the two dozen businesses that once provided work for several hundred men in San José Caben, only two remain. One is owned by Florinda, Doña Angélica's daughter, and her husband, Roberto. The couple's business is handled by four in-house looms and sixty people (half of them women) weaving out of their homes. I was initially surprised that women had entered this male domain in such force, but the explanation was understandably familiar. Florinda and Roberto said that they would prefer to use men since their experience has shown that, given female reproductive responsibilities, a woman working at home can only manage half of what a man can do. The economy of the town is so dynamic, however, that they cannot find enough male weavers! Young men eschew work at a loom, preferring to study or to earn more money in town as cab drivers. So, although they only can make about Q220 a month (approximately $36), women are lining up for this work.

In terms of *traje típico* (the traditional indigenous costume), the weaving of wearable textiles is almost completely dead as a source of women's income. Twenty years ago, I saw that *de traje* women were fewer, and that *huipiles* and *cortes* grew dusty in shops when no one could afford to buy them. What I hadn't envisioned was that even the best and busiest weavers (who still had their wealthy older clients) could not meet the demands of the increasingly higher cost of living and were abandoning their looms. Among the older women, a fortunate few are allowing their successful children to support them. Many are working with their husbands, selling the vegetables he raises in the market. Others, particularly the young mothers, are actively investing in enterprises with more economic potential, such as opening *Pacas* or carrying contraband from Tapachula.

This does not mean that women in the region no longer weave. Female weavers of the poorer, more traditional *aldea*, Santa Teresa, have inherited the bulk of the *corte* and *huipil* business. They produce for local traders to sell on the streets or on order for rural women who are still *de traje*. These women have more customers who wear *traje* and fewer demands on their income as their children are less educated, their houses more basic, their diets simpler.[9]

To get another angle on the transformation of the *traje* business, I visited Lucinda Orozco in her *mercado* clothing store. Lucinda reflects the town's evolution toward middle-class female autonomy in her status as a single, professional woman who, over the years, has had a long sequence of half-serious boyfriends. Addicted to business and determined to be self-supporting, she keeps up her mother's shop during the day while teaching school in Chamac at night.

Lucinda inherited this business from her mother, Doña Celestina, the *típica* dealer who had first taken me along on her route to Totonicapán and Palestina in the 1970s. Lucinda still buys from Toto weavers, but her San Pedro locale is decidedly slow. In fact, after sitting there all day without a sale, I wondered why Lucinda came in at all.[10] In reality, she lamented, her profit margin has been dropping steadily. She has had to pay more to keep regular weavers, but she has lost more than two-thirds of them because they cannot make any profit even at the higher rates. Now she finds herself competing with freelancing Santa Teresa weavers who sell to her and then sell on the street for the same price. So while Lucinda has to mark up a Q125 *huipil* to Q150 just to cover her overhead (rent, taxes, salaries, and electricity), the weaver's lower street price means a sale lost.

Yes, says Lucinda, there are still *de corte* women in the far *aldeas,* and rural women from other parts of the state come to buy when they have money after working the harvests on the coast.[11] But as the population grows, they are putting their daughters into skirts and blouses. Then, too, these are poor people who cannot buy the big-ticket items like hand-embroidered *huipiles* or silk *cortes* on which Lucinda might make a decent profit.

Gender Relations—The Same Old Story

Parallel to this category of struggling businesswomen, I want to include a new group—the female working poor. In the San Pedro of the '90s, girls and women have options outside cottage industry or the plaza for income potential. The town's size and the movement of commerce and people through its center translate into growing retail and service sectors, and thus a considerable opportunity for wage work. For example, while in the 1970s and 1980s there were few cafes or bars, fast-food restaurants are now opening (and closing) all the time. Unfortunately, working women cannot command very much money, and most of them complain about their small salaries. These money problems are complicated by the fact that many workers are single mothers. Time spent with women from this sector assured me that gender relations had changed little since the 1970s.

For example, I interviewed six waitresses at a local restaurant, all of them in their twenties. Each had a familiar story: they came from poor *aldea* families, and at first, most were being educated with the hope of a job and a decent income. Then each of these young women was seduced and abandoned. Juana, for example, had sex with her boyfriend three times before she realized she was expecting a baby. She says she knew nothing about her body, menstruation, or pregnancy. He left her when the baby was two months old. Santa was an orphan of fifteen, raising her two brothers, when she met her boyfriend. She became pregnant; he promised to recognize the child, but he never did. Instead, he married somebody else, left for Guatemala City, and has never seen his daughter.

The other stories are similar. Scorned by their families as *putas,* and with a child to care for, one waitress after another told of having to scrounge for whatever kind of job she could get. One worked in a sweater factory from 3 AM to 10 AM, making less than Q40 a week. Another sold *atolito de elote* (corn drink) from a jug she carried around on her head. From this work, she made so little money that there were whole days when neither she nor her baby ate. She lived like that for two years and lost thirty pounds as a result. Finally, she found a waitress job where she was required to work seven days a week. She made no money there either, but, she says, at least she wasn't carrying around the baby on her back and her livelihood on her head! Their current work at the restaurant pays a decent wage with fair benefits, but even so, by the end of the month, none of these women has enough money left to feed their children.

The same tales of struggling women and violent, irresponsible men kept coming up. In Chamac, I visited with Julieta, the daughter of Doña María Luz, the soap maker. She is now thirty, has three children, and lives with her parents. Fourteen years before, she had married Geraldo, the driver of the minibus that dropped us off at her house. Geraldo wouldn't let Julieta work in the plaza with her mother. He made her stay home to care for their cows. He beat her. He had other women. He drank. Finally, after a decade of abuse, her family helped her to leave him. She filled up a truck with her meager possessions and moved out. Luckily, he gives her Q200 a month, an extremely rare occurrence in Guatemala.

Machismo isn't limited to poor men. On this visit, Liliana told me a story about her uncle Daniel that certainly outdoes all other tales of machismo in San Pedro. It seems Uncle Daniel had women all over the country. While he traveled around visiting them, his wife, Corina, ran his business. Corina was dedicated to Daniel in spite of all his girlfriends and lovers. Her devotion was so extreme that during Semana Santa, she would prepare his favorite *tamales de carne* and send them to all his *novias* so he wouldn't miss this traditional food from home while he was away!

These stories are only a few examples of the constant soap opera of household gender relations. Unfortunately, while a few middle-class *Sampedranas* have opted out of this drama with good jobs, family support, and their own money, most women (rich or poor) are still victimized by the unreliable men in their lives. Some men cherish their families and treat their wives with love and respect, but the theme of dissatisfaction with men and marital dissolution remains. Women still expect to be mistreated by their spouses, and this brief revisit suggested their expectations often came true.

In previous work (Ehlers 1991) I have written that this imbalance of power is based on women's economic vulnerability, that women must put up with abusive and irresponsible men because their own productive efforts are so minimally rewarding. I still believe this to be true. Even where women have benefited from education and job opportunities, they are still expected to combine income production with domestic responsibilities, an extremely challenging task.

Female Entrepreneurship and the Family Productive System

Since writing *Silent Looms,* my understanding of household gender relations and women's economic vulnerability has been influenced by the work of other social scientists and feminist academics (Bruce 1989, Jiggins 1989, and others) writing about men's and women's distinctly separate productive and reproductive agendas. This literature, and my own research done in the interim (Ehlers 1998), has caused me to rethink the nature of household production in San Pedro—even to the point of arguing that a true family productive system does not exist. I no longer consider, as W. R. Smith did, that San Pedro has thrived because all members of the family work together pooling their energies and income for household consumption purposes. Instead, I now appreciate that it is women who are primarily responsible for meeting the basic needs of their children, not only in terms of reproduction, but also in income generation. I think of women not only as providers, but also as the providers of last resort. If men cannot or will not contribute to the household budget to ensure survival, women must pick up the slack however they can. It is true in San Pedro Sacatepéquez that women and men see the care and feeding of children to be the woman's job. Men's priorities lie elsewhere. *Sampedranos* in general are expected to provide basics like corn and firewood for their wives, but women must provide everything else. This may not be the rule, but, to some extent, it is the common expectation.

As Bruce (1989) and others have found elsewhere in the Third World, I believe that San Pedro, too, has two distinct production/consumption agendas in the household, one male and one female, and these agendas, while sometimes complementary, can also compete for scarce resources. Instead of Richard Smith's smooth system of cooperating family production, I see separate survival strategies and considerable tension over the allocation of money. Most women feed their children based upon what they can convince their husbands to give them, supplemented by their own small incomes. Even where women work for their husbands as day-to-day managers of stores or home businesses (the classic family production system), they are expected to turn over all the monies to their spouses. It is his decision how much allowance they receive from the receipts for household expenses. The only arena where women can be sure of controlling money is in female family businesses, and these, as we have seen, create extremely minimal returns. In short, in their role as nurturer/provider of last resort, women are coping with one economic crisis after another, with far fewer resources than their husbands.

Meanwhile, men are often living in nonfamilial worlds to which a considerable part of their earnings are directed. As in Smith's Anselmo case (and in the dozens like it that I have documented), men have their own uses for their wages or commercial income. In general, men do give their wives money, but retain the lion's share of their cash for purposes other than household consumption. Some men may drink it up, while others gamble it away or give it to other women with whom they are having extramarital relationships. In other words, they spend it on themselves. With or without these bad habits, men normally reinvest their profits in their businesses or in the conspicuous consumption of televisions, boom-box stereos, and the like.

Not surprisingly, women's consumption agenda is very different from their husbands'. Most women use their daily receipts to buy food for the household. They rarely have money to spend on themselves, nor can they keep aside cash needed for food or school uniforms to better capitalize their small businesses. Business profits directly fuel household budgetary needs instead of being used as investment for growth. With such a built-in short circuit of the rules of business, it is no wonder women's enterprises seldom thrive.

Given these parallel agendas, the real-life implications for business competitiveness and success are compelling. Imagine a woman's tomato business right next door to a man's tomato business. For the moment, we'll assume all things are equal in terms of business experience, access to credit, etc. (although we know they most likely are not). They've both just started in business. At the end of the first day, the tomatoes are gone and they've each got their Q10 of profit in their hands. The man assumes his wife will have dinner on the table and doesn't worry about food. Thus, he can put some of his Q10 into savings. Maybe he will even drink a beer or two before going home. Meanwhile, the woman puts aside her capital for tomorrow's crate of tomatoes, takes what money she has left to her neighbor's stall where she applies the rest of her profit toward the purchase of a half-pound of chicken, some noodles, and a few vegetables. Next market day, the man dips into his reserve to buy two crates of tomatoes. The woman can only buy the one. Two weeks later, he has three crates; she still has the one. Next market day, he has three crates of tomatoes and has expanded into the sale of onions. She still has only the one crate of tomatoes. The following year, no change for her, but his business has taken off.

What have we learned from this rather simplistic example of market economics? Men are buoyed by their wives' small but secure businesses which cover household expenses they don't meet. They can thus take full advantage of the marketplace, reinvesting profits and expanding their businesses. They are entrepreneurial, but their wives are definitely not.

SMALL BUSINESSWOMEN ARE NOT ENTREPRENEURS

I first understood the misappropriation of the term "entrepreneur" one day in San Antonio Palopó when I asked the mayor of the town for a list of the women he considered entrepreneurial. He quickly dismissed the notion of a female entrepreneur as misguided, saying that although they might have small businesses, women lacked the necessary talent, interest, time, and capital to be truly entrepreneurial. Besides, he snorted, women were not supposed to devote themselves to developing commercial enterprises; their work was taking care of the home.

I thought over the mayor's comment not only in terms of San Antonio, but in the more general context of highland women running the tiny domestically based enterprises I have called "female family businesses." I realized that for years I had mistakenly thought "entrepreneurial" applied equally to men and women. Now I began to understand that gender constraints impact women and their businesses in such a way that they ought to be considered an entirely separate category of productive endeavor. I have realized that being a woman in highland Guatemala means there are a great number of gender variables at work determining the kinds of businesses women choose, the way they do business, their goals, the skills they could apply, their access to resources, etc. The result is a kind of parallel business universe in which women do business very differently from men.

My point is that women's small businesses cannot afford to be entrepreneurial. Certainly, among the hundreds of women I have encountered in the highlands these past twenty years, there are some genuinely entrepreneurial women who exhibit the risk-taking, creative, hardworking behavior associated with the word "entrepreneur," but they are decidedly few. As elsewhere, when women work in the informal sector in the highlands, their businesses tend to be tiny, severely undercapitalized extensions of the domestic routine. Thus women's businesses feature skills expected in a housewife: they weave, sew, knit, cook, and sell food. These informal sector businesses provide ease of access and a certain flexibility that they believe allows for the efficient combining of productive and reproductive responsibilities. They are operations which afford immediate cash payment for services rendered. Women combine them to maximize their benefits: piecework sewing at night and a spot in the marketplace on Thursdays and Sundays.

The economically vulnerable women running these businesses cannot afford the luxury of long-term planning nor the risks necessary to grow a business. In place of the growth orientation common to men, *Sampedranas* adopt careful, conservative measures that they believe translate into the survival of their business even if this means maintaining it on a very low, stable level. The result is a fragile, barely profitable day-to-day operation. In short, *Sampedranas* work today in order to eat tomorrow.

SECOND FLOOR SHOP LADIES

An example of this strategy is found among the Second Floor Shop Ladies of the old *mercado*. Along one wall are eight small grocery stalls. The women who own these shops (most are in their 50s and 60s) are carrying on the businesses founded by their mothers and grandmothers. These women are relatives and friends who all sell pretty much the same household items (candles, rice, soups, oleo, oil, sugar, etc.) at the same prices. No one undersells anyone else or tries to woo the rare new customer walking down the aisle. In fact, instead of competing, they tend to cooperate and help each other out. Each woman has her regular patrons, but they are becoming fewer and fewer. In fact, the women agree that they are now making about one-third of last year's profit. What with the growing competition in the plaza and the illegal goods from Tapachula, some months they can barely meet their overhead.

3. Second Floor Shop Lady.

On a typical Thursday, each woman sells about Q400 ($66) in goods, but only Q20 ($3.33) of that is pure profit. On nonmarket days, they make only about Q5 (less than a dollar).

These women confirm my suspicions about female entrepreneurship. Business growth and the bottom line are not of concern to the Second Floor Shop Ladies. With or without husbands, what's important to them is that they do enough business to extract food for their tables out of the inventory. If they make a little extra, well, God has blessed them that day. Even with business declining almost to nothing, these women are content running their businesses in this way. They have made some changes when new products have become available to them, but none of them has sought out a more profitable specialty or approach to business that wasn't taught to her by her mother. They agree they will maintain this traditional management style always. The watchword of the Second Floor Shop Ladies is "status quo." They are very frank in saying they cannot afford to take risks. Sometimes, they admit, if you want more, you fail. It is more advisable just to maintain.

New Commercial Options for *Sampedranas*

During the summer of 1997, I spent a considerable amount of time researching two new businesses that have serious implications for women in San Pe-

4. Bayunquera *with Mexican contraband.*

dro. First, there were the women who smuggled consumer products into Guatemala from nearby Mexico. These goods (mostly groceries and household goods like toilet paper, Pepsi, rice, soap, etc.) are purchased at lower prices in Tapachula, Mexico, just two hours away from San Pedro. Bribing a series of border guards as they go, *bayunqueras* bring these items into the country illegally and sell them throughout the region for prices well under the going rate.[12] This allows the smugglers to make a profit on each trip, but normal businesswomen, especially those in the plaza, are dismayed at the devastation it causes to their profit margins.

The other new industry is the retail sale of second-hand clothes, a commercial venture that has offered several hundred locals a real opportunity to get rich. As they have been for years in other Third World countries, cast-off garments from the United States are now the rage in San Pedro. Stores have opened all over town, some specializing in jackets or shoes, others offering an assortment of clothes and household items. Whatever they sell, these *"Pacas"* have become part of the cultural scene, not only in terms of the clothes, but also in the encouragement of a particularly Western behavior known as "shopping."

Both of these businesses have a certain cachet not characteristic of more traditional women's enterprises. This makes them far better topics of conversation than the price of tomatoes or how to string a loom. Informants couldn't tell me enough about their trips to Mexico or the treasures they had found at the neighborhood *Paca*. At the same time, however, the *bayunqueras* and the *Paca* dealers reflect new, broader socioeconomic threats to women's businesses and their roles as providers in San Pedro. Although they offer some women exciting and challenging income-producing opportunities, each undermines long-standing relations of production and economic expectations developed over the years I have been working in the town.

TAPACHULA: THE BUSINESS OF SMUGGLING

When I first heard that the most popular new female business was smuggling, I imagined Indian women working as drug "mules" stashing cocaine or heroin (opium poppies are grown locally) into their expansive *huipiles* as they crossed over the Mexican border. The truth turned out to be far more mundane. Local women are indeed bringing illicit cargo across the border, but it is back *into* Guatemala from Mexico, and the goods are cases of ordinary household products. The smuggling part comes from the fact that they are not paying the taxes on their purchases, but are bribing the *Guardia de la Hacienda* (border guards) to allow them to slip through border checkpoints with hidden packages.

All this began four years ago when the value of the Mexican peso hit a new low against the Guatemalan quetzal. Until then small amounts of contraband were considered normal, especially in medicines which were far cheaper in Mexico. But now, while some goods are still less expensive in Mexico, it's the currency exchange that makes the difference. In 1997, five hundred quetzales were equal to 650 pesos, while before they were approximately equal. *Sampedranos* quickly exploited the potential for business in nearby Tapachula. The development of local *contrabandistas* was aided by the status of residents of the border state of San Marcos as *fronterisos*. Other Guatemalans need a visa or a passport, which takes more bureaucracy, more time, and more bribes, but *Sampedranos* don't need more than their identity cards to enter Mexico.

This business is not isolated to a few daring entrepreneurial women with the nerve to take such a risk. In fact, dozens of women travel back and forth from San Pedro to Tapachula on a regular, even daily, basis, and hundreds more make the occasional foray. It's a route to "easy money" for those who know their way around the *Guardia*'s demand for *la mordida*. How much people make depends upon their bankroll, their luck, and their markets once they return. This strategy has evolved quickly in a very few years, so that there are many different ways to be a *bayunquera*. The following addresses only the most common approaches.

First, there are acknowledged, professional, full-time smugglers, some of whom will take orders for wholesale or retail merchandise like clothes, cameras, or machinery. These women live in San Pedro, but many do not even stop there on their way out of Mexico, heading for more lucrative markets elsewhere in the highlands or Guatemala City.

Next are the wholesale food distributors who buy goods to resell to smaller female merchants in the huge San Pedro markets on Thursdays and Sundays. Many of these women go to Tapachula with vegetables to sell there, and come back with such rarities as cases of Pepsi in cans (Pepsi only comes in returnable bottles in Guatemala), or such ordinary Mexican goods as rice, soap, cooking oil, toilet paper, or cookies. People claim that these *bayunqueras* make a Q11,000 (nearly $2000) profit on every trip. Whether this is an exaggeration or not, such a considerable return is likely limited to a handful of women. It is true that there is a huge trade in contraband in the Thursday market. Some plaza women make the trip themselves, but those who do are largely from coastal cities. Locals claim that a *Sampedrana* wouldn't waste her time sitting all day with contraband in the market. Instead, she would resell it quickly in bulk elsewhere and head back to Tapachula for more.

Slightly apart from these resellers are merchants who are stocking their own stores. Ana Miranda, for example, went to Tapachula three times last year to prepare for Christmas business in her children's clothing store. While she thinks it is sad that Guatemala loses this money, she cannot afford to forfeit the profit. In addition, she says it is very difficult and terribly dangerous to go to Guatemala City to purchase inventory. Case in point: last year Ana was coming back from the capital with Q7000 ($1166) worth of merchandise piled in her car. She and her husband stopped briefly on the Interamerican Highway for a Coke, and when they went back to the car, all their goods had been stolen. I asked if they had gone to the police. "No," she responded, "we figured the thieves were probably the police anyway."

Then there are the ordinary citizens or businesspeople who want to make some money during a seasonal lull in their operations or need extra income in a hurry. These are the *Sampedranas* for whom smuggling is an economic safety valve: better-capitalized folks using their own money for goods and expenses, going back and forth to Tapachula once or twice a week. Determined businesspeople with money to invest can make a 10 percent profit on every trip.[13] Typically, a Q3000 bankroll ($500), handled properly, will yield a Q300 ($50) profit. Clearly, these people are not attempting large-scale hauls, but bring in many small, easy to hide packages. One San José Caben couple made twenty-four trips in three months during their slow season, netting Q7200 ($1200) in the sale of sweaters. They reinvested their profit in a minivan, running a shuttle service to San Pedro.

The most common category of *bayunqueras* are those small scale *comerciantes* from San José Caben who earn about Q1000 ($172) a month for their work, a decent amount locally. During the summer, there are about two dozen women going back and forth on buses, but between October and Christmas, business is so good that the number jumps to eighty or a hundred. These are women who cannot meet their rising expenses by either weaving or selling in the plaza. They supplement whatever home production they have with trips to Mexico. Many women begin by borrowing the cash from a friend or family member (at a standard 10 percent monthly interest), and might initially earn Q70 (not even $12) per trip. Profits generally grow as they learn the ropes.

Of course, ordinary shoppers make the trek to Tapachula to stock up on necessities or just for the fun of a shopping trip. The savings are considerable. For example, beer in San Pedro normally goes for Q22 ($3.65) a six pack or Q19 ($3.15) on sale. In Mexico, the same beer costs 15 pesos (less than $2).

The various investment strategies above are closely tied to a smuggler's mode of transportation. Better capitalized *bayunqueras* drive their own cars, put the goods on the floor or under the children in the backseat, merely honking and waving as they pass *aduanas*. Hired cars or taxis are normally stopped by the *Guardia* to ask what is being brought into the country. The answer is "Only corn flakes and clothes for the kids." One hundred quetzales buys their belief and safe passage.

Those who get the most trouble from the officials are those traders on the Tapachula buses, and this cheap mode of transportation is what local women normally choose. Poorer and more vulnerable than those in cars with husbands or male drivers, they are easy prey for corrupt *Guardia*. Passengers have to answer questions about their goods at least three times on the trip to San Pedro. If they lack the appropriate bribes (average Q75 [$12.50] per trip) for the officials, they lose their purchases. This is especially troubling to women who had to borrow the cash for the trip, but they attempt to make up for their loss by trying again the next day.

Impact of the *Bayunqueras*

Although smuggling can be a source of much-needed income for strapped *Sampedranas* (not to mention the adventure of it all!), it has its downside as well. The impact of the *bayunqueras* has been to seriously threaten the stability of many different kinds of existing businesses in San Pedro. Local shops and stalls selling food, clothes, tools, CDs and tapes, even veterinary supplies, simply cannot compete with the low prices of Mexican goods. Most merchants now understand that they must take part in the hated process just to stay open. They do this by preordering wholesale amounts of goods for their shops or buying individual items in the Thursday plaza for resale in other markets.

Edulina and her family used to live well on the Q3000 ($500) of comestibles (sugar, salt, beans, corn) she sold every day to wholesalers out of the shop. Of that, Q100 was clear profit (3 percent). Now, for the last eight months, she's been selling only Q400 ($67) daily, with only a Q25–30 ($4–5) profit. The main reason for this severe drop is that wholesale buyers are spending their money with *bayunqueras* (e.g., Q60 per hundred pounds vs. Q80 for Guatemalan corn), and Edulina now sells only retail. The profit margin is double that of wholesale, but the Q400 daily volume barely yields a decent income.

In the plaza, it is the same story. Stalls that had been in the same spot for generations have gone under in just the last year or two. Francisca cannot find buyers for her normal wares of rice, beans, noodles, corn, or oil at prices up to Q1 more per pound than any *bayunquera* charges. Furthermore, products that were staples for her can no longer compete, for tastes have changed with the new imported goods. Mexican corn, for example, sells faster than Guatemalan because customers say it has a better flavor. Mexican Mazeca (corn meal) is handier than buying corn in bulk: no firewood, no *nixtamal* (corn boiled in preparation for grinding) to watch, no carrying the corn to the mill, etc. On a typical Thursday in 1997, Francisca sold Q200 ($33) in her plaza stall, down from Q500 a few years before, and a small percentage of her Q1000–1500 Thursday sales in the 1980s.

The government's response to rampant smuggling has not been to catch and punish corrupt border officials, but to attack the small-time *bayunqueras.* The week before I arrived, the *Guardia* teargassed the San Pedro Thursday plaza in order to roust the people selling contraband and seize their products. This terrorized hundreds of innocent residents, shoppers, and *comerciantes,* and did little to discourage determined *controbandistas,* who were back the following Thursday in their same locations.

My sense is that there is little locals can do to stop the Tapachula trade, and most are not really pressing the issue. Although businesspeople are suffering from this wave of clandestine competition, many are adapting by including some of these goods as part of their trading strategy. Indeed, smuggling has proven to be a critical fall-back business for hundreds of women, and consumers certainly benefit. One wonders just what people would do if the government really did crack down on *bayunqueras!*

PACAS: THE SECOND-HAND CLOTHING BUSINESS

In the 1980s, I wrote that modernization and the high price of *traje* were pushing women away from wearing clothes that identified them as old-fashioned, traditional, or indigenous. Instead, they were donning what I've since labeled "Kmart specials," i.e., flimsy polyester or cotton dresses, blouses, and skirts quickly sewn up by local dressmakers. In many ways this was a dismaying transition. It marked the further entry of San Pedro into the global market economy, and at the same time signaled the erosion of the female production base. On a more personal level, I found the new clothing options ordinary, cheap, and unattractive, especially when compared with the gorgeous, delicate handiwork of the *huipil* and *corte*. My investigations had proven that although it cost more initially, *traje* was a better investment (Carlsen 1997). Traditional woven garments lasted longer, especially when clothes were washed with harsh soap on rocks or in cement sinks. So, in terms of work, practicality, and aesthetics, the choice of "Kmart specials" was hard to comprehend. It took me months of fieldwork and years of socio-economic analysis to understand the implications and motives of the turn away from *traje*.

When I returned to San Pedro in 1997, however, the new move to *Paca* clothing was a flagrant, obvious, easy-to-understand fact of life.[14] On any day, mountains of very affordable, well-made used clothes were being moved into stores named after *pacas,* the 1,000-lb. bales in which the goods were packed for shipment. The suppliers of these goods are middle-class (and, from a look at the labels, wealthy) Americans whose cast-offs are exported to Guatemala from the U.S.[15] Since American affluence translates into a constant seasonal turnover in fashions, the supply of last year's garments is steady.

While the finest second-hand clothes (the "A" classification) are not shipped to San Pedro due to their higher price tag, the "B" *pacas* are still full of goodies. In only ten minutes' search through the various piles in one *Paca* I found a bridesmaid dress (dark blue), four Notre Dame sweatshirts, a Harris tweed jacket, Liz Claiborne pants, Polo pullovers, a pair of Levi's with bleach spots, Wranglers for Women, Gap turtlenecks, a practically new sweater from Jones New York, Dockers shorts, a brand new DKNY skirt with the tag still on, a tan Bill Blass jacket, a brightly colored Carole Little silk sweatshirt, two L.L. Bean wool sweaters, a Bloomingdale's pink cotton sweater, a jean jacket with warm pile lining, and a canvas book bag from Doubleday.

The allure of clothes like these (and the hundreds of brands I didn't recognize) is palpable, and hours before shops open a new *paca* bale, hordes of people line up to get into the shops. *Pacas* are omnipresent; they are found on every commercial street in San Pedro, sometimes two or three to a block. Most of them are tiny, dark storefronts on side streets, but successful merchants have expanded into larger and better-situated locations. The buyers are of two kinds: the first is the ordinary shopper, most of whom have a garment or two in mind when they come in. Some go from shop to shop asking, "Do you have any warm jackets?" or, "Are there any children's shoes this week?" These are the retail customers who might spend a dollar or two at a time.

More central to the success of the *Pacas* are the wholesale buyers, the *mayoristas*. They spend several hundred dollars on Thursday market days buying dozens of pieces for resale in rural communities or even in Mexico. Customers tend to be loyal, and it is especially important for *Paca* owners to develop good relationships with their *mayoristas* so that they can count on those large sales every market day.

My personal introduction to *Pacas* came on the first day of my visit when it turned out to be windy and colder than I had remembered for June. I lamented my absentmindedness, as I had lived in this town before and knew there had been nowhere to shop for a warm sweater or a jacket. "Oh, that's easily remedied," replied my friend Angélica. "Let's just go across the street to Doña Nedia's *Paca*." I was skeptical, but off we went. Sure enough, there in the *Paca* were piles of sweaters and racks of jackets, all with familiar American brands, most in good condition. I fished out a Gap wool sweater quite similar to one in my own closet at home, paid my Q3 (50 cents), and stayed warm for the rest of my fieldwork.

Paca Basics

I quickly learned that *Pacas* were a well-established fact of life in San Pedro. This extremely visible, popular business intrigued me, and I spent time learning as much about them as I could. It wasn't just the irony of finding my own clothes on the backs of people anthropologists consider exotic "others." I was immediately convinced that embedded in *Pacas* are many of the central socio-economic realities of both the town I had studied before and its newer 1990s incarnation.

In the first place, *Pacas* fit into my restudy because more than half the town's *Paca* owners are female, and women also manage many of the *Pacas* held by their spouses. Most of these women are young, high-school educated locals. *Pacas* have become a very clear expression of how educated *Sampedranas* have redirected their professional goals toward the town's signature economy—commerce. Many chose the *Paca* route when they could not find jobs with degrees as teachers, accountants, or nurses. Others worked at those jobs for a while, but found the salaries or the distant rural assignments unsatisfactory. They did not opt for plaza sales or market stalls even though most of them learned those businesses at their mothers' sides as children. Instead, they leveraged their own budding entrepreneurism, putting it together with their parents' confidence in them, and financed this new, modern business mostly with family money. Clearly, investment in a *Paca* is an accepted avenue for a young, educated woman, and it had the cachet of being American, modern, and quickly profitable.[16]

While *Pacas* seem very "cutting edge," in many ways they represent the persistence of a decidedly female way of doing business. Doña Yolanda, for example, defers to her husband on business decisions although they work in side-by-side storefront *Pacas,* each doing the same retail routine all day long. Like most female *comerciantes,* every day Yolanda extracts what she needs from her cash drawer to buy food, but little else. While this expense money might be considered Yolanda's salary, it is strictly dedicated to household expenses. She has no other money of her own, and at the end of each day, she gives her husband the money which he takes to the bank. She explains this by saying she's just "helping" her husband, despite the fact that the *Paca* had been started and then shared by the two of them.

At the other extreme of this model of female conservatism are the female *Paca* owners who, while not making much money, are independent and mobile businesswomen. Doña Julieta is a legendary entrepreneur who owns two of her own *Pacas* in San Pedro and two in coastal towns. She buys thirty *pacas* a week in Guatemala City, selling six in her shops and wholesaling the rest. I believe that one of the secrets of Doña Julieta's success is that she is unmarried. There is no need for her to oversee a household, and, in fact, constant business travel means she is seldom at home. She has hired help to run her San Pedro stores and to cover all the childcare needs of her newborn

5. Owner of a "Paca" used clothing store.

baby. In short, being unencumbered by a demanding spouse means Doña Julieta can completely devote herself to making money.

A few *Pacas* opened for business about ten years ago, but beginning in 1991 the number of stores began to mushroom. Today, there are more than fifty full-time *Pacas,* plus a number of them which come and go in the plaza on any Thursday. The basics of the business are fairly standard. The *pacas* (bundles of clothes) weigh about one thousand pounds and cost about Q4000 ($666) each. Shop owners open one *paca* every Thursday when they know that customers will be pouring into town for the weekly market. Most owners purchase their *pacas* from one of three local wholesalers who buy dozens of bales in Guatemala City, then truck them to San Pedro. Each *paca* contains two to three thousand pieces. The prices are consistent, and no allowance is made for brand names or fashion. All skirts go for Q6, for example. By the following Tuesday, the inventory has been picked over. The *saldos,* or leftovers, are sold to one of a handful of men from Xela who pay about Q800 ($135) for what usually amounts to half a *paca.*

Pacas started out being very profitable, but as more and more secondhand clothing shops have opened, owners are making less. In a normal month, the sale of one *paca* a week nets about Q1600 profit ($265), a figure that compares quite favorably to monthly salaries of Q290 for a nurse or Q800 for a beginning teacher. In fact, the *Paca* bottom line of about Q400 per *paca* looks even better for women when you take into account that it represents a 10 percent net profit (after rent, utilities, workers, and even the *gasto* is taken out of the *Paca* cash box).

The *Paca* Impact

Over the last few years, *pacas* have seriously undermined women's clothing businesses already vulnerable to the inroads of modernization and tighter budgets. Weavers have lost many of their few remaining *Sampedrana* and *aldea* customers as women abandon their *huipiles* for much cheaper *Paca* blouses. *Cortes* are still worn by traditional women, but more and more they prefer combining them with *Paca* tops, t-shirts, and blouses. Even machine-embroidered *blusas,* a popular alternative to *huipiles* in the '80s, are expensive (approximately $20) compared to the cost of less than a dollar for a blouse from the *Paca.*

But it is not only the traditional operations that are impacted by inexpensive used clothes from America. Machine sweater-makers report that their home businesses, already on the wane because they couldn't compete with sweater factories, are now completely dead due to *Pacas.* Retail stores specializing in baby's and children's clothes have lost half their business where nearly new outfits for kids arrive in the *pacas* at a fraction of the cost. Women who sell fabric for clothes ("Kmart specials") are hanging on by a thread only because of customers who sew their own dresses or blouses, but seamstresses can barely afford to keep their doors open.[17] I originally described these *costureras* as a growth industry that was taking off as women switched from *huipiles* to cheap dresses, but now even their comparatively affordable prices are less attractive.

Paca Customers

It seems that everyone in town shops at the *Pacas.* Shoppers know what they want. Teenagers are regular customers, and their new suburban U.S. look is due in large part to careful consideration of the *Paca*'s brand-name clothes they recognize from TV and magazines. Well-off and educated locals regularly search the piles for quality merchandise not normally for sale any-where in Guatemala. In fact, the *Pacas* have become quite a habit for many consumers—mostly women—who might drop in a few times a week just to look. Status-conscious housewives, shop-owners, and businesswomen, however, rarely buy clothes in the *Pacas* because they would be embarrassed to acknowledge that they are buying second-hand. If they are passing by, they might stop in to ask for towels that can be turned into mops, but little else. Meanwhile, when I admired the sweater worn by my good friend, the English-speaking doctor, he proudly announced *"Paca!"* as if to say, "I got such a deal!"

If the *Paca* customer base is variable, there is little doubt that those who have benefited the most from good-quality used clothes are not the wealthy doctors, but the poor *campesinos*. Rural people can now purchase clothes that make work and day-to-day life easier and more comfortable. For the first time in their history, geographically isolated highland Indians can take ad-vantage of the textile industry's scientific innovations, even utilitarian space-age garments. A young *aldeaño* shopper told me his prize possession was his L.L. Bean Polartec vest which he wore against the winter chill at 9,000 feet. Yes, it was somewhat ratty when he bought it at the *Paca* for $2, but it cer-tainly did the trick in a household without a fireplace, where even blankets are scarce.

I counted ten Mam-speaking men in one *Paca* buying jeans or shirts for themselves and baby clothes for their children. They were from several far *aldeas* and had come to town—without their wives—to buy and sell in the market. Each one had some items in mind when he came in and knew what he could afford to spend. Clearly, they had been in *Pacas* before. One young man carried a *Jurassic Park* canvas bag, and another sported a fashionable mauve Polo t-shirt.

I was fascinated by a toothless old man whose pants had been mended many times before. Over and over, he examined a pair of Levi's, measuring the waistband around his neck to approximate his size. These pants—hardly worn—were of such sturdy denim that I thought they would likely last the rest of his life. Finally, he approached the owner and began to negotiate in earnest for the jeans. She had a price in mind and stuck to it for a minute or two, seemingly ignoring his efforts to bargain. In the end, she took his money with a grin when he quietly asked if he could please have them for Q7 ($1.25), because at that price he would still have his bus fare home.

Although many traditional women have taken to wearing modern *Paca* clothes in combination with *cortes,* some have abandoned *traje* entirely for

American garments. I could identify these women as Maya because even in their western garb, like most Indian women, they still wear their hair in one long braid and carry their babies in papooselike sheets on their backs. In that sense, they are maintaining the outward signs of their ethnicity. Their clothes, however, express none of that history. Again, I wondered, does this decision to abandon *traje* emerge from economic exigencies and the availability of alternative clothing? Or is it a more complicated turn away from an indigenous way of life?

A few hard-learned rules of clothing and ornament still apply. For example, most poor women *de traje* have two, or at the most, three *huipiles:* one for work, one for church or fiestas. Although *Paca* clothes are cheap, *aldea* women still only own one or two blouses which they wear until they disintegrate in the washing. Thus, you will see a woman in the same clothes day after day. Some women still own *huipiles,* but they only put them on for special occasions.

Women may occasionally buy *Paca* blouses or sweaters for themselves, but their children's clothing needs are far more pressing. Indian women spend a long time going through the piles of children's shirts, pants, dresses, and shoes. Maybe they will only purchase one item after a twenty-minute search, but the effort suggests the importance of the choosing. Clearly, theirs are children for whom indigenous clothing is not to be.

In sum, my observation of the *Paca* phenomenon demonstrates that as far as dress is concerned, the inroads of modernization and the pressures of stretching one's income have finally reached beyond the changing town to San Pedro's far *aldeas.* Until quite recently, indigenous identity and traditional rural way of life had been the crucial determinants of their dress. Now, I watched as women dressed themselves and their daughters in western clothes whose meaning was derivative and foreign. Pushed away from *huipiles* by the high prices and pulled into the *Pacas* by the low cost and high quality of the product, they were abandoning *traje* before my very eyes.

A Last Word

In this revised edition of *Silent Looms,* I want to welcome old and new readers to San Pedro Sacatepéquez, San Marcos, Guatemala. Looking back on what I have observed over twenty years, I am confident that what I wrote in the first edition of the book applies equally to women in the 1970s and to women today. Although specific economic scenarios have been somewhat transformed, I believe that *Silent Looms* continues to be an honest assessment of the problems women face when development undermines traditional productive and reproductive strategies or adaptations.

The last paragraph of *Silent Looms* is an optimistic scan of San Pedro's future where I suggested that women could be incorporated into the development process if they were more integrated into profitable external markets and businesses. This has not happened, and I was naïve to think that somehow it might. Unequal gender relations have persisted, denying most women a chance to benefit from the possibilities of modernization. The traditional foothold of female family businesses has ended in San Pedro, replaced with little more than minimally sustainable jobs or commercial ventures. Daughters who once supported women's enterprises by their labor are in school or struggling on their own to make a living in so-called modern occupations. Thus, women of all ages continue to find themselves on the margins of change, working on their own but without the skills, opportunity, or time to engage in potentially beneficial endeavors. Although new businesses like *Pacas* or Tapachula smuggling may appear to have promise as income-producing opportunities for some women, we have seen how both have far broader and potentially serious negative repercussions.

Since 1977, I have personally examined issues of gender and development not only in San Pedro Sacatepéquez, but also in San Antonio Palopó, Guatemala, San José, Costa Rica, and in Denver, Colorado. In each setting, I have focused on women whose productive efforts are circumscribed by their relegation to the domestic arena which severely constrains them as potential players in the wider business world. It is a daunting challenge for women to try to juggle production and reproduction, and although more and more women are participating in income-producing jobs and businesses, domestic responsibility means few realize the economic benefits accruing to men. As such, female participation in decision-making at the household and community levels is seriously diminished, thereby cutting short any attempt at establishing gender equality.

In the end, the question that emerges from this research is whether "women's work" must, by definition, be merely dead-end, labor-intensive extensions of housework. What kind of economic transformation would have to occur for *Sampedranas* to be pulled and/or pushed out of the house in significant numbers? I am not necessarily advocating the introduction of *maquilas,* where job opportunity is usually translated into exploitative labor conditions. Instead, I am wondering whether there is anything inherently valuable about "traditional" female businesses. New work and new relations of production can emerge that better serve women's needs. The challenge is to change the structure of production and the sexual division of labor so as to afford women the chance to take advantage of these new activities.

Tracy Bachrach Ehlers
Department of Anthropology, University of Denver
May 1999

Notes

1. All names used in this introduction are pseudonyms.

2. Although Richard Smith and I approach women and development from quite different perspectives, I clearly remain in his debt for first turning me in that direction.

3. Guided by this philosophy, in 1983 I gained sixteen pounds in eight months of fieldwork in Iowa where I was studying female farmers.

4. In 1987, I paid a visit to the military base in San Marcos to announce my presence in the town. The presidency of Vinicio Cerezo provided a façade of peace, but the army was still a force to be reckoned with. Although anthropologists were returning to Guatemala, we had to consider the safety of informants. In my case, I did not want to arouse any suspicion about my purposes, so I decided to be perfectly straightforward with the military as to why I was in town, a plan my *Sampedrano* friends thought would be advisable. I went to the base to present my credentials from the University of Denver, the City of Denver, and (via my representative, David Skaggs) the Congress of the United States. I confess to being nervous around so many guns, but mostly I was frightened of confronting the reality of the military presence. The experience ended up being a model of my own gender analysis of Guatemala. The *comandante* interviewed me in a room filled with personal souvenirs and photos of him doing active counterinsurgency in the region. But war wasn't on his mind. He used the visible evidence of his own masculinity to ask me to dinner. Meanwhile, I was trying my best to be as inconsequential as possible, explaining that all I was doing there was studying textiles and women weavers. In my nervousness, I forgot my speech about the value of social science in a changing world. Instead, I folded my hands and tried to look like a boring academic. Then, when he stopped talking (and puffing on his cigar) long enough to afford me the opportunity to speak, I made my excuses about dinner, saying I would, of course, be back. Then I got out of his office and off the base as fast as I could.

5. In an amazing series of events, the social chaos of the highlands became all too real to me during this fieldwork. For weeks, stories of lawlessness in the countryside dominated the papers. They had a common thread: despairing of ever finding justice or even a fair hearing for their complaints, citizens of small Mayan communities had taken the law into their own hands. Suspected trespassers, criminals, and thieves were being handcuffed, flogged, and even executed. Towns were demanding legal sovereignty (i.e., their own courts) for indigenous conflicts and crimes, a concept that confounded the chaotic, corrupt Guatemalan justice system. The odd word *"linchamiento"* told the whole story.

The shocking account of such an action in San Antonio Palopó (my second field site) awakened me to the urgency of these appeals.

The first TV news story said that three thieves had been caught by the locals about midnight. They had handcuffed them, but two ran away. A crowd gathered and set the last one on fire by pouring gasoline on him and striking a match. The next day, I saw the photo of the charred cadaver on the front page of the *Prensa* and realized, much to my horror and surprise, that the thief was a local! He was wearing the Tuneco *traje!* I recognized many faces standing around this victim of the *linchamiento*. They had burned alive one of their own.

It turned out the "thieves" were just drunken teenagers who had fallen from their barstools into the neighbor's patio below. Apparently, the resident had a long-standing grudge against these boys whom he suspected of robbing him earlier. In fact, the town had drawn up a list of local incorrigibles for the state authorities, and these young men were on it. Nothing had been done to stem the alarming tide of juvenile insubordination and crime. Angry and alarmed by this, the crowd made an example out of this wayward teen. They knew the police weren't going to do anything. Not only were there too few officers to cover petty crimes like theft, but criminals could escape punishment by paying off authorities anywhere along the line. People were frustrated enough to take the law into their own hands.

6. But these municipal figures underestimate the growth of fundamentalism considering that evangelical churches often spring up around self-proclaimed pastors who hold worship services in their homes without specifically signifying them as "churches."

7. My own attempts to even meet with a pastor (to whom I had an introduction from his sister) were stonewalled by his secretary. After grilling me about my own religious affiliation, she kept me waiting for more than an hour and then, without explanation, abruptly cancelled the meeting.

8. This troublesome trend toward indulgent middle-class status is clearly not applicable to everyone in the *municipalidad,* since only a third of the total population of approximately 73,000 lives in the city. Survival strategies that were true almost everywhere twenty years ago persist in the *aldeas*. For example, a 1996 study done by the city shows that, on the average, *aldea* children start working at age nine. Even thirty minutes from town, fifty percent of kitchens have dirt floors, eighty percent of births take place in the house, and forty-five percent of women over fifteen are illiterate, compared to fifteen percent female illiteracy in the *centro*. Still, forty-one percent of rural people own televisions, and in the three nearest *aldeas,* between fifty and eighty percent of households are viewers.

9. As to whether the *Paca* business (see below) will undermine the Santa Teresa weaving endeavors, we shall have to wait to determine.

10. Actually, Lucinda must be in her store to buy product. When her busy season begins in November, she must have at least one thousand *cortes* in inventory, so she needed to be available to weavers delivering their goods.

11. Lucinda's term for these rural women was *"amarillos,"* a term I found somewhat disparaging. She was referring to their traditionally yellow *cortes,* but I had never heard this word used to describe rural Indians. My sense of a class-based prejudice against those still living a traditional life was strong in this store as well as in other shops run by

educated people two generations or less from *traje*. For example, one afternoon I witnessed Lucinda's helper taunting a poor old woman interested in buying a simple cotton *corte*. The helper started by calling the woman *"abuelita,"* a personal diminutive term, to which the woman responded, "I'm *not* your grandmother! In fact, I'm a señorita and I don't have any children!" This made the young woman howl with laughter and only increased her delight in tormenting this customer. Oblivious, the woman asked to see some other *cortes,* but she was not to be accommodated. Only this one was right for her! This disrespect continued as the helper and a nearby friend teased the woman about the quality of the prospective purchase, insisting it was silk, when clearly it was not. The woman finally got fed up and fled, followed down the aisle by the mean-spirited laughter of the two young women.

12. My best information on the origin of this word is that it has been associated with low-status *comerciantes* or businessmen from El Salvador.

13. Good businesses in San Pedro can normally turn a profit of between eight and twelve percent. However, women's businesses are used to making quite a bit less, e.g., three percent. Thus, it is easy to understand the lure of the *frontera* and its easy money.

14. The term *"paca"* has two references. One is the bale of clothing itself *(paca)*. The other is the store where the clothes are sold *(Paca)*.

15. According to a *Los Angeles Times* report (Wilson 1997), there are more than one hundred used clothing dealers in U.S. port cities who have created a multimillion-dollar business exporting discarded or slightly damaged garments. Up to sixty percent of clothes donated to agencies like the Salvation Army and Goodwill are, in fact, sold to these middlemen who in 1996 sent 481 million pounds of second-hand clothes to Third World countries. In some areas, used clothes account for more than one-third of all clothing purchased (Haggblade 1990), and the trade is growing. The total value of used clothes traded internationally has risen from $229 million in 1984 to $782 million in 1993 (Bigsten and Wicks 1996), seventy percent of which takes place in Third World countries. According to Wilson's figures, Guatemala ranks tenth in the world in amount spent in the used-clothing trade ($1.53 million), and fifth in the world in metric tons of clothes imported.

16. One unanswered question about *Pacas* is why, in this overwhelmingly Catholic town, about half the owners are members of evangelical churches. Other scholars have written of the affinity of Guatemalan *evangélicos* for business (Annis 1987), but I believe the explanation lies neither in the Protestant work ethic nor in a new moral order, but in social status and word of mouth. *Pacas* are clearly an entrepreneurial niche that satisfies the search of many evangelicals for an economic expression of the social mobility suggested by their church membership. *Paca* ownership has spread to fellow church members through mutual support networks. In many ways, it is the same kind of pattern that explains why fifty percent of *Paca* owners have relatives in the same business.

17. The same is true of *sastres,* or tailors. Pants from the *Paca* cost about Q7 ($1.25) plus some small alteration, versus Q15–30 ($2.50–5.00) a yard for fabric and Q25 ($4.15) for labor at the tailor's shop.

1

Introduction

GLORIA FUENTES'[1] BABY lived long enough that people said it cried, but then minutes after birth it was dead. Infection from the anesthesia, they said. And now Gloria was gravely ill, bloated and feverish. I had gone to see her in the hospital as soon as I heard the news. She seemed near death. Yet she managed to whisper to me: "We'll have to celebrate later." No one had told her that her son had died.

We brought the dead baby home to prepare it for burial. In the car, I held the tiny, still warm body. Gloria's father, Braulio, brought a small coffin. In a short time, the living room was filled with mourning female relatives. The men—Gloria's teenage brothers and her uncles—had silently slipped away from the house. We dressed the baby in the white wool sweater and cap Gloria had crocheted. Calmly, the women passed the dead baby around, kissing him, touching his face, remarking how much he resembled Gloria. Then Tia Eli tied his hands in prayer, preparing the body for the makeshift religious services to come. The priest was away; we would have to say the words ourselves. Curtains were pinned up to erect an altar; the child laid upon it, his face covered. For a long time, everyone sat around quietly sighing or sobbing, saying little. It seemed I alone wondered why the baby had died so unexpectedly and why his well-fed and healthy mother was now so ill. The family refused to place blame, it being God's way to decide these things. Suddenly, Gloria's mother fainted and was revived with a sharp-smelling onion, some oregano and Tia Eli's coaxing to drink spoonfuls of water. Some time later, the baby was unofficially baptized Roberto Emanuel Jesús. Everyone went to sleep in little groups, sad, tired, and fully clothed.

Roberto would have been the first Fuentes Velásquez grandchild, under normal circumstances a cause for rejoicing in any Guatemalan family. But Gloria's pregnancy had not been celebrated. Instead, it had been an embarrassment and a source of dissension among family members. Her unmarried status alone was not problematic because so many women in the town bear their children out of wedlock. What set Gloria apart was that she had been the one to veto the marriage. She had been a teacher in a coastal school, coming home on weekends when she could. She had entered the affair out of loneliness and naiveté, but soon recognized the man's failings, all too familiar to Guatemalan women. He drank. He was jealous and covetous of her attentions and insistent on her devotion only to him. He, too, had been a teacher, but was now mostly unemployed, relying upon her to support him. He was needy, lazy, and demanding. In contrast, Gloria was hardworking, ambitious and independent; she had planned to go to college on Saturdays and Sundays in order to secure a better teaching job closer to home. She had a carefully designed future, and she could see that living with this man would ultimately destroy it. So when he suggested marriage, she refused. She came home and announced her decision to her astonished family. Then she set about preparing for her baby, oblivious to local gossip and the persistent advice of relatives and friends. She continued to teach, waiting out her pregnancy by helping with the various family businesses on weekends, and obsessively knitting and crocheting baby clothes.

I sensed that other women both respected and pitied her. They doubted that she would ever have another chance for marriage since few men wanted the responsibility of another man's child. But they understood her defiance of the normal pattern of unsatisfying sexual relations, followed by pregnancy and a quick marriage. They knew too well that life with men often resulted in conflict and separation. Nonetheless, they accepted that women were supposed to suffer, and indeed, Gloria Fuentes Velásquez fulfilled that anticipated and appropriate role with the death of her son.

Gloria survived her long illness, and eleven years later she is a respected teacher in a San Pedro school. She has been enrolled at the university in Quezaltenango, and has earned several advanced degrees. But while she has an active social life amid friends and fellow educators, she has never had another boyfriend. Nor have I ever heard her—or anyone else in the family—mention her dead baby.

Gloria is not a martyr to a patriarchal system; nor is she by any stretch of the imagination a crusader for female independence. Rather, Gloria is an example of the contradictory expectations for female roles in the home and in the workforce. Women in her town are expected to subordinate themselves to male domination, while at the same time being skillful and independent workers. They are socialized to accept a secondary status, to be obedient, and nurturing. Yet the family productive system is often based around their work, their cottage industry, and their market trade. Gloria herself expresses this contradiction. Over countless cups of coffee, she has told me again and again that although San Pedro has a proliferation of irresponsible husbands, they are not to blame for mistreating their wives. Instead, one should look to the failure of women to control and direct their own potential. After all, she has suggested, when a woman's whole life is bound up in her kitchen and her children, who can blame her husband for seeking out someone more interesting?

This book is about the women of San Pedro Sacatepéquez, a highland Guatemalan town. The town is a busy Indian commercial center, and its women, called *Sampedranas,* supply the majority of its traditional labor force. The book is about working women like Gloria, the women of her family, her neighbors, and co-workers; the woman who washes her clothes, the girl who sells her mangoes, the old grandmother who hobbles from house to house selling cheese. It is about the female family businesses that sustain San Pedro households: weavers, knitters, marketwomen, shopkeepers, traders, and the value of children to an economic system based upon the production and trade of petty commodities. It is also about love, sex, the ideal Latin American model for gender relations, and what sustains these roles. And it is about a changing and developing world where once autonomous women producers are being transformed into a dependent working class.

What originally interested me about San Pedro Sacatepéquez was the remarkable persistence of the family productive system, supported to a great extent by child labor. I wanted to study the value of children in rural and urban families. But after a few weeks in the town, I realized a more telling and critical picture would emerge if I refocused my anthropological lens. The reasons were simple, even obvious. As I became accustomed to the town's frenetic pace, I saw that many family productive systems—cottage industry, market activity, and commercial trade—hinged not on the labor of children but on the managerial efforts of women. It was a woman's job to bear children, serve her husband, and maintain the efficiency of the family's income producing efforts. To this end, she directed the labor of her children either to assist in production or to take care of the house and babies while the parents worked. Although I still wanted to examine the value of children, I decided to do this within a larger framework that concentrated on women. To do so meant that a new light might be shed on the impact of development on the town's women, and on its men as well. What roles, for example, had

Sampedranas played in the developing economy of the town? How did the entry of a modern consumer economy affect female interaction with men and influence productive activity? And, finally, were women able to take advantage of existing opportunities for increased economic and social power?

Because they were ready to step into marriage and the responsibilities of a family, post-pubescent women were the focus of my study. I emphasized their work, interactions with men, family lives and histories, and connections with other women. Of these, the first two—work and men—were most important both to *Sampedranas* and to me. Indeed, I spent the overwhelming majority of my time talking with women about the continuing struggle (*la lucha*) of earning a living and the constant battle of dealing with men.

The Town

Gloria Fuentes Velásquez and fourteen members of her family live in downtown San Pedro Sacatepéquez, in the state of San Marcos in the western highlands of Guatemala. San Pedro (urban pop. 15,000) is a successful and expanding Indian commercial center. Compared with the generational continuity found in most traditional highland communities, the contrast between the Fuentes family in 1938 and 1988 is remarkable. Before World War II, Gloria's grandmother walked forty kilometers every week to the busy market in Quezaltenango to sell her hand-woven textiles. Today, Gloria's brothers and sisters include three teachers, an engineer, a doctor, an agronomist, and a highly placed government civil servant. When they travel to Quezaltenango it is for college classes or to buy supplies for their successful farm. They may catch one of the dozens of buses stopping in San Pedro on its way to Guatemala City or travel in one of the three family cars. By any standard, the Fuentes Velásquez family is middle class. Two generations beyond itinerant textile traders, they continue to express the strong work ethic characteristic of the town's Indian population, but their hard work is quite richly rewarded. What is compelling about their professional achievements and consumer acquisitiveness is that they are not unusual *Sampedranos*. Their success story is one of hundreds, or to a lesser degree, thousands in the town, an anomalous and fascinating circumstance amidst the chronic impoverishment of the Guatemalan highlands.

Since World War II, San Pedro Sacatepéquez has experienced an unprecedented level of socioeconomic expansion. The form development has taken is the elaboration of local and regional trade, integration into the national and international market system, and the expansion of a transport network, which, taken together, has afforded the town's population a prodigious rise in its standard of living, particularly in terms of capital investments and personal consumption. In his book *The Fiesta System and Economic Change,* Waldemar R. Smith traces the town's dramatic growth curve and its impact on traditional religious organization, focusing on the entrepreneurial energies and fortunes of male informants. My study is more intimately female. I have written this book to show how the town's transformations have affected the lives of the women of San Pedro Sacatepéquez.

Early in my fieldwork I realized that San Pedro's rising standard of living, though an obvious measure of economic modernization, did not necessarily distribute the benefits of development equally by sex or class. In addition, growth did not always permit women to maintain whatever economic independence they had previously. It was also clear that a decrease in economic control for women led to a similar decrease in influence over other social relations. When women lost their customary autonomy in the handling of business or productive transactions, they lost influence in the exchange economy and became more dependent upon the productive efforts of men and subordinate in social and family life.

Closely linked to decreasing female status in San Pedro is the transition away from the "female family business." A clear consequence of development in San Pedro has been the replacement of traditional cottage industry with piece-work employment, and the relocation of business and small industry to sites outside the home and thus away from traditional family productive systems. The shift from female-controlled cottage industries to piece-work or jobs in factories, shops, or offices is accompanied by a re-evaluation of the value of children's contributions in monetary terms rather than their cooperative labor. Families recognize that by sending their children to school, their sons and daughters will some day bring home the salaries and prestige of teachers, accountants, and managers. As women lose their daughters to the jobs of a developing economy, they may be forced to abandon their independent businesses and may themselves become employees of more modern enterprises.

But modernization does not happen overnight. Data from the town and three nearby *aldeas* or villages—San José Caben, San Isidro Chamac, and La Grandeza—show that women continue to be active in the local exchange market, selling goods and services as a means to feed their families. Although the development of the town has provided continued access to profitable market relations for men, most rural women are too undercapitalized to exploit commercial opportunities effectively. In addition, rural women are handicapped by their persistence in traditional cottage industries and low-level trade relations that have few long-range returns. Thus, while men have energized their own small businesses through cooperatives or investment in transport, women have not been able to take advantage of these options.

This is not to say that development in San Pedro has not helped women at all, nor that women are not taking advantage of the diversity of productive opportunities that comes with modernization. To the contrary, women in the town and its *aldeas* continue to make a living by exploiting the multifaceted commercial relations that have made the town an economic oasis in the highlands. Women are by necessity intimately connected to the town's commercialism and they are most certainly aware of the importance of their hard work for the family's survival. Furthermore, as San Pedro has evolved away from traditional indigenous patterns and become more oriented toward western values, women have changed as well. In the last fifteen years, they have become enthusiastic students, even traveling an hour or more to night classes at the university; they have learned new skills appropriate to modern, semi-industrial businesses; and they have diversified their market trade to satisfy the more sophisticated tastes of the town's consumers. One must be impressed with the ability of these remarkable *Sampedranas* to adapt to whatever economic contingency occurs.

However, in spite of the eager participation of women in the town's developing economy, a problem arises when we take a closer look at the crucial variables that measure women's status, reflected here in terms of female control of production.[2] My research shows that with the town's increasing integration into the national and international economy, women in San Pedro encounter obstacles that prevent them from gaining or maintaining economic independence. In spite of their motivation to continue to contribute to the family income, women find that they no longer play as significant a role in production as they once did. Not only is their economic influence abating with the decline of the market for traditional female-based goods, but control over their own production—and the production of their children—has been diminished as well.[3] Those women who are benefiting from the town's economic changes tend to be middle-class, educated, and urban. Although the availability of education acts as somewhat of a class leveler that spreads the advantages of development to the rural poor, the process has been slow, and the pay-off in jobs disappointing. In short, although at first glance women seem to be successfully adjusting to the commercialism and vitality of the town through a multiplicity of new jobs and cottage industries, the appearance of effective adaptation is illusory. Some women are profiting from new opportunities, but for the majority, changing relations of production have actually deprived women workers of the economic control they once had.

To a certain extent, women maximize their productive potential by forming partnerships with men. In terms of male-female interaction, marriage in San Pedro is—practically speaking—the basis for successful economic survival. Marriage is based on the demands of the family productive system for workers—both adult and juvenile. Teenage infatuation initiates the cycle of illicit courtship, premarital sex, and pregnancy that propels couples toward marriage and the rapid development of a working family. Women take advantage of their children's labor—especially daughters—to enhance their small businesses, sometimes juggling three or even four income-producing activities. Men, who are far more commercially successful, play a lesser role in meeting the immediate needs of the family, because they tend to keep their monies for business and personal needs. As such, most women carry the lion's share of the responsibility for the household budget, and it is this need to feed and clothe the family that obligates women to work as hard as they do.

Overall, male-female relations in San Pedro are, for Guatemala, idiosyncratic. The town's ethnic and historical roots emerge from the traditional Mayan community, and a sizeable percentage of its rural residents live by and maintain those values. Moreover, the Mayan productive system, where couples are interdependent and mutually supportive, is still characteristic of many *Sampedrano* homes. At the same time, however, development is moving the urban population away from traditional modes of production and toward modern employment and increasing levels of female dependency. In line with this cultural dichotomy, *Sampedrano* marriages lie somewhere between the mutual complementarity and relative equality of marriages among traditional Mayan peasants[4] and the full-blown *machismo* that characterizes marriages of middle-class *ladinos* in which men maintain dominance through female economic dependence.[5] All indigenous *Sampedranos* work, and to one extent or another, the sexes rely upon each other. But the marital waters are muddied by social mobility and the adoption of national values more representative of their new affluence. The town partially expresses its evolution toward being middle class by encouraging *macho* behavior, and, to a lesser extent, the near *aldeas* follow suit. Although men and women acknowledge the need to cooperate, there is also a mutual antipathy in their interaction. Thus, while men respect their wives as hard workers without whose efforts most families would starve, they eagerly anticipate the day when their economic success will be measured by the complete dependence of their nonworking wives. For their part, although women know they must marry and have children, they mistrust men and expect the worst from them, and although there are stable and happy marriages in San Pedro, many men— urban or rural—live up to the *macho* image of unreliability, philandering, drinking, and wife abuse. After years of witnessing and comforting women in distress, I have reluctantly concluded that women are enculturated to passively accept psychological and physical abuse from men not only for the status suffering provides, but more importantly, in order to keep men around long enough to father their children. By enduring the sexual relations they fear, women become pregnant, a much-desired status that assures them future material aid and emotional stability. They know that while men may come and go, they can always rely upon their children's labor and their love.

Not all *Sampedranas* are forced to exploit male virility in this way. As the case of Gloria Fuentes illustrates, development has afforded educated and economically mobile women the advantage of being able to reject unsuitable men because they can rely upon their own productive potential. In a community where marriage is a normal part of a woman's life, voluntary spinsterhood or single parenthood seems like anomalous female social rebellion, but it may become a viable alternative to marriage for those with sufficient resources to go it alone.

Being in the Field

During much of my San Pedro research I spent long hours comfortably chatting, laughing, sympathizing and watching silently while *Sampedranas* went about their daily activities. I worked with dozens of women in town and the *aldeas,* but it was as a member of the Fuentes Velásquez household that I had a particularly favorable seat to witness the drama of local family and social life. The household centered around a widowed sister in her late fifties, her middle-aged brother, his wife, and their three daughters (15, 21, and 28) and four sons (17, 19, 22, and 27). It was a fortuitous circumstance for me because the family was educated, upwardly mobile, and epitomized the transformations taking place in the town. I was witness both to the pressures to spend money and the constraints of constant debt. I watched while jobs and domestic responsibilities were juggled with long bus rides to an urban college and midnight bus rides home. On another, more intimate level, the tensions and tragedies of their family life were always open to me. My closeness with family members meant I was privy to the courting rituals of the teenagers, the hidden but seething hostility between wife and sister-in-law, and to the hurried deliverance of a diagnosis of Don Braulio's terminal cancer by a doctor on his way to lunch.

In order to put this sort of personal reality into a cultural context and to provide some systematic historical framework, I also conducted extensive archival research. In Guatemala City I found the national censuses still being compiled and analyzed by hand. For many long. dusty hours, I rummaged through two hundred years of San Pedro church records on marriages and baptisms to establish precedents for single motherhood. My research afforded me entry into the town's vital statistics usually kept under lock and key. Educators cheerfully handed over chronicles that documented dramatic growth in female school attendance. And the town's only gynecologist allowed me to copy his careful records of every hospital birth since the 1960s. I formally surveyed one hundred women from San Pedro and five *aldeas,* and collected nearly fifty life histories. In addition, I was fortunate to have access to the surveys and computer analyses done by Smith and Wilson in 1973, which complemented (and occasionally corrected) many subjective generalizations developed while in the field.

On my return visits to San Pedro in the summers of 1987–88, I visited dozens of informants to bring my data on women and the town up to date. I walked every street and three *aldeas* to chronicle the physical changes, in particular the development of non-traditional commercial enterprises. The civil servants in the office of the Christian Democratic mayor, a family friend, took an interest in me and were very helpful. Ten years before, I had had great difficulty extracting civic records, but the new mayor—elected with Cerezo in 1985—made the archives available. I also administered a follow-up survey in San José Caben on profession, costume, education, and marriage status.[6]

What had been a difficult and lonely trip through the fieldwork maze in 1977 seemed a comfortable visit with family and friends ten years later. I was also older, had other fieldwork experiences, and felt more relaxed about the direction I knew my work was taking. The second time around, I did not feel compelled to "grill" the women I visited. Time was no longer a rare commodity that would run out on me before I wrested from them every fact I sought. We caught up, gossiped, and enjoyed each other's company.

Being a woman had a distinct influence on my fieldwork. I never consciously attempted to be an asexual fieldworker (Bujra 1975), but being a married North American without her husband in a Latin American country did complicate my role as a researcher and added to my already misunderstood status. The first time in the field, I lived alone in an apartment upstairs in the Fuentes household for almost twelve months, although my husband did visit me at regular intervals. While (and perhaps because) my status was somewhat ambiguous (i.e., alone but married, adult and student, thirty but childless, woman and scientist), I gained access to almost every area I cared to investigate, which included witnessing the midnight birth of a baby, participating in nine prayer nights of a *novena,* and even taking part in planning the rescue of a kidnapped child. Women would confide in me their problems, fears, hopes, and doubts that many never dared express to others. I think this was largely because I asked questions about their lives that no one had asked before and because they were curious about me, based on rumors of *gringo* stereotypes and the fact that in my work I flagrantly violated many rules set down for married Guatemalan women. Part of this rule-breaking behavior was discussing all kinds of inviolate topics with men as well as women.

Despite baseless warnings from friends living in Guatemala that working closely with men would compromise my reputation with women, I always spoke to men, be they husbands, relatives, friends of my female informants, or casual acquaintances. The local officials and professionals were exclusively men (with one exception, a woman lawyer), as were many merchants and weavers. Access to men was not as straightforward as it was to women, and initially, I was often exasperated by bureaucrats who failed to keep appointments or businessmen who brushed me off when I arrived for a scheduled interview. Rural men were consistently polite and helpful. Where I faced difficulties was with upwardly mobile men, particularly *ladinos* who often were uncomfortable talking to me as an equal. I persisted, believing that over time I would establish my credentials so that even the busiest or most highly placed official would make time for an interview. Indeed, by my third month in San Pedro, bank officers, lawyers, and government officials were polite, available, and very helpful.

Aloof and distant informants were not my only problem with men. I also confronted the character of the *macho* Guatemalan male, who treats women as sexual objects. This embarrassed and confused me and quickly became a nuisance. In a sense, having to deal with men in this way helped me appreciate the exasperation of *Sampedranas* and Guatemalan women in general about *los hombres latinos*. Very few women had anything good to say about men, most seeing them as irresponsible liars who could be counted on to chase other women, drink to excess, and gamble away their money. They were said to exploit the hard work of their wives and children, whom they treated like slaves, and were generally of no use whatsoever. Although I found women tended to exaggerate in their negative assessment of men, I could not help but empathize with their helpless, frustrated sense of martyrdom.

Because I am a woman who could be both social scientist and confessor, my approach was characterized by access to the personal intimacy of the female world. In examining first hand the dynamics of romance, sex, and the economics of the male-female relationship, I looked at Guatemalan society from the bottom up. A poignant story illustrates this phenomenon.

It all began in June, 1977. I had been in Guatemala City for the weekend, and as I emerged from the bus, I encountered my neighbor and friend, Doña Beatriz Ochoa, who was in a state of near-hysteria. She tearfully explained that while I was gone, it had been disclosed that César—her youngest and handsomest son—had impregnated his *novia,* Ana Gabriela, and worse, they had been married at the insistence of her family. Ana Gabriela was at this time six months pregnant and the gossip about the couple had finally reached her mother's ears. César's father had been immediately summoned to Ana Gabriela's home by her father—one of the town's leading citizens—to receive the news and to agree to an immediate wedding. As it turned out, everyone later agreed that this was the worst possible choice of action. Hindsight provided several honorable and practical alternatives such as Ana Gabriela's moving to her relatives' house in Guatemala City to have the baby, who would then be raised by Ana Gabriela's mother. Had this happened, Ana Gabriela would have gone to the university as planned; César could have finished high school and then accepted the scholarship his mother had procured to the Guatemalan West Point. As it was, they were banished from her family's good graces and came to live in César's already overcrowded family home.

At age 16, César had to forego his hopes for higher education and a career as an army officer in order to support his wife and daughter. Ana Gabriela, a pampered and spoiled child, now came under the direction of an angry and hostile mother-in-law who blamed her for shattering a mother's dreams for her son's future. The situation was exacerbated by Ana Gabriela still being "very much a girl" in her new family's eyes. Their bedroom, for example, was filled with pictures of movie stars. She was inappreciative of the sacrifice the family was forced to make for her, and, when the baby was born, she was inept at caring for the child or helping in any of the family businesses. For fear of getting pregnant again and because sex held no interest for her ("it was over so fast"), for a time she refused César's sexual advances. (Surprisingly, despite her education and sophisticated family, Ana Gabriela knew almost nothing at all about birth control.) So Beatriz cried every day, her daughters "tsked" constantly and speculated as to the future of this liaison, the two families seemed permanently estranged, and the couple was resentful of the severe limitations each placed on the professional and personal future of the other.

This unpleasant conflict seemed on the way to an ordinary recovery by the following year when I paid a brief visit. By that time what had seemed an unendurable heartbreak for both families had been accepted, absorbed, and pushed into the background in time for another crisis, the serious illness of Ana Gabriela's father, Don Julio. Indeed, when I returned to San Pedro in

1985, I found a very relaxed and happy Ana Gabriela running the Ochoa's store and taking care of her young daughter and baby son while César went to law school in Quezaltenango! Since then, this young and initially flighty couple have spearheaded the development of a sophisticated wholesale vegetable business that has added considerably to the family's income. César has become a lawyer but, because he spends most of his time at their vegetable gardens in Chamac, has not opened a practice. Instead, when people from that *aldea* need legal advice, they may seek him out at home where the success of his business allows him the luxury of treating them at no cost. Ana Gabriela has given birth to two more children, but still manages childcare, housework, and retail vegetable sales. She is a reader of fine Spanish-language fiction, watches American movies on TV, and handles all the store's financial matters. Ironically, in light of his past indiscretions, César has become the head of the Ochoa family. Although he has two older brothers, his leadership in developing the family business has positioned him well domestically. A marriage begun in teenage passion has flowered into mutual respect, sincere concern, and open affection rare among Guatemalans.

What emerges from this and countless similar episodes is the passion and yet the ordinariness of the daily scene. Indeed, it is the frequent repetition of similarly catastrophic and melodramatic events that provides the key for unraveling the mystery of social interaction in San Pedro Sacatepéquez.

The Political Background

In the decade after Gloria Fuentes lost her baby, the Guatemalan people were confronted with a dramatic and tumultuous political situation from which they have still not emerged. From 1978 to the election of President Vinicio Cerezo Arevalo in 1985, the country was ruled by a series of brutal military governments. To isolate insurgents and their presumed grassroots supporters in the Indian highlands, three successive generals—Romeo Lucas Garcia, Efrain Ríos Montt, and Oscar Mejia Víctores—launched campaigns of terror against their own people. Nearly 200,000 were killed or "disappeared" in the process of undermining what the military labeled Communist-inspired revolutionary activities. Also targeted was what Sheldon Annis has called the social fabric of the country:

> Scores of mayors and anyone foolish enough to be called a "leader" were shot. The cooperative movement, which had been built over nearly twenty years with funding and technical assistance from AID, was decimated. The previously ubiquitous local structures of *técnicos, promotores,* and village-level *comités*—the most common means used

by private voluntary organizations and even government ministries to transfer resources for village-level activities—were suddenly invisible or paralyzed, unable to implement even the most mundane of development activities. (1988:7)

The events of the last ten years have witnessed the demise of the popular movement, personal atrocities, the destruction of the countryside, and the displacement of nearly one million people who sought safety in the mountains, in camps in Mexico, and as refugees in American cities.[7] The election of Cerezo occasioned much valuable debate on the possible rebirth of a legitimate political movement amidst persistent human rights abuses (Painter 1987). Elsewhere, writers have focused on some unexpected repercussions of the guerrilla war (C. Smith 1988, Torres-Rivas 1985, Stoll 1988, Earle 1988, Manz 1988). New work documenting the changes wrought by this decade of violent repression appears regularly.

This relatively recent chronicling of the impact of military presence is particularly welcome because until 1987 when Cerezo's civilian presidency was well established, it had been difficult for researchers to work in Guatemala. Death squads and government forces potentially dangerous to informants and friends made extensive fieldwork more than difficult. Since so much anthropological work was focused in the volatile western highlands, many targeted communities were well-known to ethnographers. Each of us had horror stories from our villages and towns to recount. Colleagues living in Guatemala more or less permanently had fled during the early 1980s, fearing that they were next to be kidnapped, tortured, and murdered. The establishment by the government of paramilitary civilian patrols in rural communities, to search locally for "subversives" divided these communities against themselves. Given this climate, many researchers feared not only for their safety but for the lives of local people who by association with Westerners might generate unwarranted suspicion. So, until the last few years, many of us involved in Guatemalan social research had discouraged one another from attempting more than brief visits and, accordingly, switched our emphasis from fieldwork to sociopolitical analysis and human rights advocacy (see Davis 1983, Paul 1986, Brintnall 1983, Stoll 1983). Now, after nearly a decade, anthropologists—myself included—are returning once more to Guatemala.

San Pedro Sacatepéquez in Ten-Year Perspective

I first went to live in San Pedro Sacatepéquez in December 1976. I stayed a year and later made some predictions about the demise of female family business and the resulting decline in the status of women (Ehlers 1980, 1982). Curious about the veracity of my forecast and eager to see firsthand how San Pedro had fared amidst the political and socioeconomic turmoil of the past decade, I returned in 1985, 1987 and again in 1988. What I found is that San Pedro is different from many other towns and villages in the highlands in that it has emerged largely unscathed from military attacks on the indigenous population. This surprised me since San Pedro finds itself just outside ORPA (Organization of the People in Arms) insurgency operations on the *fincas* and among the smaller community of the coastal plain.[8] I had anticipated that like towns in Quiché and Huehuetenango, San Pedro's close proximity to an area of military-guerrilla activity would severely affect the town. What I found was quite different. In general terms, the considerable army presence three miles away (a military base for three thousand troops was established in 1983) creates an atmosphere of nervousness and suspicion, but the military itself is not the most crucial variable for explaining change in San Pedro. In fact, the consensus is that relations with the military are much better than they have been for years. In the early 1980s, almost everyone in the town had heard or read about torture and massacres as nearby as Tumbador or Tajumulco, and many people had had personal contacts with uniformed "bandits" who attacked and robbed them on the highways, a sign of the lawlessness endemic in the highlands. Encounters with insurgents were, as now, limited to people in cars being stopped on the road to hear political messages, and little more.

Three prominent citizens were assassinated in 1980. One, Rosalinda Cabrera, was a lawyer with whom I had worked in 1977. Her brutal murder by automatic weapon fire in front of her young children still baffles *Sampedranos*. The second victim was José Luis Juárez Romero, the mayor of the town, who had a history of supporting the rural poor with loans and civic improvements. Then-President Lucas Garcia had summoned public employees to Guatemala City to demonstrate in support of his government. In all likelihood, Juárez' public opposition to that order had marked him for death. Later, the leader of a teachers' strike in the neighboring town of San Marcos was also killed, and the strike postponed.

Currently, the town's apprehensions regarding the military have to some extent diminished. Citizens are still hesitant to go out alone at night; raucous, drunken soldiers have been rumored to attack lone youths and women. The presence of armed soldiers, or "*cuques*" as they are called, in the market or at dances always occasions some negative reactions. Nonetheless, the town has grown accustomed to—if not actually welcomed—the army, in part because the army spends nearly seventy-five percent of its food budget locally. In addition, the construction of the base was a much-needed tonic for the local economy; three hundred people from the San Pedro-San Marcos area are still employed there as drivers, nurses, administrators, seamstresses, cooks, typists, and laborers.[9]

While on the local level, the military appears, at least for the present, to be playing an innocuous role in the town's affairs, on the national level, this is certainly not the case. The hard currency the government spends on weapons and counterinsurgency operations, combined with a serious trade and monetary crisis begun in the early 1980s, has plunged Guatemala into an inflationary tailspin. The consequences of this fiscal miasma (discussed more fully in Chapter Two) have been widespread in the highlands, and they have not sidestepped San Pedro.

In 1977 I noted a downturn in traditional female cottage industry taking place within a context of a remarkable growth in commercial activity. For the last twenty years, the movement away from traditional indigenous behavior and values in San Pedro Sacatepéquez has been fueled by growing media access and a popular national and international orientation. Recently, however, the town's tendency toward assimilation has been rapidly accelerated by national economic patterns beyond its control, specifically, the 1985 drop in the value of the national currency, the *quetzal*,[10] and a concomitant rise in the cost of living. This situation plunged thousands of marginal domestic producers of all kinds into desperate straits, essentially curtailing the upward mobility that had seemed within their grasp and forcing them to scramble for survival. In particular, producers of the indigenous *huipil* (who were slowly losing their market share during my early fieldwork) were quite suddenly out of business. With retail prices quadrupled to meet the nearly exponential rise in costs of imported threads, no one was buying *huipiles*. *Sampedranas,* whose mothers and grandmothers wore the locally produced Indian costume, were now buying only cheap polyester blouses produced outside the town. In short, the anticipated long-term direction of sociocultural change my research had predicted ten years before came to pass in a few tumultuous years.

This description of the local implications of national military policy may seem somewhat anticlimactic given more dramatic accounts of counterinsurgency campaigns from Quiché or Huehuetenango. Neither this brief narrative nor the book that follows deals with genocide or dislocation. Nor does it provide a backdrop for understanding massive political rehabilitation or religious conversion. I leave that work to those who have studied communities heavily and immediately affected by military repression and/or the socio-political changes often connected to it. But San Pedro does not exist

in a cultural or economic vacuum. Although the military seems to be playing a relatively benign role in the town's affairs, the sociopolitical consequence of national military policy has been extremely relevant here, responsible for a serious deterioration of the town's most crucial variable, economic
potential.

Guatemalan Gender Studies

Like the unusual and idiosyncratic nature of the town, this book on the women
of a Guatemalan community is a departure from traditional Mesoamerican
anthropology. Until recently, Guatemalanists neglected the status of women
as a legitimate subject, turning their attention to females only when examining life cycle events such as birth and marriage in which women cannot
easily be ignored (Bossen 1983, 1984). Perusing the ethnographic material
on Guatemala, one sees women as peripheral actors outside the areas where
anthropologists have traditionally concentrated their efforts, namely religion, economy, or ideology. Within these larger topics, women were not
studied because, more often than not, researchers assumed these to be exclusively male concerns. Critics point to western androcentric biases to explain this, but in part it may also be due to the inability of anthropologists—
male or female—to utilize Mayan languages to communicate with women
who, more often than men, are monolingual (Tumin 1952). For example,
Bunzel admits in *Chichicastenango* that her major informant's wife was a good
friend, but because the anthropologist did not speak Quiché, the two women
could not really converse (1952). Another reason may be that Guatemalanists rarely employed women as informants, even when they recognized their
authority and expertise (LaFarge 1947).[11]

In spite of the marginalization of women as subjects, some small gems of
information about female roles and statuses can be gleaned from classic texts.
The subordinate position of women in Indian communities often emerges,
particularly in the analysis of marriage patterns (Oakes 1951, Wagley 1949)
and in the maintenance of ethnic boundaries (Tumin 1952). Occasionally,
female status based upon the monopoly of economic resources is addressed,
for example in Reina's (1966) examination of Chinautla's pottery industry,
which allows women to produce cash surpluses large enough to make them
major donors to church rituals. Unfortunately, in spite of these few illus-
trations, discussions of male/female relations have been theoretically unin-
formed and cursory, resulting in superficial and often contradictory analyses. This intellectual gap in the development of women as valid topics for

study is a sad reminder of many lost opportunities for research. Nearly two generations of acculturation, national political conflict, and change have erased many of the traditional patterns described in these early ethnographies. So we may never know why female *chimanes* (shamans) disappeared in Todos Santos (Oakes 1951), or whether men in Chichicastenango did indeed whip their wives during hard deliveries to punish them for their sins (Bunzel 1952).[12] Not a research priority decades ago, understanding of sexual inequality among these Maya remains elusive.

A few ethnographers have focused on Guatemalan women, but briefly, and in a manner peripheral to their main body of work. For example, with more than forty years of fieldwork in San Pedro la Laguna, the Pauls produced two articles on women (L. Paul 1974, Paul and Paul 1975); both were useful, and it is lamentable that more has not emerged from that Tzutujil town. From the same geographic region on Lake Atitlán, Tax's *Penny Capitalism* is somewhat exceptional for including several valuable descriptions of women's work as agriculturalists, petty commodity producers, and traders in Panajachel, as well as a brief but fascinating analysis of the marriage patterns of rich and poor women. Tax differs from many other Guatemalanists of his period in that he treated women as equal members of the community whose pattern of production, inheritance, and wealth he wished to investigate. Yet, many topics central to an explication of women's status in Panajachel are not addressed.

More recently, it is especially disappointing that attention has not been paid to Guatemalan women in light of the country's dramatic evolution away from its Indian identity since World War II, and the personal and social disorganization that has accompanied the demise of the traditional way of life (see Brintnall 1979, Hinshaw 1979, Colby and van den Berghe 1969, Hill and Monaghan 1987). Bossen, reviewing this literature (1983), criticizes many contemporary writers for this bias, yet she suggests that the scarcity of information on women's roles and status may be turning around. She points to Maynard (1963), Chinchilla (1977), Ehlers (1980), and Irías and Alfaro (1977) as writers interested in the analysis of female roles in Guatemala. Each considers women as members of a labor market with evolving productive and familial options within the developing nature of the Guatemalan economy. But these works are few, and I agree with Bossen that for this period,

> Taken together, the corpus of information on Guatemalan women is thin; the search for information leads to data that are fragmented, incomplete, and frequently laced with generalizations for which supporting evidence is not provided.

Since Bossen's 1983 review, several new ethnographic books and articles dealing with Guatemalan women have appeared. A few, like Bossen's own investigation of the status of women in four communities, take place outside the critical period of the military repression and terrorism (the *"situación"*) begun in the late 1970s. Researched in 1974–75, *The Redivision of Labor: Women and Economic Choice in Four Guatemalan Communities* proposes that sexual differences in the Third World are heightened as result of capitalist development. The most ambitious and thorough study of Guatemalan women and development to date, Bossen's book compares the status of women and men *within* each of four communities, while also contrasting the degree of sexual stratification *among* the four, "each representing important socioeconomic segments of Guatemalan society" (1984: 14). By examining women's roles in a rural Mayan village, a coastal plantation, an urban middle-class neighborhood, and a squatter settlement, Bossen provides ample evidence suggesting that the further the society is from subsistence level, the more women's work is minimized with development and the more dependent women become.

Sheldon Annis' *God and Production in a Guatemalan Town,* based on fieldwork during the late 1970s and early 1980s, takes as its theme one of the indirect consequences of highland counterinsurgency: the rise of Protestantism in San Antonio Aguas Calientes. Annis acknowledges the tense period in 1982 when General Ríos Montt instituted his infamous "Bullets and Beans" policy that brought a reign of terror to the countryside. Mainly, however, he is interested in Ríos Montt's born-again Protestant zeal, which opened wide the doors to fundamentalist missionizing and conversion throughout the highlands.[13]

The focus of *God and Production* is the linkage between Indian identity and Indian economy, and its unraveling in the 1980s, an event that parallels the rising popularity of Protestant sects. But where do women enter the picture? Annis' choice for the most "emblematic" element in indigenous culture, most imbued with the meaning of Indianness, is backstrap weaving. Because women are traditional weavers, two chapters of the book are devoted to their work as producers and textile entrepreneurs. In asking why women weave, Annis is filling in the Catholic/Protestant dichotomy he establishes early in the book. Using the ancient relation between religion and production as his metaphor, the author coins the term *"milpa* logic" as an expression of what it means to be Indian. Since the colonial period, *milpa* logic has been associated with Catholicism and, among other things, the value given to weaving as a symbolic Indian act and ethnic expression. Meanwhile, there are anti-*milpa* forces working to undermine community identification, specifically Protestant *"suelo del cielo"* thinking that rejects indigenous communalism in favor of individual achievement. In terms of weaving, Protestant personal gain is expressed in the emphasis on the commercial potential of woven goods.

Despite Annis' comfortable familiarity with women—he apprenticed himself to two weavers, one Protestant and one Catholic—his analysis is tantalizingly abbreviated. For example, the question of who wears *huipiles* and who does not, as he sees it, is based upon religious preference alone. In fact, as we shall see, it is only one variable among many.

Because of the turbulent times, many newer works deal with human rights violations and the impact of military repression on highland Indians. Of these, one focuses exclusively on women, and in this case, it is a life history of a revolutionary woman from Quiché, Rigoberta Menchú. Edited by Elisabeth Burgos-Debray, *I, Rigoberta Menchú* faithfully describes Rigoberta's struggle, often in agonizing detail. Beyond Rigoberta's role as a participant in grassroots insurgency and a witness to highland atrocities (her brother's public torture, her mother's death), what makes the book especially valuable are the chapters on a woman's life in a traditional Maya village. For the first time, we are privy to the exigencies of impoverishment and isolation as well as the meaningful continuity of tradition from a female perspective. In her recounting of the death of a dear friend sprayed with insecticide while picking cotton on a coastal plantation, she says,

> And that friend of mine had left me with many things to think about. She used to say that she would never get married because marriage meant children and if she had a child she couldn't bear to see him die of starvation or pain or illness. (88)

In a chapter titled "Lessons taught her by her mother: Indian women and ladino women" Rigoberta vividly relates her own enculturation about what women can and should do:

> My mother had the same idea of women as our women had had in the past. They were very strict and believed a woman should learn her womanly occupation so that she could live and face many things. And she was right. Because we can see a difference. My father was very tender and always protected me. but it was my mother who coped with the big problems in our family. (219)

Later, Rigoberta decides to forego marriage while involved in political activities, despite the fact that

> . . . for us marriage is something joyful (because the concept our ancestors had was that our race must not die out and we must follow our traditions and customs as they did) . . . (223)

Her reasons are clear:

My idea is, though, that there will be time enough after our victory; but at the moment I wouldn't feel happy having a *companero* and giving myself to him while so many of our people are not thinking of their own personal happiness and haven't a single moment to rest. (225)

In all, *I, Rigoberta Menchú* provides long-absent information on Guatemalan women and some of the richest ethnographic detail available on the Maya. The vitality of the narration is remarkable, particularly in her consistent and passionate remembrances of the ancestors' guidance. Furthermore, it reminds us that Mayan women are not a generic type of mother, midwife, or weaver. Rigoberta, by her own account an ordinary woman from Quiché, rose above the limits imposed upon her by history, culture, and poverty to become a heroine, a leader, and a spokesperson for her people.

Previous Studies of San Pedro Sacatepéquez

Very little ethnographic research in Guatemala has been about highland towns like San Pedro Sacatepéquez. Overwhelmingly, Guatemalan anthropology has emphasized small-scale, isolated, indigenous communities (e.g., Tax 1953, Tumin 1952, Oakes 1951, Bunzel 1952, Reina 1966, Paul and Paul 1963). When social change or economic development oriented the work, the village still remained the focus of analysis (e.g., Nash 1958, Brintnall 1979, Annis 1988, Warren 1978, Colby and van den Berghe 1969, Hinshaw 1975). Some attention has been paid to markets in towns (e.g., Goldin 1986, Swetnam 1973, McDowell 1976), but Tax's (1937) early article on *municipios* aside, few writers have studied towns larger than 10,000 people. Carol Smith's voluminous writing on Totonicapán is an important exception to this trend (see Smith 1977, 1978, 1983, 1984, 1988). Based on research since the early 1970s, Smith has generated theoretical and economic models of how commerce, ethnicity, and history can combine to provide an Indian town with a successful economic life-style amidst many poorer communities. Overall, Smith attributes Totonicapán's economic vitality to the lack of lower-level competition, resulting in the town being able to service a wide area (1977). As such, commercial stagnation in its hinterland benefits the entrepreneurs of Totonicapán. Ironically, amidst a thriving market for cottage industry, locals exacerbate this skewed commercial relationship by exclusively utilizing indigenous workers. Smith asserts that Totonicapán's sense of community, class consciousness, and ethnic solidarity prevent individual employers from maximizing their own economic interests by hiring cheaper external labor (1984).

The parallelism of San Pedro Sacatepéquez to Totonicapán is not lost to Carol Smith. She ascribes the same reasons for the towns' commercial supremacy, although San Pedro remains for her on a lower level in the larger highland commercial network. W. R. Smith's (1975, 1977) explanation, while comparing the town's diversity and growth with economically stagnant villages in its region, downplays their commercial linkages. He is more concerned with San Pedro's large size and its fortuitous geographic location between highland and lowland markets where it has been able to take advantage of transport needs. In addition, motivated by intercity ethnic competition, *Sampedranos* have utilized their family productive systems and the entrepreneurial tendencies of the population to successfully wrest control of commerce and industry from neighboring *ladinos*. The result has been an Indian monopoly on commercial endeavors. Not only have commercial weavers, traders, and truckers greatly expanded their businesses since World War II, but employment and educational opportunities for their children have burgeoned as well. Smith argues that the effect of this change in less than two generations has been a cultural orientation more in line with national *ladino* values. At the same time, he suggests that because they can take advantage of socioeconomic mobility within the confines of their own Indian town, *Sampedranos* do not find it necessary to identify themselves as *ladinos* in order to get ahead.

W. R. Smith's work on San Pedro Sacatepéquez made a major contribution to our understanding of economic development and sociocultural change in Mesoamerica. His work on the relation between ethnicity and economic mobility, however, focuses entirely on male entrepreneurs, and his informants are almost exclusively men. Smith neglects women as economic actors, despite the prominent role they play in petty commodity production and trade. His conclusion about the positive impact of development is based upon an assumption common to many androcentric writers that if men are beneficiaries of economic mobility, those benefits can be generalized to the entire community (Nash 1976). My study complements Smith's analysis by showing that while development means a higher standard of living overall, it also results in a disproportionate *decrease* in female status in terms of economic control.

John Hawkins' book, *Inverse Images: The Meaning of Culture, Ethnicity, and Family in Postcolonial Guatemala,* approached San Pedro Sacatepéquez from a completely different, one might say "opposite," perspective from Smith's economic analysis. Hawkins applies semiotic structuralism to an examination of what it means to be an Indian in San Pedro in relation to what it means to be a *ladino* in neighboring San Marcos. Hawkins tries to contrast ethnic beliefs and behaviors as being based on inverse ideologies developed during Spanish domination of Latin America. Thus, he argues that being Indian acquires meaning only in opposition to being *ladino,* and vice versa. The basis for this theory is Hawkins' supposition that Indian culture is not derived from the pre-Colombian Maya, but is instead merely a negative interpretation of Spanish-*ladino* ideology. For example, *ladino* is high status, Indian low status; *ladino* is urban, Indian rural. *Ladinos* are adaptable and open, with wide-reaching affiliations; Indians are atomistic and restricted within the ideational and political isolation of the closed corporate community. Hawkins, unlike Smith, devotes several pages of his book to women's work and family life. His examination, however, is sketchy at best. At times, he admits that his analysis (with regard to marriage patterns, for example) is mostly speculative and/or based on flawed census or survey data. Also, in most of these discussions, women are categorized as secondary producers and earners, helping husbands in their work while managing their own minor businesses as a sideline. This skewed perspective is consistently reinforced by citing males alone as heads of households, a particularly short-sighted assessment in a town so thoroughly based upon female petty commodity production and trade within family productive systems. Finally, Hawkins' analysis of women's contribution to family income in relation to marriage instability is marred by his attempt to support his "inverse ideology" theory by setting women's supporting role in opposition to men's dominating role. He states:

> The respect for the woman's labor power and the value of her income counterbalances the centrifugal force of her ability to be independent. Apparently, as a result the conjugal failure rate balances out at about the same level as that of San Marcos. Rather than less divorce or separation, the San Pedro woman gets more respect. (317)

But as I will show, male-female interaction is far more volatile, reflecting the dramatic socioeconomic changes that are seriously altering the town.

The approach of this study of San Pedro Sacatepéquez is at once ethnographic and personal. My curiosity about and affection for the women of San Pedro, nurtured over more than a decade, encouraged me to write about them as real people who are players in a larger cultural reality as well. This book attempts to do that in the context of women's relationship to the rapid expansion of the town's economy and its modernizing worldview. The title, *Silent Looms,* specifically refers to the traditional weavers who have been especially impacted by development and social change. As the town's economic profile evolves toward a cosmopolitan and national model, ethnic identification expresses itself in new ways too. The silencing of looms means more than women being put out of work. In the implicit rejection of indigenous clothing as no longer relevant to the new, more worldly *Sampedrana,* it also says that with development the town has taken a decisive step toward a new future. The chapters ahead examine the implications of that step for the women of San Pedro Sacatepéquez.

Notes

1. Names and personal details of all my informants have been changed in order to protect their privacy. I retained the surnames common to the town (e.g., Fuentes, Orozco, Velásquez, Ochoa), but did not attribute them to people from those families.

2. The issue of female status is a complex one, further confused by the seemingly interchangeable use of the terms "stratification," "inequality," or "female position," and "women's role." Since there seems to be a great multiplicity of views on the meaning of status and since it is desirable to avoid some of the problems inherent in imprecise terminology, the following definition of female status has been adopted for this study: Female status is the ranking, in terms of prestige, power or esteem, accorded the position of women in comparison with, or relative to, the ranking—also in terms of prestige, power, or esteem—given to the position of man (Buvinic 1976). In this view, sexual stratification is seen as primarily a response to relations of production. Accordingly, the indicators necessary for the evaluation of women's status are selected as economic considerations involving female control of production of socially necessary goods and services, specifically, control over access to raw materials, control over the technology of production, disposition of work time and work schedules, place and mode of production activity, and disposition of the products of labor (Harris 1971). The operationalizing of this definition is achieved through the measurement of female control of production by how and to what extent women have gained, or maintained economic control as modernization transforms their society.

3. By its nature, economic development relieves women of their contribution to production by devaluing and weakening artisan production in favor of commodity production outside the home (Safa 1977, Chinchilla 1977). Since women are primarily responsible for traditional cottage industry, they lose power in the economy as wage labor becomes increasingly important and males assume principal responsibility for supporting the family (Saffioti 1977). There is a sizeable literature on women and development, and for references to the concepts and the debates, as well as many of the works, I refer the reader to Charlton (1984), Buvinic (1976), two valuable bibliographic sources; Boserup (1970), an early definitive analysis; and Benería (1982). Nash and Fernández-Kelly (1983), and Staudt and Jacquette (1983), post-Boserup analyses that broadened and strengthened the perspective.

4. The discussion of male dominance among Latin American peasants contains many fascinating theoretical and methodological twists and turns. While most writers analyze

gender relations in terms of the exaggerated masculinity known as *machismo,* others argue that there is less sexual stratification among indigenous peasants whose economic well-being depends upon mutual support between spouses. See for example, Bossen (1984) for an introduction to some of the relevant Guatemalan literature on male/female complementarity and gender equality among Mayan peasants. The dynamics of gender relations under conditions of stability and change are addressed in Rothstein (1983) where she points out that what the authors called male domination in several classic studies in Mexico—Lewis' (1963) work on Tepoztlán and Beals' (1946) study of Cherán—actually are cases of male/female cooperation. In Tepoztlán, however, the relatively egalitarian nature of gender relations seems destined to be toppled as increased female economic participation ushers in male resentment at the loss of their productive edge.

5. There is voluminous writing on the concept of *machismo.* Some works that focus on the relationships between Latin American men and women under conditions of male dominance include Gissi Bustos (1976), Kinzer (1973), Collier (1986), Slade (1975), Lewis (1964), and Levine et al. (1986).

6. Much to my embarrassment, during these return fieldtrips I was treated like visiting royalty in the town and in its nearby *aldeas* where I had many friends and informants. I later realized that what seemed like ministrations to a very important person were just the ordinary attentions normally given to a man! For instance, *aldea* women served me at a table while they fussed with the food around the fire. I was called with the men for the first sitting at the crowded Fuentes table, and then urged to eat again when I stayed to chat with the second- and third-shift women. It was, I must admit, a luxurious and fascinating fictive status.

7. See McClintock (1985), Schoultz (1983), Davis and Hodson (1982), Inter-American Commission on Human Rights (1981, 1983, 1985), Americas Watch (1982, 1984, 1986), and Krueger and Enge (1985).

8. Part of the following discussion originally appeared in Ehlers (1987).

9. I should add that because they have so little information about insurgency and counterinsurgency operations and because rumor seems to be the most powerful medium for news, *Sampedranos* are quite ignorant and confused about the role of the military or the intentions of the guerrillas. Ironically, several thousand people only got their first good look at the problem several years ago when the American cable television channel Home Box Office (HBO), widely available in San Pedro, showed "*El Norte.*"

10. A word about money. Before 1985, the value of the *quetzal* to the dollar was 1:1, an historically stable ratio that made conversion extremely simple and allowed writers to use dollars or *quetzales* in their discussions without confusion. After 1985, however, the relationship of the *quetzal* to the dollar dropped, but by 1988 it appeared to have stabilized at 2.70:1. These fiscal fluctuations make it somewhat difficult for the reader to follow changing prices or the cost of living over a ten year period. This situation is made even murkier because some of my information was gathered before the devaluation of the *quetzal,* and some after. What I have done to make monetary matters simple is this: All prices are quoted in *quetzales* and are pegged at the pre-1985 *quetzal* to dollar value of 1:1 unless the information is dated: If a date appears in the discussion, that is a reminder that the value of the monies has changed to approximately 2.70:1, and that in-

flation has reduced the local buying power of the consumer as well. A more complete discussion of this trend appears in Chapter Five, Cottage Industry.

11. An interesting exception to the exclusive use of male informants is Wisdom's (1940) use of a Chorti woman among his four main informants, perhaps explaining his considerable attention to women's productive contributions.

12. June Nash reports that in Cantel, a midwife of "reformed" practices told her that other midwives did have the husbands beat their wives to induce birth (personal commun.).

13. For a description of social and economic strife in San Antonio Aguas Calientes during the Lucas Garcia period, see Annis' "Story from a Peaceful Town" in Carmack (1988).

2

Ethnographic Sketch

SAN PEDRO SACATEPÉQUEZ, San Marcos, is located in the extreme western highlands of Guatemala near the Mexican border, four and a half hours by first class bus from Guatemala City, within commuting distance to Quezaltenango, Guatemala's second largest city, and easily accessible (two to six hours on a truck or third class bus) from dozens of smaller coastal and highland towns and plantations. Surrounded by luxuriant green hills, San Pedro lies in *El Valle de la Esmeralda* (The Emerald Valley), so-named when Spanish conquerors founded the town in the name of the crown in 1595. *Sampedranos* trace their cultural heritage to the Mam-speaking Maya who for centuries have inhabited this part of the western highlands. Although Mam is rarely spoken today, even in the far *aldeas,* the connection to indigenous culture remains. It is expressed symbolically in the traditional yellow skirts and richly woven *huipiles* worn by rural women, and formally, in cultural festivities that serve to remind the townfolk of their bloodlines.

Each year *Sampedranos* recall their cultural roots in plays, poems, and speeches during the week-long celebrations of the town's saint's day, June 29. A *Reyna Indígena* (Indian queen) is selected, marimbas play traditional tunes, women dance the ancient dances, shuffling about on pine needles marking the solemnity of the occasion.

I have watched these performances many times from my seat among the teachers in their business suits. Sometimes I attended with barefoot women in *huipiles* from the near *aldeas* who carried their babies slung across their backs. The audience, remarkable in its diversity and numbers, is also known for its patience and endurance since the festivities start late and last long past midnight. Like reenactments of the first Thanksgiving by North American children, these pageants reinforce the memory of long mythologized origins and revered traditions. Yet every year—as if in celebration of the town's economic mobility—they become more sophisticated and elaborate, an ironic mixing of slick media-hype with heritage.

For the last few years an effusive emcee has been imported from the capital to keep the evening's pace brisk and stimulating. His sonorous baritone and his enthusiasm impart a certain beauty contest feeling to what had previously been an attempt to recapture traditional values embodied in the *Reyna Indígena*. But no one seems to mind; in fact, the pageant's popularity grows annually. For many viewers, rural and urban alike, this is the only proximity they have during the year to their ancient Mayan roots. And modern technology makes the occasion easily accessible, since it is videotaped and replayed for weeks on the local public access television station.

To a certain degree, San Pedro Sacatepéquez represents a substantial departure from Guatemalan Indian communities characterized by progressive impoverishment and proletarianization.[1] San Pedro is one of a handful of highland towns that have advanced into a competitive position in the national economy as major centers of Indian entrepreneurship and self-sustaining economic growth. The congregation of 15,000 Indians in a commercially viable town is rare in the highlands, where the majority of Indians are rural agriculturalists. Most situations of concentrated economic power in the highlands remain in the hands of minority *ladinos* who populate most urbanized areas.

It seems certain that San Pedro has been able to avoid the downward spiral of over-population, market dependence, and agricultural decline found elsewhere in the region partially because it is a town. As such, it can exert economic power based on a large specialized population which is, in this case, Indian (W. R. Smith 1975). In order to explain the incongruity of an affluent and complex Indian community among many hundreds that are resource-poor, several other factors may be isolated, the most salient of which are San Pedro's strong family productive system, and a history of active commerce which pre-adapted the town to take advantage of economic growth when appropriate opportunities occur. The readiness, flexibility, and skill of the populace to fill special labor niches in the expanding commercial market is just one example of the viability of the town's market enterprise that frees these Indians from the demands of seasonal migrant labor endemic in other highland communities. Smith has outlined the history of San Pedro's economic takeoff which provides some background for the genesis of its progressive character. He points out (1977) that before World War II, Indians in San Pedro were peasant producers whose commercial networks were largely regional. The Indian economy was based on agriculture, mule trade, and cottage industries although some wealthier *Sampedranos* owned coastal plots where they grew cash crops and raised cattle. The town's fame as a trade center had long been established as was its reputation for handicrafts and textile production. By their own definition, most people were *naturales* or Indians leading traditional lifestyles.

Until 1950, the progressive sector in the town was monopolized by European immigrant entrepreneurs who were the town's elite. These foreigners established San Pedro's external trade connections and started general stores and wholesale businesses which eventually led to the town's successful commercial expansion. The foreign entrepreneurs never intermarried with the indigenous population, and with their gradual disappearance, an Indian bourgeoisie has risen to take its place of commercial dominance. While the number of truly wealthy families is relatively small, the middle class has expanded quite rapidly, partly as a result of the opportunities development affords in business and wage labor, and partly because schooling is so readily available as a secure sign of rising social status.

The tenor of the town is of never-ceasing activity. The main market day on Thursday draws thousands of buyers from all over Guatemala and from Guatemala's three neighbors (Mexico, Honduras, and El Salvador). A half-market is held on Sunday, but in fact, there is plaza activity all week long. When I first arrived in San Pedro in 1976, the plaza was empty between market days. Twelve years later, vendors set up every day hawking fruits and vegetables, cooked food, baskets, live chickens, ceramics, plastic pans, soap, or flowers. But the plaza and its indoor version, the *mercado central,* while the focus of trade, are by no means the only bustling businesses. *Sampedranos* are continually preoccupied with money-making projects. Based largely upon cottage industry and family productive systems, the diversity of business is astounding. And, as the following cases illustrate, *Sampedranos* will travel to make a sale.

- Doña Julieta is a baker who spends three days making a hundred pounds of *shecas,* San Pedro's traditional bread, then travels by truck to coastal markets to sell, returning to prepare another load for San Pedro's Thursday market.

- Don Juan Ignacio buys fruits and live chickens on Thursdays, then travels three hours by bus to sell them in small highland markets.

- Women weavers produce belts, blouses, and skirts that they sell to Doña Celestina, a dealer who resells them in San Pedro on Thursdays, at the large Indian market in Totonicapán on Saturdays and in tiny, nearby Palestina on Wednesdays.

- During the three month mango season, Don Felipe's truck, bulging with the pulpy orange fruit, arrives daily from the coast to wholesale to small-time female traders whose baskets ring the outside of the market.

- Cement from the capital is trucked in by Doña Juana's small company twice a week and sold to people from all over the state who are building houses. (Many customers haul away the hundred pound bags on their backs to await the next bus home!)

While merchants previously walked an entire day to reach the large market in Quezaltenango, sold for a day and walked back the next, transportation by bus, truck, or car has now made it possible to trade in three or four different locations each week and still participate in San Pedro's lucrative Thursday market or half-day Sunday market. In addition, merchants do not rely only upon coastal fruit and vegetable dealers, but now also contract with local truckers for regular weekly buying trips into Guatemala City where produce is cheaper and credit easier. Every week *Sampedrano* textile brokers travel five or six hours on second class buses to the capital with fabric, clothing, and tablecloths for export or for the urban middle class. In short, investment in accessible transport has facilitated much of San Pedro's commercial activity.

Downtown is a beehive of vehicular activity more reminiscent of midtown Manhattan than highland Guatemala. Ten-ton Mercedes trucks must constantly be dodged. Noisy, overcrowded vans line the sidestreets to load shoppers for hourly trips back to the *aldeas*. Top-heavy Blue Bird buses with goods piled in huge string bags (*redes*) on their roofs bring traders to and from the coast and the highlands. The noise of the traffic is constant, as is the smell of the exhaust. But all this does not bother the *Sampedranos*. To them it is the sound of business and, better yet, the smell of money.

To get a clear picture of the town's productive activity, consider the following occupational analyses. A 1987 study by City Planners from San Carlos University counts fully eighty-five percent of San Pedro's urban population working in the commercial sector, mostly as self-employed entrepreneurs (Rivera and Yoc Pérez 1987). Included in this figure are all manner of trade and sales establishments, and the artisanal sector (carpenter, shoemaker, tailor, stonemason, tanner, builder, weaver, knitter, etc.), accounting for nearly forty percent of workers, and a small semi-industrial sector comprising sweater factories and other partially mechanized businesses.[2] A San Pedro Public Health survey shows that fifteen percent of the town's heads of households are professional (teachers, agronomists, accountants, government workers), and twelve percent agriculturalists (San Pedro Sacatepéquez *Centro de Salud* 1986). In contrast, the latter study notes that three-quarters of

rural families either farm their own land, rent land, or do agricultural day labor. In addition, rural residents who live near the town combine agriculture
with commercial activities. The data from nearby San José Caben is indicative: although more than fifty percent of this *aldea*'s household heads said they
were farmers, thirty percent said that their primary work was as artisans.[3]
In short, studies show an intensive active economy that is vigorously drawing upon its labor supply, both urban and rural.

A long-established relationship between commerce and transport is crucial to the apparent boom economy in San Pedro. Being only an hour and a
half from the Pan American highway near Totonicapán is certainly an asset.
More important, however, is the easy access to Quezaltenango, only an hour
away. This road was paved only eighteen years ago, opening commercial and
educational linkages that had been difficult to establish before. There are
more than a dozen daily buses that go to Quezaltenango or pass through it
on their way to Guatemala City. Most *Sampedranos* use the buses so often that
they know the schedules by heart. Filled with students on their way to San
Carlos University in Quezaltenango, merchants hauling cargo, or seamstresses needing just the right shade of lace, the buses rumble through town
long into the night. On market day, getting back from Quezaltenango to San
Pedro means waiting hours for an empty seat and then being packed sardine-
like into buses quickly over-filled with eager traders. The possibilities afforded by a well-developed system of transportation may be seen in the
events of one midnight escapade. Thieves burglarized a local shop and, like
so many highlanders, not having an automobile for transport, they made
their escape aboard the 3 a.m. third class bus to Guatemala City! Local police
alerted the authorities in the capital, and the thieves were arrested as they
stepped off the bus.

Part of the reason for recent improvement and development of roads and
transport in the area is that San Pedro is the geographic twin of the depart-
mental capital of San Marcos. There exists between these two towns great
animosity and rivalry. Though the towns are nearly contiguous, they seem
on the surface to ignore each other's presence. Ethnic differences would
seem to be the cause of unfriendly relations, but there is a class distinction
as well. San Marcos (urban population 6,000) has a largely *ladino* citizenry
reflecting its civil services and offices, while San Pedro is Indian and commercial. Residents of San Marcos are mostly salaried and white-collar with
fixed incomes, easy consumer credit, a car, and a color television.

In contrast, money-making in San Pedro invariably involves some commercial enterprise, even as a second, third, or fourth income. Rare is the
Sampedrano—laborer or professional—who does not have a store, a loom,
or a sewing machine to turn to after work. The enthusiasm *Sampedranos* have

for trade is belittled by *Marquenses* (residents of San Marcos) as a fixation with money, and there are endless San Marcos stories of how Indians work day and night and then drink and gamble away their profits. Antipathy toward San Pedro has increased since 1985 when inflationary woes shrank San Marcos' own commercial profits and stymied entrepreneurial efforts. Frustrated and broke, *ladinos* constantly complain that they are economically stagnant because they cannot compete with their neighbors. They decry child labor as uncivilized, and bitterly attack *Sampedrano* tactics of working at cost just to stay in business. *Sampedranos* shrug off *ladino* objections. They laughingly point out that San Marcos is such a dull place that one might walk naked through the main streets and no one would be around to notice (W. R. Smith 1975).

Despite hostility between the towns, they do interact regularly. This is clearly evident in the bullish ten-cent-a-person taxi business between them. On a non-market day, ten or fifteen taxis travel the mile between town centers, and on Thursday market days, that number more than doubles. Although both towns provide most goods and services (churches, doctors, stores, movies, radio stations, etc.), each has its specialty. As the state capital, San Marcos houses the state hospital, the judicial center, the jail, and government bureaucratic offices. San Marcos also has the best private schools, and, until 1985, the only banks. San Pedro, however, has its market and its hundreds of shops, drawing from San Marcos many customers who cannot resist the low prices and variety of merchandise. Even on non-market days, San Pedro shopping rivals that of its twin city. San Pedro also has the only two legal houses of prostitution and, ironically, the only gynecologist.

Despite a seeming stand-off between the two towns, San Marcos clearly dominates in terms of a style of upward mobility to which more and more *Sampedranos* aspire. The most obvious manifestation of these rising aspirations is the relatively recent availability of scores of consumer items imported from Guatemala City, the United States and Japan. Four or five neighborhood stores opened during one recent year in San Pedro, offering stereos, cassette decks, electric typewriters, and furniture. The terms of purchase are invariably based on time payments, often with no down payment required. T-shirts are also very popular, especially those bearing the logos of American universities or the likenesses of rock stars. Blenders have been around for some time as have pressure cookers, but large-screen color televisions, designer jeans, and digital watches are more recent entries in the consumer market.

I introduced the first portable radio–tape deck, and the first sleeping bag in 1978, and a requested Ward's catalog was a tabletop favorite for months.[4] Since then, however, longing for consumer goods not available in San Pedro has been partially ameliorated by frequent shopping trips to Tapachula, a medium-sized city just across the Mexican border. The dramatic drop in the value of the peso since 1982 has made the two-hour trip popular, particularly for the purchase of clothing and shoes. Other larger items, like furniture or electronic equipment, are better purchased in town since credit, the preferred payment plan, is not available in Tapachula.

Another measure of consumer acquisitiveness is the increased desire to buy Japanese-model cars and pick-up trucks. Where twenty years ago there were but two automobiles in San Pedro, now hundreds of cars line the streets. It is interesting that San Pedro trucks and cars were initially used primarily for commerce while San Marcos vehicles were more often for convenience or pleasure. Owning a car in San Pedro usually meant operating a taxi at least a few afternoons a week. This seems to be changing. Motorcycle ownership is up, as are purchases of luxury cars, suggesting a possible trend toward previously *ladino* priorities in spending.

Television has also made a big difference in San Pedro's expanding national and international perspective. I remember the first black and white set that the Fuentes family bought in 1977 when a transmitter was built outside of town to relay TV signals from Guatemala City. The family quickly abandoned their animated and, for me, informative discussions over meals, focusing their attention instead on soap operas from Mexico City. In 1986, an enterprising appliance dealer put a parabolic dish atop his house, and automatically became the cable franchisee for the town. Charging a Q17 initial fee, and then Q11 a month, he has wired nearly two hundred homes to receive seven channels: HBO, the Disney Channel, Cinemax, *Univisión* from Miami, and three Mexican stations. The Fuentes family now owns four color television sets, located in the living room and in the bedrooms of the married children. Meals are uninterrupted by foreign melodrama, but afternoons and evenings are spent huddled in front of American English-language movies that everyone loves, but no one understands.

There are many other signs of mobility and change. When I first came to San Pedro in 1976, there was one doctor and a handful of lawyers. A dentist visited twice a year to pull teeth at the *Centro de Salud*. Twelve years later I counted twenty-two doctors, twenty lawyers, and six resident dentists. There used to be only one phone, at the Guatel (Guatemala Telephone Company) office in San Marcos where making a call consumed most of a morning. Today there are 385 telephones, 84% in private homes. Funerals, too, have changed. Until recently, the family and friends slowly marched to the music of a small band from the church to the cemetery a mile away, allowing the entire town to join the ritual from their doorsteps and stores. As of 1988, a funeral home had opened complete with black limousines whose tinted windows now deprive onlookers of their chance to participate or even to catch a glimpse of the mourners.

Perhaps the best indication of the changes in the character of the town are the new types of businesses lining the streets of downtown San Pedro. Here are a few examples of shops opened since 1978. No businesses like these ever existed before.

- 13 shoe stores
- 2 record/cassette shops
- 5 auto parts stores
- 2 fresh chicken shops
- 2 film and film developers
- 5 bluejeans and separates stores
- 2 banks
- 4 photocopiers
- 6 TV and radio sales, and electronic repair
- 2 designer eyeglasses
- 3 unisex hairdressers
- 4 health food stores
- 1 fast-food chicken restaurant

In addition, there has been rapid expansion in competition among existing stores. For example, where there were two sweater factories, there are now more than twenty. Eleven new drug stores (five owned by one family) line San Pedro's streets, while ten years ago there were only three. I counted hundreds of small stores selling everyday necessities like corn, rice and beans. These *tienditas* have always been a commercial mainstay, but their numbers are now five times what they were before. Stores selling cheap western-style clothes appear to have grown exponentially. Bakeries selling scores of different breads and sweet rolls have a long history in town, but today there are two specializing only in cakes, and four making French pastries. The list of new street-level businesses goes on. For example, where there was only one hardware store, now there are five. And, most important, the director of the market proudly announced to me that there are now two thousand traders in the Thursday market, twice as many as there were ten years ago.

There are several lessons to be learned from this surge in commercial outlets. What is clear is that it reflects a diversifying population with a growing middle class and money to spend.[5] Two generations removed from wearing *huipiles* and speaking Mam, San Pedro's urban sector is educated and relatively affluent. Many families have been able to send their children to high school and even to college so that they can become teachers, engineers, social workers, agronomists, doctors, and lawyers. The fact that the University of San Carlos is only an hour bus ride away in Quezaltenango has made it easier for *Sampedranos* to earn college degrees. They wear Western clothing, own appliances and cars and express clear preferences for rock and roll and *salsa* over traditional marimba music. Conspicuous consumption seems to escalate with more schooling and a monthly salary. As the size of the middle class has grown, so has the town's profile adjusted to reflect a more national and international orientation.

The Fuentes Chicken Business

In his book on San Pedro, Smith tells the story of Marcos Fuentes, a native who rose from poverty to become an internationally respected agronomist. Marcos, the son of itinerant traders, was not supposed to go to school beyond the sixth grade, but when the government offered a scholarship to the National Agricultural School in Quezaltenango, good fortune smiled upon him. Just ten days before the award was granted, brothers from a different family who were the best students in the class had to leave school to help in their father's fields. So the award went to Marcos instead. Meanwhile, the two boys who had had to forego education grew up as manual laborers, earning less than fifty cents a day, and humbling themselves before the embarrassed Marcos when he returned in later years for visits. The irony of his good luck is noted by Smith, who says:

> The lives of these three men of similar background and intelligence diverged radically because of a chance event in 1928. Had the Fuentes [no relation to Marcos Fuentes] brothers stayed in school but another few weeks, one of them, rather than Marcos, would have benefited from free higher education and become the confident, self-assured individual. Confined by their menial occupations, the unfortunate Fuentes brothers retained the humility of their forebears. (118)

As soon as he could, Marcos helped his younger brother, Braulio, to go to school, and he, too, became an agronomist. Thus, the Fuentes family began to learn the value of a good education, a lesson that was passed onto all the children who were to come. In the years ahead, all seven of Braulio's children went to school, and each in turn to college. Today, they are all salary-earning professionals. Together, the family is a productive system working on projects and businesses that sustain them beyond what they earn as engineers, doctors, teachers, and agronomists. Their story is similar to other poor or middle class *Sampedranos* who constantly strategize to maximize their cooperative productive energies. What makes the Fuentes family special is the level of sophisticated management they apply to their endeavors, particularly to their poultry business.

The chicken project began in 1980 when newlyweds Miguel and Liliana bought twenty-five chicks to raise in the yard of the family's downtown house. The business quickly grew to eight hundred chickens. They were selling two hundred on Thursdays alone. But Miguel admits in the beginning he made a big mistake: he got greedy. So when a woman from the coast wanted to buy all his chickens for resale, he agreed. This meant he could buy more new chickens from other producers to increase his total sales. Some of the new chicks were sick, and the disease killed his entire stock. He lost everything, but was philosophical about it, thinking "*Se murió el chucho y se acabó la rabia,*" a Guatemalan saying that means "if the dog dies, you have gotten rid of the rabies," i.e., his devastating failure cured his greediness. He went back to concentrating on his medical studies.

Meanwhile, his wife supported them and their two children by making and selling the town's most elaborate pies and cakes. Her business was so good that when he finally graduated, and was making Q200 a month, they were able to save most of it. When they had saved Q1000 his brothers came to him with a plan. They would start another chicken business behind the house, but as soon as there were any profits, they would develop the land their father had left them in La Grandeza. Miguel decided to commit eighteen months to the project, figuring the chicken profits would allow him to open up a clinic in the *aldea* which did not have a doctor. So he bought one hundred chicks, and then two weeks later two hundred more. The first day he slaughtered fifteen chickens and only sold seven because no one knew about the store. He worried. Then, little by little, the word got out. Soon they were selling fifteen a day, and twenty-five on Sundays, and the business was off and running. By the time they were selling six hundred birds every two weeks, the neighbors were complaining of the smell, and the health department gave them a month to move out of town. On August 7, 1986, they moved to the *aldea* La Grandeza.

The costs involved in setting up a business on their land were enormous. Installing electric lines cost them Q4000, the two main buildings were Q3000 each, and the big one more. Salaries for laborers were Q150 a week, plus what they had to pay the workers who built the barns. To capitalize they borrowed Q5800 from Liliana's godmother who had a considerable fortune tucked away from her small grocery business. From Miguel's design, they built feeders that allowed feed concentrate to flow out as the chickens ate. To buy feeders would have cost Q19 each, but they built ninety for less than Q8 each. The oldest brother, Jorge, an engineer, made the eleven water drips himself for a third of the retail cost. In all, Miguel and Jorge were the brick-layers, carpenters, chicken farmers, and peons. The workmen basically copied their work. When all the labors were over, the chickens began dying because the floor was cold. So they built a rudimentary incubator with light bulbs to keep them warm. That, too, worked, and it saved them the Q1000 it would have cost in Guatemala City.

In 1988, the brothers built four new barns to house the ten thousand chickens they now keep in La Grandeza. Expansion has proceeded smoothly, and along the way they have developed systems for using everything. For example, they feed the unsellable chicken innards to six pigs who live near the barns. Although there is little money in fattening so few pigs, they can turn a reasonable profit every few months. Miguel sells all the chicken excretions to farmers for fertilizer, and it is so popular that he has contracts nine months ahead. Nothing is wasted.

Sales at Pollos Santa Teresa are so good that its normally understated manager describes business as "*excelente.*" Every week about a thousand chickens are sold to people from towns and *aldeas* in half-pound, pound, and two pound lots. The family does a healthy business with restaurants too, but most sales are over the counter. In the first year of business, the Fuenteses promoted their fresh chicken outlet—the first in town—with contests and raffles for free birds. This year they have no need for gimmicks as sales are brisk. In just two years they have doubled the number sold. The profit from each chicken is about ninety *centavos,* a figure they have carefully derived from calculations of depreciation on buildings, equipment, feed, amortization and fuel. The only labor costs are those of the six workers at the farm; family labor is contributed, or in the case of Miguel Fuentes, who works full time as manager, immediately reinvested in the business.

It is largely due to Miguel's sophisticated business sense that the enterprise is flourishing. Based on years of entrepreneurial experience in family cottage industries operated from their little store, Miguel applies a managerial style that any farmer—or businessperson—would admire. He subscribes to six poultry journals in three languages, is invited to industry meetings in Guatemala City or San José, Cosa Rica, and regularly declines job offers from larger competitors. While Miguel's managerial skills and entrepreneurial vision keep sales climbing, other family members are also integral to the accomplishments and the expansion of the enterprise. Everyone in this large family contributes time and energy to the business.

The Fuenteses' division of labor is drawn largely along sexual lines. The three sons manage the land in La Grandeza where they have built six chicken barns. The storefront off the house is run by the women, especially Miguel's wife, Liliana, and his mother, Doña Ofelia. The system, carefully worked out over the first two years, is as follows. Every morning at 4:30 a.m., Miguel and his brothers leave to direct the slaughter and dressing of the day's first chickens. They return by the 9 a.m. opening, with plastic crates of chicken ready to be sold, and a pick-up full of live chickens to be killed and cleaned in the courtyard by an *aldea* family hired for that purpose. The doors open promptly. Usually there are customers already waiting outside. Doña Ofelia dons her apron and starts cutting up chickens into pound lots, with a new digital scale assuring accuracy. Customers get chicken parts, dark and light together. If they want only breast, it costs more; if gizzards are all they can afford, the price is lower.[6] Liliana takes orders, darts back to where Ofelia is chopping to announce the customers' requests, returns with their chicken in small plastic bags, takes the money, throws it into an old sewing machine drawer, and gives them their change. Large bills are kept separately, and there is a chart posted with the prices so time-consuming multiplication is unnecessary. The women keep track of larger orders on a clip board that lets them know the size of the order and when it is to be ready. There are no quantity discounts: restaurants pay the same Q1.80/lb as do regular customers.

When Ofelia's daughters return home from their work as teachers, they don aprons and pick up a cleaver to assist her. What is particularly interesting about this arrangement is that none of the daughters has any money invested in the business. They help out because their mother and the family benefits from their labor. It would be unthinkable to not be helping in this or any of the other income-producing activities that take place in the Fuentes household.

Meanwhile, the family is planning its next venture. They have the education they need, the capital, and the experience. Based on their cooperativeness, hard work, and ingenuity, they are ready to take advantage of any opportunity, or more likely, to originate a business plan, and see that it succeeds. Right now they are considering expanding the chicken idea to Coatepeque, a large town on the coast. Ricardo, the youngest brother, has just graduated as an agronomist, and there are plans for him to begin an export agriculture project. Miguel envisions developing real estate and housing in the *aldeas*, a kind of Guatemalan Levittown for the *Sampedranos* whom he imagines are as economically mobile as the Fuentes family.

Aldeas

At the same time that many *Sampedranos* are developing a marked middle class orientation, the majority of San Pedro's citizens outside the town retain the life-style of their parents and grandparents. San Pedro has seventeen *aldeas* or small villages which, while at varying distances (from one to thirty kilometers away, some highland, some coastal), are legally part of the *municipio,* tripling the urban population of 15,000 to more than 45,000 for the entire township. These *aldeas* represent traditional input into San Pedro. For example, *aldeanos* are still farmers while in the town hardly anyone makes *milpa* anymore. Most *aldea* women continue to wear the traditional *Sampedrana traje* (costume), and, depending on the *aldea,* might weave, raise chickens or cows for their eggs and milk, sell radishes or onions, or process a great variety of foods for sale in town.

The majority of flowers and edible goods sold in San Pedro's market are carried in baskets on the heads of *aldea* women who grow or produce them at home. Many coastal *aldeanos* trade avocados and other vegetables once a week, arriving by the truckload or on foot early enough on Thursday to get their regular places in the cheaper areas of the plaza. Others from the far *aldeas* have not developed any trade connections with the town, neither produce nor textiles, and are forced to supplement their inadequate *milpa* production as seasonal *finca* workers on coastal plantations. They, however, are in the minority in this relatively thriving economy.

Migration between *aldeas* and town is not a common occurrence. *Aldeas* are largely endogamous, so marriage between *aldeanos* and townfolk is relatively rare. Nor do young couples relocate when they marry. Instead, they move in with the boy's parents, and later build their own houses nearby. Clearly, jobs outside of San Pedro in the capital or in other cities call for making a permanent move, and that is becoming somewhat more common with rising levels of education.[7] Employment opportunities do not draw *aldeanos* to San Pedro, however, as most workers are urbanites or relatives of urban entrepreneurs who are being apprenticed. Those rural folk who do find jobs in town are most likely from the near *aldeas,* and can commute. People tend to move only when smart business planning or economic good fortune make it a necessity. What might cause a move is a cottage industry that expands, or busy traders needing better access to the market. In these or other circumstances, only the well-capitalized can afford to relocate. The migrants, then, are the most successful *aldeanos* who, once they are in town, try to improve their economic fortunes even more. This case study illustrates the process.

Rosario and Edulina Ramirez live in Chamac with Rosario's parents, but they will be moving out as soon as they finish building their new house in town. Over the last fourteen years, this uneducated, rural couple has been able to save Q5000 by investing their considerable energies in plaza trade. Between them they have had nearly a dozen different businesses. Edulina learned to make soap from her mother-in-law, but she also sells factory-made soap and detergent at her plaza stall. Her other products include three kinds of sugar, salt, plastic bags, and nylon by the yard. At night, after she has put her four children to bed, Edulina makes babies' hats on her knitting machine. Meanwhile, on Mondays and Fridays, Rosario rents a pick-up truck to buy thirty or forty pounds of fat for soapmaking, forty-five minutes away in San Juan Ostancalco, where he sells finished soap balls in their market. These and other businesses take up all their time. Aside from going to mass on Sunday, Edulina says she never takes any time off. They wear old, tattered clothes, and eat sparingly, because they have been saving.

By 1987, their sacrifice began to pay off. They made a down payment on a plot, and began to build their house. A year later, they had only two rooms completed, but were hopeful of moving in soon. Their plans are to open a wholesale grain business in front where they will also store the other products they bring to market.

Edulina and Rosario are, in many aspects, a typical *Sampedrano* couple. Like others, they live to work. In this case, however, they have invested in a product—homemade soap—that skirts the price fluctuations common in the plaza. As such, they have been able to combine hard work and personal sacrifice with consistent market activity to create a small nestegg. The next step for them was to expand into wholesaling with a storefront operation downtown. While they will leave behind their families—and the hard work of soapmaking—they anticipate a small measure of success in their new urban endeavors.

Although, like this couple, many *Sampedranos* were born in an *aldea* or own land there, a certain disdain for *aldeanos* exists among townfolk. They are considered to be dirty, ignorant, poor *inditos* (a derogatory *ladino* term for Indians), even if, as in some cases, they are one's parents. In reality, *aldea* populations vary extensively. Not all of them are poor; nor are they characteristically illiterate or unkempt. But what is true is that their levels of prosperity (and westernized behavior) rise the nearer they are to town. The reasons are relatively obvious. The closer *aldeas* tend to be more economically secure because they can exploit the market easily through their home products and in turn be exploited by the town as a source of cheap labor. Secondly, if the *aldea* is a good distance away from town, it will not be able to invest in education, particularly higher education, thus minimizing its development potential. Only three or four of the *aldeas* are geographically close enough for their children to attend a junior or senior high school in San Pedro. Further away, even where the local schools are within walking distance, one does not sense the overwhelming push toward education that seemingly pervades the town and the near *aldeas*. For example, one finds girls from the distant *aldeas* of San Pedro Petz or Chim who do go to school, attend elementary school for only three years and then quit to take care of smaller children at home. Ten years ago, this was also characteristic of near *aldeas* where daughters' labors were needed in cottage industry. But no longer. Today, in three of the near *aldeas,* the majority of girls attend school at least through the sixth grade. Many go on to junior and senior high school, and a few have gone to college. Clearly, the proximity of a thriving economic center has had positive educational and economic implications for some of its hinterland. The *aldea* that best exemplifies this is the near *aldea* of San José Caben.

SAN JOSÉ CABEN

Within a week of arriving in San Pedro, I traveled to San José Caben (pop. 3500), an *aldea* famous for its industrious weavers. The walk was hot, hilly, and long. I remember saying then that an anthropologist would have to be crazy to do fieldwork in a place that was so inaccessible. Of course, two months later, I found myself working every day in San José Caben studying women weavers. It had quickly become apparent that urban women wove less and less. Most of the *huipiles* were made in *aldeas,* and the best ones in San José. The walk which had been so daunting at first became much easier over time, especially when I had many stops to make along the *aldea*'s two streets. I came to see San José, only a forty-minute walk (or a fifteen-minute bus ride) from town, almost as a suburb of San Pedro. Like those of Chamac and La Grandeza, two other near *aldeas* whose populations are also decidedly rural, San José Caben's productive efforts and educational goals are intrinsically connected to the nearby town's commercialism.

Weaving has been an important activity in San José Caben for generations, but only in the last twenty years has it come to dominate the economy. For years, the community's emphasis on weaving afforded the village a relatively stable, if minimal standard of living. But as San Pedro's commercial development advanced, the *aldea*'s fortunes burgeoned. The transition was simple. With modernization, urban women were evolving away from weaving *huipiles,* emphasizing other commercial activities instead. *Huipil* traders were seeking new weavers to supply their market stalls in town. Many women from San José took advantage of this opening to move into weaving, and in doing so developed a veritable monopoly on the production of fine

Table 2.1 *Female Occupations in San José Caben (1988)*

Jobs*	Sample (n=80)	Mothers (n=73)	Daughters (n=63)
Weaver	42 (52.5%)	22 (30%)	35 (55.5%)
Seamstress	24 (30%)	1 (1.5%)	10 (15.87%)
Merchant		10 (12.5%)	
Breadmaker		6 (7.5%)	
Soapmaker		6 (7.5%)	
Teacher			8 (12.69%)
Housewife	31 (38.75%)	28 (35%)	7 (11%)
Other	10 (12.5%)		3 (4.76%)

*These figures were obtained by asking women what their major occupation was now and what it had been previously. For this reason, and because many working women describe themselves as housewives as well, there is considerable overlap in totals.

traditional blouses. Occupational figures reflect this newer trend. In a 1988 study of women in 80 San José households, I found that 52.5 percent had worked as weavers of *huipiles* (Table 2.1). In comparison, only thirty percent of the mothers of these women had been weavers, and almost all were back-strap weavers, a technique that is far less commercial. Also, the productive efforts of the older generation were much more diversified. Nearly thirteen percent were market traders, and fifteen percent bakers and soapmakers. This change to concentrating about half the female productive activities on weaving paid off handsomely. Women were able to marshal the labor of their daughters to weave as much as one labor-intensive *huipil* every week. Their contributions to family income increased steadily and, in many cases, financed diversification into a new male industry, the weaving of cotton yardgoods.

Both men and women in San José know how to set up a loom, but this was not always true. Historically, men spent most of their time in the fields or as laborers in town. After 1960, however, their productive efforts began to be directed more toward weaving tablecloths and bolts of fabric, an industry that characterized San Pedro as well. An essential component in their work was the sewing of clothes cut from the woven fabric. Women who did not weave bought treadle machines and became seamstresses. By 1988, thirty percent of my sample were sewing the cloth into garments and accessories (skirts, bags, dolls, pants, shirts, etc.) which the men sold in Quezaltenango, Guatemala City, and for export. The novelty of this work is clearly reflected in the fact that only 1.25 percent of the sample's mothers ever did this kind of work.[8]

Table 2.2 *Schooling of San José Caben Children (n=281)*

Sex	Elementary	Junior High	Senior High	College
Boys	84 (30%)	27 (10%)	27 (10%)	3 (1%)
Girls	105 (37%)	18 (6%)	16 (5%)	1 (0.4%)

The strongest indication of San José Caben's emphasis on social and economic mobility is that one hundred percent of the 80 women I sampled (mean age 41) had sent their children to school (Table 2.2). Sixty-seven percent of the children had primary school training; many were continuing. Sixteen percent had enrolled in junior high in San Pedro, fifteen percent were currently attending or were graduates of high schools in San Pedro or San Marcos, and 1.42 percent had been to college in Quezaltenango. It is noteworthy that while the figures show more boys than girls go on to secondary school, girls represent nearly half the educated children nonetheless. Meanwhile, fully seventy-one percent of their mothers—the study sample—had had fewer than three years of schooling (Table 2.3). Thirty-five percent had never been to school at all, and only one woman had been to high school. Nonetheless, in the last twenty years, these overwhelmingly illiterate women had produced twenty-five teachers, two lawyers, and a doctor.

Why are *Sampedrano* families sending their children to school? Smith isolated education as one of the first profitable resources uncovered by *Sampedranos*. Beginning in the 1930s, and intensively since the 1940s and 1950s, the townfolk have fulfilled their desire to reap economic benefits and community esteem through education. Smith showed that schooling not only breaks down class distinctions, but is one important source of the cultural transformation spreading throughout the town and into its hinterland. The dramatic growth of educational options since the 1950s is evidence of the local demand for information, skills, and a more worldly perspective.

Individual urban and rural *Sampedranos* are prospering in part because they are educated. Smith tells many stories of professional men who rose from poverty to material success and public acclaim because of the years they dedicated to earning a degree. Women have also utilized schooling to become teachers and professionals, and in the process are achieving an unprecedented level of economic mobility and independence. Moreover, since many well-educated locals remain in their home town to work or establish a business, schooling has become a crucial element in the development of a vital, pluralistic society. Recently, formal education has been exploited as an alternative to traditional skills previously imparted within the family. As in-

Table 2.3 *Schooling of San José Caben Women* (n=80)

No school	<3 years	3rd grade	6th grade	High School
35 (44%)	22 (27.5%)	17 (21%)	5 (6%)	1 (1%)

digenous crafts and home industries decline in the face of a more modern life-style and orientation, *Sampedranos* recognize they need new proficiencies and productive tools best provided through schooling. While schools continue to offer vocational courses appropriate to artisan trades, more students are seeking high school diplomas and college degrees as avenues to success.

As the case of San José Caben illustrates, San Pedro's immediate hinterland expresses both the town's entrepreneurial energies and eagerness for the tools education can provide. Many *aldeanos* from villages as close as San José have fostered trade and production partnerships that afford them some financial security, or even allow them to prosper. Those in the nearer *aldeas* have been able to strategize better than others because more business opportunities are immediately available. As such, they send their children to schools not just because they are close to town, but also because the success of their cottage industries and/or jobs permits them to release some child labor.

The differences between successful near *aldeanos* and poorer distant ones are clear to most rural people. Rosario and Edulina, the successful merchants from Chamac, for example, cluck their tongues judgmentally at the way the poorer *aldeanos* live. Although electricity, proximity to water, and passable roads are relatively recent in their own *aldea,* these distinctions reflect their own newly found status, far above what they describe as the lowly condition of Chim, an *aldea* only an hour away. Class distinctions like these play a role in San Pedro that, while subordinate to the larger categories of Indian and *ladino,* are integral to group identity nonetheless.

Class Distinctions

To a certain extent it is true that the populace of the entire *municipio* of San Pedro Sacatepéquez shares in what Smith called the "unprecedented prosperity" of the urban section of the town, but they do so with different degrees of success due to extremely variable access to opportunities. Most town people have improved their economic status only since 1950, and while a few *aldeanos* may have combined entrepreneurship and ingenuity to achieve a fair measure of security or affluence, the majority of rural people—near or far—are still forced to muster the productive efforts of all family members just to make ends meet. To some degree the rural/urban dichotomy reflects certain recently imposed cultural class distinctions. Class in this case is based upon adherence to a traditional versus a modern life-style, as well as the long-standing economic measure of ability to accumulate capital and property.

The economic and cultural criteria overlap significantly since the town's wealthiest truckers and merchants—the first generation to be economically mobile—tend to have traditional rural ties and are minimally educated. One doctor and a few lawyers approach the incomes of these prosperous men, but the social gap between the two groups is so large, they rarely interact informally. Increased wealth, however, brings status to the children of the newly rich, who usually acquire solid middle class tastes and behaviors through extensive schooling and familiarity with national values.

In spite of any imprecision in the assignment of social status, it is important to understand how the fruits of development are distributed to local men and women, and part of that process must include examination of the constraints of class. With this purpose in mind, an outline of San Pedro's own cultural class designations is offered to facilitate analysis of a population that includes (among others) rural peasantry, upwardly mobile ex-peasants, urban students and working people. Life for all these people is changing so rapidly that the precise markers of class identity described here (e.g., consumer preference, degree of economic mobility) may have already begun to change. Nevertheless, they do form a schematic background for examining roles in a developing town, and, as such, offer a basis for analysis.

Among themselves, *Sampedranos* have designated two broad classes of people: *gente civilizada* and *gente natural*. In the town, a majority has adopted the *civilizada* personification of their social and economic growth pattern, and indeed, a few of them are quite learned. Some are very affluent. *Civilizadas* wear Western clothing; donning *típica* (Indian costume) is stylish only for formal photographs harkening nostalgically to their Mayan ancestors. They are educated. Many are high school graduates or have been to college. *Civilizada* families have a tendency to be overextended in terms of credit, owing for material possessions bought "on time" and for short term loans from the bank. They own televisions, frequent movies and dances, eat salads, hamburgers, and fast-food chicken sandwiches. In short, they have all the visible manifestations of Western living, expressed keenly in a distinct preference for conspicuous consumption. Included among this group are a very few *ricos* who are the town's leading citizens and professionals.[9]

The *gente natural* is a large and somewhat diverse lower class category which applies to most of the men and women of the *municipio*, that is, all of the *aldeanos* and poorer urbanites. It includes all *de corte* women who still wear Indian skirts (*cortes*) although the majority of poor Westernized women are also considered *gente* for purposes of this discussion. In terms of education, some *gente* women have three or more years of schooling, but most are illiterate nonetheless. In spite of these common characteristics, there exists tremendous variety among women as to their life-styles, material possessions, and occupations. Many would resent and reject this grouping, considering themselves too upwardly mobile to be thrown into a category "with the rest of those *inditos*." However different one woman might appear to be from another, the similarities in their low standard of living and high incidence of malnutrition, for example, are general enough that all are grouped together as *gente natural*.[10]

A scan of ten years of medical statistics accumulated at the San Marcos State Hospital illustrates the difficult situation of most poor women. These figures, while not representative of the entire population (affluent *civilizadas* go to private hospitals elsewhere), do show an uneven distribution of the benefits of development on a local level. For example, birth statistics show that 98% of the women entering to give birth are severely malnourished. The ramifications of the inadequate diet of most women is reflected in the extremely high number of babies and mothers who die before leaving the hospital, a figure local doctors ascribe primarily to malnutrition or to lack of prenatal care. In 1976, six of every thousand women entering the hospital died in childbirth or within a few days of giving birth.[11] This figure is up from four in a thousand in 1967 and five in a thousand in 1971. The dramatic nature of these figures is clear when they are compared with the United States' figures for 1975, which show only 0.12 maternal deaths per thousand live births (Vital Statistics of the United States 1977). Furthermore, only a small percentage of the *municipio*'s births (27%) take place in the hospital. Most are homebirths attended by midwives for which we have no comparable data. Licensed midwives from relatively accessible areas do rush their patients to the hospital when complications arise, but many births take place in distant *aldeas* where no emergency medical help is available and public health officials can only speculate as to the unrecorded deaths connected with homebirths.[12]

Some of the side effects of chronic female malnutrition come to light during and after pregnancy. For example, the widespread tooth decay of relatively young women is first spotted by dentists in pre-natal examinations locally known as *control*. This system of check-ups started in the early 1970s when public health authorities began to draw pregnant women into clinics by offering free weekly allotments of CARE food products to all mothers in *control*. Dental check-ups are part of this program and since their inception, dentists have had to extract thousands of rotten teeth in the belief that this may prevent dental infection from spreading to the fetus.[13]

After birth, malnutrition immediately devastates the newborn baby when insufficient nutriments are supplied in mother's milk. Health and religious personnel encourage poor women to supplement their milk with soft foods and cereals, but the custom of only breast-feeding for the first year is still common, especially when mothers can barely feed themselves. Consequently, babies who have been undernourished from the womb are further weakened by breast-feeding and are therefore subject to any passing illness.

In spite of a growing middle class, local statistics from 1987 on malnutrition and infant mortality are unchanged from 1977 and, as such, continue to be dismaying. According to the director of public health, ninety percent of the children from San Pedro and its *aldeas* are malnourished. Of every thousand new babies born, fifty die before they reach one year, a figure that although high, compares "favorably" with the national average of over sixty! Western medical care is far more available than it used to be, yet a doctor's visit costs more than a day's business profits, and the cost of drugs and patent medicines has risen nearly four hundred percent.

What this discussion clearly shows is that while San Pedro may be a prosperous Indian community by any standard, great numbers of *aldeanos* and townfolk struggle nonetheless. It is common to hear women say "*Luchamos para vivir como somos pobres*" (We struggle to live because we are poor). While it seems customary for everyone in San Pedro to proclaim that they are poor, or make only a slim profit, for many, this statement is all too true.

History of San Pedro as a Weaving Town

The bulk of early twentieth-century analysis of Guatemalan weaving comes from the work of two women, Lilly deJongh Osborne (1935, 1965) and Lila M. O'Neale (1945), who as early as 1905 and 1936, respectively, traveled to Maya towns and villages, chronicling the weaving techniques, costumes, and textile trade of dozens of communities.[14]

I mention their work because O'Neale's and Osborne's observations and those of other writers who worked in Guatemala before World War II (e.g., Bunzel 1952; Tax 1953) help establish the history of San Pedro's textile industry. Analysis from the 1930s, for instance, describes the excellence and intricacy of the town's local costume, as well as its production of extraordinary textiles and embroidery for trade. Osborne notes that although one-piece *huipiles* were rare in the highlands, "the most beautiful are those made in San Pedro Sacatepéquez (Mam country)." (19) And, "these *huipiles* . . . are a good trade-article, as they are totally covered with silk designs, giving the whole a really spectacular appearance." (87) In O'Neale's discussion of materials, she also points to the town as a distinctive example of silk weaving.[15]

> The women's skirt materials at San Pedro Sacatepéquez (San Marcos) are handsome fabrics whether new or old. Most of them are all-cotton weavings, but more than a few have crossbands of yellow silk—which fades to a fine canary yellow—and jaspe (tie-dyed) yarn. These skirts represent a use of the greatest amount of silk employed in the weaving of the basic material to be found today in the highlands. A huipil heavily brocaded in colored silks completes the costume. (18)

San Pedro made its name in the textile trade with more than its own impressive silk costume. External trade was based upon the ability of *Sampedrano* weavers to copy the authentic designs of other towns and villages (Bunzel 1952). Its professionally made collars were also widespread, as were its belts. Factories dotted the town producing patterned lengths of silk and cotton for skirts, machine-stitched shirts, brocaded *huipiles* made on large draw looms, tablecloths and pillow tops (O'Neale 1945).

Like other Guatemalan towns (e.g. Totonicapán, Huehuetenango, Quezaltenango, Momostenango) that have historically engaged in commercial production of woven articles, the volume of San Pedro's textile trade has for many years been based upon utilizing the four-harness footloom introduced to the region by the Spanish in the seventeenth century. The production of fabric on a footloom (also called the treadle loom) is rapid and simple when compared to its predecessor, the stick or back-strap loom (*palito*). Not only is the fabric produced often twice as wide, the manipulation of the loom itself is easier. Once footloom weavers learn the design, they can turn out quantities of the distinctive regional patterns in far less time than it takes local stick weavers.[16]

Despite the consensus in San Pedro that footloomed fabrics were clearly inferior to *palito,* today the stick loom has been completely replaced except for the commercial weaving of thin belts. The reason seems to be pure economic prudence. Basically, the forty-day time investment necessary for the production of one *huipil* makes stick-loom weaving impractical for entrepreneurial activity. It simply cannot compete with the more ordinary, cheaper footloomed fabric produced in one-quarter the time. Although as recently as 1977 a few women still wove specialty *huipiles* on *palitos,* the footloom has been the basis of San Pedro's weaving trade. Footlooms transformed traditional weaving into an industry for the centralized commercial production and distribution of fabric, providing clothing and household items to non-weavers and to those stick weavers who did not have the time, inclination, or appropriate skill (O'Neale 1945).[17] The dominance of the faster, more efficient technology has never sidelined San Pedro's traditional back-strap weavers. Instead, it has allowed hundreds of women to transfer from domestic, low-volume weaving to marketable commercial enterprises. By using the footloom, women who had previously had little to trade could become textile entrepreneurs. One eighty-year-old textile trader told me that in 1935 there were only twenty *palito* weavers making *huipiles* to sell. By 1950, however, many more weavers were exploiting a new and expanded local market based on the changing character of family productive systems. In the late 1940s and 1950s, as more and more women moved into income-producing work, *Sampedrana* weavers stepped into a growth industry by quickly and cheaply producing the clothes other *Sampedranas* could no longer weave themselves.

In spite of the diverse and changing technology, the traditional weaving cottage industry has always been monopolized by women. Historically, men were usually connected to the textile industry only in a trade capacity, leading their mule trains along established routes to market. On the other hand, until quite recently, all women knew how to weave. Female domestic responsibilities that kept women more localized than men did not stop at cooking and childcare; skilled weaving was a prerequisite for marriage. Stories from Osborne's highland visits in the 1930s illustrate the rigorous marital requirements of a *Sampedrana* trying to master the various difficult weaving techniques and to be able to market her products as well:

> With weaving she must be able to make enough money to buy a first-class wedding costume for her fiance, a costume which is store-bought and quite according to modern fashions. (1965:225)

Should a woman fail to satisfy these expectations as proof of the marketability and excellence of her craft, "she may be beaten by her husband and her future in-laws, if not actually returned to her parents . . ." (Osborne 1965:226). A more personal story refers to a San Pedro woman who had been engaged for more than a year and a half and could still not marry because she had not yet mastered the weaving techniques, "despite the wealth that her fiance boasted in mules and his trade reputation" (Osborne 1965:62). Information from the girl's mother suggested there would be an additional six month delay before the wedding since the bride could only weave simple patterns but not the more complicated brocade design which was the pride of the town.

Sampedranas are no longer required to learn to weave. Their economic and education opportunities have greatly expanded, and now that almost every woman has a marketable skill or craft, weaving is no longer a preferred female occupation. To the contrary, women are moving away from this type of home industry, primarily because the market for San Pedro textiles has shrunk dramatically in the last fifteen years. There are many reasons for the decline. Locally, as the town turns away from its indigenous symbols, women are abandoning their *traje* in favor of cheaper Western dresses. The money that had previously been invested in costume as an outward expression of ethnicity is being spent instead on consumer items. On the regional level, competition from better-capitalized factories in Quezaltenango has squeezed San Pedro out of its commercial textile trade. And, as I will discuss in Chapter Six, the final blow was struck in 1985 when inflation and the falling value of the *quetzal* made the San Pedro costume far too expensive for most consumers. In place of the weaving of Indian textiles has come the male-dominated manufacture and sale of yardgoods, an industry that has completely replaced female weaving as the town's major occupation.

Women and the Economy

Today, the majority of female money-making occupations in San Pedro are in the various aspects of retail and wholesale trading, as well as cottage industry. Locations vary from home to plaza to market stall to store to warehouse. Female income is often a secondary or tertiary source of money in the family, but one also finds many rural families depending upon the work of its female members for most of its food. This is true even in cases where there is a male head of household since traditionally the money earned by men is used only for corn and firewood, forcing the wife to develop her own income in order to provide for other family necessities. This financial arrangement has become extremely demanding for men as well, with less and less highland land available for cultivation. With an average of seven *cuerdas* (1 acre = 9.4 *cuerdas*) of land, men find that their *milpa* does not suffice for a year of corn and they are forced to find additional income in order to supplement what they can grow. This partially explains the increasingly large number of men who quickly take advantage of opportunities for investment in trade, transport, and commercial weaving.

Female economic development has been hampered by the fact that women have found themselves utilizing traditional skills and market connections first established by their mothers and grandmothers. Rarely has a woman ventured into learning a new kind of work unless, as in the case of

Table 2.4 *Three Generations of Women's Work*

Jobs	Generation 1 (grandmothers) n = 107	Generation 2 (mothers) n = 109	Generation 3 (daughters) n = 77
Traditional	41 (38%)	51 (47%)	22 (29%)
Modern	5 (5%)	25 (23%)	44 (57%)
Housewife	61 (57%)	32 (30%)	11 (14%)

Source: Smith and Wilson (n.d.)

the knitting machine, new technology literally sweeps through the town, enabling hundreds of women to produce garments at home in whatever spare moments they might have. With this one exception, the otherwise complete reliance on traditional skills has limited the economic growth of women, relegating them largely to a singularly female labor area, undercapitalized and with no long range returns.

But with the town's development, women's emphasis on these traditional female family businesses seems to be changing. Analysis of Smith and Wilson's (n.d.) research on San Pedro families in the mid-1970s shows that within the last generation women in town and its near *aldeas* have moved away from traditional cooperative women's work and toward modern employment. The following figures show an increase of nearly 35% in jobs daughters (generation No. 3) elect outside family enterprises. At the same time, the figures indicate an overall rise in income-producing work for women with far fewer married women stipulating "housewife" as their primary occupation. These figures support Smith's (1977) contention that socioeconomic development since 1945 has resulted in more employment, but the trend seems to be for the female population to be occupied outside the home and apart from the female family businesses.

Analysis of the implications of modern or traditional employment will be taken up in the next chapter, Female Labor and the Family. For now, suffice to say that while modern occupations may expand female money-making potential, they restructure the worker-product relationship so as to deprive women of the control of their own labor, a critical element in traditional work. Furthermore, extradomestic jobs in the modern realm seriously disrupt familial labor arrangements which afforded women easy dispersal of household and job responsibilities.

The availability of modern employment should not be misinterpreted. There are modern jobs for women that afford them economic mobility, social prestige, and secure monthly salaries many times higher than what their mothers earn. Teaching, the most popular position, pays Q240 a month to start, and the job provides secure employment and government benefits. A smaller fraction of professional women work as nurses or social workers and a few are civil servants. Because the basic requirement for these jobs is a high school degree, professional women are overwhelmingly urban and middle class, but the spread of education is making them more accessible to rural *aldeanas* as well. However, analysis of high school graduates in San Pedro shows that compared to men, women occupy a narrow range of jobs. While men are found in more than fifteen different positions, female high school graduates are segregated into only a few employment categories, particularly teaching, where they hold more than half of the more than two hundred classroom positions in the town and its *aldeas*.

The lack of variety in female job opportunities is mainly a result of cultural expectations about the kind of work women ought to do, and the assumption that their most important job is at home taking care of the family. As such, they are tracked into only a few "helping" professions while still in school. Currently, it is extremely difficult to find a teaching job, but women are not being encouraged to train for non-female careers that are more in demand. By confining women to only a few professional options, the result is that they are not as prepared as their male counterparts to take full advantage of the opportunity schooling provides.

Similarly, the expansion of the external trade market has mainly involved men; women neither own trucks nor supervise commercial looms. Wherever a woman is working, she is commonly connected only to the internal market or is on the piecework end of the labor market. She sees a small amount of cash at the end of each transaction, whether it be through the sale of textiles she has woven, flowers she has grown, or *tamalitos* she has cooked. It is difficult to say whether the much-touted investments in education will afford women more opportunities for improving this situation. I know of dozens of high-school graduates who cannot find employment. In short, it seems that as modernization sweeps through the town, women are not able to jump on the "marimba wagon" as fast or as easily as men.

Work and the Family

Sampedranas brag that they "live to work." For all but the most ladinoized, hard work and its accompanying suffering are marks of social prestige that status-hungry women are reluctant to give up. Women like to think of themselves as constantly occupied and although they may linger over coffee and rolls now and again, or perhaps catch a moment of their favorite television soap opera just before bed, it is rare to find many women sitting still for very long without some kind of work in their hands. In addition to their income-producing extradomestic businesses and cottage industries, *Sampedranas,* like all Guatemalan women, continue to fulfill primary roles in household labor as well. Local women rarely differentiate between work for income and domestic housework, combining them instead under the rubric of *la lucha,* i.e., what a woman must do simply to keep her family alive from one day of hard work to the next. The self-generated stereotype surrounding the tireless efforts of women at work has much basis in fact in San Pedro. Women do not exaggerate their efforts; they really do work all the time.

Few women manage *la lucha* without assistance. It seems a rule of thumb in the Guatemalan highlands that female children—all but those of the very rich—work in the home from very young ages. Generally speaking, even a five-year-old will be able to help out if only to feed the chickens and pick herbs out of the *milpa.*[18] By the time she is nine years old, a daughter may be carrying the baby around on her back while chopping vegetables for lunch. These simple tasks are at first carefully supervised, and through endless hours of observation, mimicry and lessons, young girls are socialized into their domestic responsibilities. By adolescence most *patojas* (teenagers) cook and clean with considerable deftness and confidence. Furthermore, they have developed a passion for children and can always be counted on to entertain visiting youngsters for as long as the guests remain. The mastering of these domestic tasks is basic to a *Sampedrana's* education; no girl could anticipate marrying without them. Indeed, it is expected that the move from her natal home to husband's home will be a smooth transition from one set of *oficios domésticos* (domestic labor) to another.

While it is clear that female orientation to and practice in the *oficios domésticos* is critical for her future role as a wife and mother, on a more immediate level, the execution of domestic responsibilities by daughters serves an important household function in terms of the efficient division of female labor. It frees the mother and older girls from routine housekeeping and permits them to devote themselves to their income producing businesses that keep the family financially stable. This is not to say that all household responsibilities are dumped Cinderella-style on the youngest. A sufficient number of daughters gives productive mothers the option of being full-time workers and of utilizing the labor of older daughters to maximize that extra-domestic work. At the same time they may be secure in the knowledge that in their absence, meals are being prepared and the toddler is being bathed.

Child labor in this case can free adult females from personally having to execute all domestic and extradomestic labor when it is necessary to do so, and as such, plays an extremely important role in family maintenance.

While on the whole *Sampedranas* seem to enjoy a higher standard of living and consumption level than most rural Guatemalans, the expansion of capitalist options has certainly not been an even one. Most people continue to work hard to survive, but rewards and control over resources fluctuates not only by sex but by class. Thus, townswomen tend to be more elite in their habits and values, approaching the national levels of education and consumption, while to a certain extent rural women maintain the life-style and spending patterns of their parents and grandparents. In spite of the diverse nature of their daily lives, the proliferation of the benefits of development has meant that upward mobility is a feature of most families, rural or urban, although again, it is realized in vastly differing degrees.

Overall, in spite of their relatively favorable economic status, with increasing modernization *Sampedranas* are undergoing a restructuring of their productive options typical of women in situations of development. For example, as the international market network expands, access to a diversity of consumer goods makes traditional female cottage industry effectively obsolete, forcing thousands of previously independent producers to rely upon low-paid piecework as an economic alternative. And, in the burgeoning San Pedro commercial economy, male access to credit and export networks has permitted capitalization of an increasingly complex commercial transport and trade system, but women have been unable to enter this field which is considered an exclusively male domain.

Highland Oasis?

San Pedro, like any market system, has been vulnerable to economic trends beyond its control. Since 1985, many of its positive steps toward a secure standard of living have been stymied by Guatemala's dismal national economic profile. Brought on by sagging international markets for Central American agricultural products and soaring interest rates, the problem has been exacerbated by the incurring of nonproductive debts to finance military operations. The country began to feel the crunch in 1984 when the *quetzal*-to-dollar value—which had been 1 : 1 since 1925—began to drop until it reached 4 : 1 in 1985. Since then it has stabilized at 2.7 : 1. In the meantime Guatemala has lost more than $1.1 billion to the US in foreign exchange. Sources in the Bank of Guatemala report that reserves sunk to negative $602 million in November 1988, a drop of nearly $300 million from 1987 (Central America Report December 16, 1988). By its own analysis, Guatemala is confronting a serious fiscal crisis. The government announced that cotton exports alone were down by more than $100 million in 1986, putting fifteen thousand families out of work with a loss of $40 million in wages (Enforensa 30 Jan. 1987). Exports of coffee, sugar, and cardamom were all down for 1987, but the price of imports took a fourteen percent jump (Central America Report August 12, 1988). According to the Bank of Guatemala, inflation was more than forty percent annually, and the jobless rate was between thirty-five and forty percent. Real wages dropped by thirty-eight percent between 1981 and 1986, and government per capita spending was down fifty percent in the same period. Rural workers still make only one or two dollars a day, while the prices of basic goods have risen 105 percent between 1985 and 1988 (Noticias de Guatemala, January 1989). One impact of all this is that protein consumption dropped by at least fifteen percent, caloric intake by sixteen percent, and the per capita intake of eggs, meat and fats was reduced in ninety percent of the population (Guatemala News in Brief 1987).

This fiscal crisis has affected San Pedro. Opportunities to buy and sell in the bustling market or in dozens of regional markets have long provided viable careers for some, subsistence for others. But inflation and the dropping value of the *quetzal* in overseas markets exacerbates the already existing problems caused by increasing population and the evolution away from traditional cottage industries (see Chapter Six for a full discussion of this trend). Lower sales in home-based production have forced people to fall back upon market trade,[19] and in the last few years local commerce has become a very crowded way of life.

Competition in the market—both daily and weekly—is intense and profits are low. Merchants who for years have run successful stalls and shops on less than a ten percent profit margin fear they will have to close their doors as dozens of competitors spring up to undercut their prices and claim their clientele. The work week is of necessity seven days and nights. One sign of prosperity is to take off Sunday afternoon. Even so, few families have only one business, and the coupling of trade with some other industry or job is *de rigeur*. In one extended family of fifteen, I counted five salaries and eight separate money-making activities. If a customer knocked on the door wanting a shroud, paper flowers for a grave, a birthday cake, a bottle of soda pop, oil for the car, or a legal opinion, business was transacted. The hour of the day or night was immaterial, with even the meager profit of one late-night sale not to be lost. *Sampedranos* have always been proud of their work ethic, but

Table 2.5 *Prices in 1977 and 1987*[20]

Item	1977	1987
black beans	.08 −.14/lb	.70
corn	.05/lb	.22
rice	.15/lb	.75
soap	.04 each	.22
meat	.75/lb	3.75
chicken feed	8.40/100 lb	33.80
milk	.08 liter	.50
salt	.03/lb	.20
chicken	.29/lb	1.80
sugar	.08/lb	.30−.32
bread	6 for .05	.04 each
carrots	.40/doz	1.00
shrimp	1.20/lb	8.00
tomato paste	.15 each	.75
hot sauce	.10 each	.50
gasoline	.95/gal	2.95
electricity	.07/kwh	.21
antacids	.05 each	.15
private school	4/month	15.00
bus fare to Quezaltenango	.50	1.50
teacher's salary (beginning)	240/month	372/month
laborer's salary	1−2/day	2.50−3.50
maid's salary	12/month	40/month

in the last few years, it has become necessary for survival. Rampant consumerism may be characteristic of enough *Sampedranos* to support several hundred shops and services, but the overwhelming number of people must work overtime to buy anything as expensive as a monthly pound of meat or three yards of fabric for a school uniform.

Over the last decade, the cost of living has escalated dramatically. Table 2.5

illustrates the repercussions that the national economic crisis has had on the prices of daily necessities in San Pedro. With income not keeping pace with inflation or actually declining, there is no doubt that here, as nationally, the quality of life has seriously deteriorated.

The costs of daily necessities clearly have increased fivefold in a decade, without corresponding increases in wages and salaries. One obvious result of the price increase is that people's diets suffer. With many families existing on a combined income of Q4 daily, few people can afford to buy what they would like to eat. Ten years ago, the ordinary diet of the rural *Sampedrano* included cereal or eggs for breakfast, and meat once a week. Today only the wealthiest people can afford meat on a regular basis, a situation that has resulted in the bankruptcy of nearly a dozen butchers in only four years.[21]

Summing up, San Pedro Sacatepéquez can be described as an anomalous highland Guatemalan town where access to an expanding market economy affords the local Indian population opportunity to support themselves and their families. Clearly, commercial success is available to *Sampedranos* in varying degrees. Only a few people (between ten and fifteen percent of the urban population) may be characterized as middle class, although many more aspire to *civilizada* status through education and the acquisition of consumer goods. The majority of the people are poor by any standard but are still able to employ economic strategies like cottage industry and trade to free themselves from seasonal migratory labor so typical of Guatemala's rural Indians. Until recently, the town's economic good fortune was expanding, assuring many more people a secure economic future. But since 1985, national fiscal problems have somewhat curtailed development, stalling the growth of prosperity that had characterized the town. As will become clear, those whose futures are particularly imperiled by this kind of economic instability are women. I wrote in 1980 that San Pedro's development diminished the importance of work that is characteristically female and predicted the demise of cottage industry run by women and their children (Ehlers 1982). What I did not realize was that the end might come quite so quickly.

Notes

1. The story of underdevelopment in Guatemala today may be told in a brief list of figures. Seventy-five percent of the country's population is rural, and eighty-two percent of rural inhabitants are illiterate. More than 400,000 rural families hold parcels of land too small for subsistence. Landless peasants make up one-fourth of the rural workforce (Davis 1988). Thirty-five percent of the population cannot satisfy its basic needs,

and forty percent have inadequate diets (Oxfam 1984). Infant mortality is sixty-five deaths per one thousand live births (World Bank 1987). Seventy-five percent of all children under five are malnourished. Over half the total number of deaths are children under five years old (Painter 1987), one reason why rural life expectancy is only forty-one. The national doctor-patient ratio is one per 3,600 but since eighty percent of the country's health services are in the capital, the adjusted ratio is closer to one doctor per 23,000 people outside Guatemala City (Jonas and Tobis 1974).

2. Hawkins (1984) found 52.8 percent of urban *Sampedranos* worked in crafts (carpentry, seamstresses, tile and brick makers, etc.), but since he has many disclaimers amending his analysis, even suggesting that the survey be "read with some caution" (147), I hesitate to utilize his figures.

3. Since this local survey neither allows for dual occupations nor includes nonhousehold heads, i.e., women, it offers only a partial picture of rural labor patterns. To supplement it I did an informal survey of fifty-nine families from the six nearest *aldeas* and found that more than half the workers were dedicating their labors both to agriculture and to artisanal production as weavers, embroiderers, brickmakers, bakers, tailors, tanners, or traders. They did this by either dividing the work, e.g. husband farms, wife weaves, or by each household member doing a number of jobs.

4. Anthropologists tend to flinch when they witness consumer acquisitiveness in an indigenous community, while among *ladinos* it is considered normal behavior. Yet why would one assume that Indians do not desire these goods if everyone around them has them — and the modern status they signify? Margolies addresses this issue in her work on Indians in San Felipe when she suggests that though Indians may be stoical about property and frank about their impoverishment, they do not by any means worship poverty. To the contrary, progress is conceptualized in personal terms as improving one's economic situation and living better (1975).

5. Based upon a number of informal indications of affluence such as a varied and nutritious diet, a telephone, cable TV, a car, and at least one child attending university classes, I estimate that between ten and fifteen percent of San Pedro's urban population may be defined as middle class. I should point out that this classification, while clearly arbitrary, is also, to a certain extent, relative. I learned this when my American middle class father visited me in San Pedro in 1977. We were invited to dine with a family of successful merchants, who satisfy all the requirements I have listed above. In addition, they had a large house with at least one idiosyncrasy with which suburban Americans can identify. That is, there was one room, never used, whose pristine furniture was carefully preserved under plastic covers. After a large meal featuring the biggest pork loin I had ever seen, three vegetables, rice, soup, many bottles of whiskey, and a delicious mango dessert, we staggered home to bed. On the way, thinking my father most certainly had been impressed with the quality of life among the town's middle class, I asked him how he had enjoyed his visit. He turned to me with a look of immense sadness, and said, "My God, those people are so poor!"

6. Because very few people have ovens, and because long cooking over a fire uses expensive fuel, the preferred method of preparing chicken is boiled, or in a soup.

7. As in most Guatemalan communities, there are more high school graduates in San Pedro than professional job openings. In other Latin American and Third World coun-

tries, the underemployed and jobless often migrate to large cities in an attempt to remedy the situation. Indeed, well-educated members of San Pedro families have relocated to Quezaltenango and Guatemala City for jobs, but their numbers are small. Instead, *Sampedranos* prefer to work in town or in San Marcos, even if it means temporarily putting off professional positions. A young architect I know, for example, has decided after six years of college to join his family's bakery business rather than open a practice in another town.

8. In Chapter Five, I compare these two occupations, showing how *costureras,* who work for their husbands or other men, have lost the productive autonomy that *huipil* weavers still maintain.

9. There are many male/female discrepancies in the attribution of status and class. I will discuss this in Chapter Six. For now, it ought to be noted that few women have achieved *rica* status themselves; most are the wives of successful men. *Civilizadas* are not considerably different from the *gente* in terms of male oppression of women, nor are educated women able to take advantage of new opportunities as easily as educated men.

10. W. R. Smith refers to the *gente natural* as *naturales* and while I am using the local referent *gente,* we are talking about the same social category.

11. These statistics were accumulated in 1977 through examination of hospital records. In 1988 I was unsuccessful in persuading the new hospital administration to allow me access to those records. However, discussions with the obstetrician in charge tells me that the figures are basically unchanged from ten years before.

12. It has been suggested to me that the high maternal mortality rate may be because women who anticipate a difficult birth go to the hospital, while better nourished, healthier women give birth at home, and that homebirths would then show a lower mortality rate than hospital births. This may be true for some individuals, but informant opinion and data from Public Health nurses and doctors imply that the trend is just the opposite. While there are many myths and negative stereotypes about the hospital that tend to scare rural people away (e.g. hospitals are where one goes to die), more poor and malnourished women are giving birth in the hospital every year. One obstetrician told me that in 1959, when he became the second doctor—and only gynecologist—in the state, only fifty women came to the hospital to give birth, but by 1987 there were nearly 1500 births a year. Because the population is overwhelmingly poor and malnourished to begin with, the rise in numbers of hospital births would naturally mean that there would be an increased frequency in associated illness and death. Attendance in a maternity ward alone is no insurance against catastrophe. A better strategy is to have regular check-ups as the pregnancy proceeds so that complications are diagnosed and preparations made for whatever difficulties lay ahead. Doctors point out that *Sampedranas* who have been examined during their pregnancies almost never die in childbirth. Unfortunately, except for the small number of women in *control,* most expectant mothers have no pre-natal care.

13. Despite the free food given away to lure women to pre-natal health care, the program has had only minimal success. A 1984 study of the patients in the gynecological wing of the state hospital in San Marcos showed that for the last six months of that year, only 22% of women giving birth had been in pre-natal *control* programs (Orozco Fuentes 1985).

14. O'Neale included one hundred ten communities in her study, Osborne eighty. Although many books are now available on the topic (e.g. Rowe 1981, Anderson 1978, Conte 1984, Bunch and Bunch 1977), none rival the comprehensiveness, depth of analysis, or historical import of O'Neale or Osborne. The later work of Carmen L. Petersen (1976) is a considerable addition—and in a sense, a complement—to the descriptive analysis of O'Neale and Osborne. Pettersen, a painter, explained that her book came about when, after fifty years of a relatively isolated existence on a coffee plantation, she realized that the quality of Guatemalan weaving was fast deteriorating under the impact of roads, missionaries, tourism, and transistor radios. She was determined to record as many costumes as she could. To this end between 1970 and 1974, she painted and commented on twenty-one men's costumes, sixty women's costumes, and thirteen children's costumes. Although she painted *in situ,* Petersen borrowed the costumes from the Ixchel Museum in Guatemala City, and had local people model them. Thus, although her work was done in the 1970's, the clothes she painted were far older.

15. Imported silk was a common material in highland textiles during the twentieth century, especially from 1933 to 1935 when its popularity peaked. But from 1935 to 1940, there occurred a dramatic shift to rayon, and thereafter silk is very rarely found in textiles. The best analysis is that this abrupt change was probably due to the war in the Pacific and the corresponding difficulty in producing and distributing silk (Carlson and Wenger: n.d.).

16. Analysis of the museum collections shows treadle-loomed textiles as long ago as the 1880's, e.g. a one-piece San Pedro *huipil* from 1901 in the Peabody Museum's collection (personal commun. Robert S. Carlsen). Unfortunately, the relative recency of textile collecting makes evidence of earlier footloom work elusive.

17. Backstrap weaving continues to be very popular throughout Guatemala today. Skirts are commonly produced commercially on treadle looms, but among the *de corte* indigenous population, most clothing is produced at home on the *palito.*

18. O'Neale writes of encountering highland children as young as four years old assisting in the arrangement of their mothers' looms, and six-year-olds designing and executing their own weavings (1945). I first learned about the usefulness of young children in 1977 when I was teasing an informant about taking her adorable five-year-old home with me to Colorado. "Oh no, Doña Terry," she said, "she already knows how to wash dishes!"

19. Carol Smith, in her analysis of a similar problem in Totonicapán, calls market trade the "last-resort employer" (1988).

20. Market prices of basic goods in Guatemala vary by the region, fluctuate almost daily, and have a regular seasonality as well. Thus this price list suggests an inflationary trend as it appears in one highland town rather than a precise index of change over a ten year period.

21. Guatemalan beef, like coffee, is almost entirely an export crop, and its domestic scarcity has added dramatically to its very high price.

3

❧

Female Labor and the Family

IN SAN PEDRO, THE USE OF daughters as female workers has been one important way for women to combine their roles as housekeepers and domestic or extradomestic businesswomen. Daughters act to free mothers of the sole responsibility of cooking, cleaning and childcare, thus opening the way for mothers to concentrate on developing market relations and entrepreneurial activities. Also, daughters are socialized to the income-producing work their mothers do and are useful in maintaining and increasing production. This may be done initially by their taking over the monotonous or preparatory tasks, permitting the mother to emphasize more skilled or practiced techniques, and later on daughters may work alongside their mothers to increase saleable output through parallel production. Similarly, trade opportunities grow as daughters are brought into the business to diversify products or expand markets. Moreover, since women must mobilize their available resources and capital in order to fulfill the family's domestic needs, the more workers in the home—particularly female workers—the greater the financial security during the lifetime of the mother. In addition, the daughters will have a functioning enterprise to take over upon their mother's death or retirement.

The organization of female labor into a potent working force is best expressed in what I have called the "female family business"; trades, shops, services and cottage industries that are owned and run by related women for the family's financial betterment. There are many kinds of female family businesses. Many are only nominally female family owned because almost all profits go to the mother who employs younger female kin only as helpers or apprentices. Others are divided into separate and personal enterprises housed under one roof, with each woman having her own share. And a few are similar to collectives, with all work and monies divided evenly. But no matter what percentage each woman owns or manages, all female family businesses are alike in that they maintain a certain stability or financial solvency on the basis of the exploitable family labor used for the day-to-day running of things. Very few of these businesses can afford hired help. What makes family labor attractive is that related women do not pay themselves for their labors; most are essentially working *gratis*. Women stopping to analyze the dollars and cents of their enterprises never speak of money earned by the hour or day, nor do they include the value of their time in figuring out how much to charge. Female family business is seen by *Sampedranas* as "women's work," just another non-paying responsibility which, like domestic housekeeping, falls to women as part of family caretaking.

The family businesses which do take on non-related apprentices or wage laborers are the rare, well-capitalized ones. The majority are minimally financed. Profit margins are very small and net income rarely exceeds the average per capita income of a dollar a day. Many female family businesses are too small to function on a daily basis and some suffer from seasonal fluctuations that cause them to be periodically abandoned, often at a loss. Thus, over a year's time, the majority of producers cannot be assured of more than a small return on their labor.

The recruitment and organization of female labor varies to some extent, but in general, the traditional model has been one where daughters help their mothers in the latter's business and in the process learn enough to initiate the same kind of business after they marry. Thus it is easy for a trader's daughter to open her own stall and for a weaver's daughter to buy a loom and begin weaving on her own. Over years of apprenticeship each has developed skills and expertise (as well as some potential customers), and they have the confidence that their work will generate some income for their new families.

Girls usually start out in business at age nine or ten when they can be helpful doing menial jobs such as winding thread or stacking oranges. When it is necessary for the mother to be away momentarily, she may leave her small daughter in charge of her shop or stall. By puberty, daughters are valuable assets to almost any businesswoman, since by that time they are competent and efficient workers who can be trusted to manage things on their own. It is during the teenage years that the mother-daughter system flourishes and production is at its peak. Daughters often set up parallel businesses which either double output or add variety to the selection of products. They may be sent on trips to Guatemala City or Quezaltenango, where they develop skills in bargaining and negotiating with suppliers and other businesspeople. With the girl's marriage at age nineteen or twenty, the mother-daughter arrangement ends as the new bride turns her attention to her new home, and the mother must rely on the younger girls. Due to patrilocal residence patterns, after marriage, mothers-in-law often benefit from the addition of new female labor into the home. No matter what productive skills the bride may have developed as a girl, her mother-in-law will probably try to incorporate her into her own business. For some women, marriage means a cessation of all business activity for at least a year or two while they concentrate on their new husbands and their first baby. The return to income-producing work most often goes in one of two directions. The bride may take advantage of skills developed in her mother's work to open her own business, or she may enter into a new and modern occupation. If she chooses traditional work, the system continues. If, as so many women are doing, she opts instead for contract piecework production or employment outside the home, female family business comes to an end.

Monetary contributions from daughters (and sons) who are working must also be considered for a complete picture of female resources, but while remittances from Guatemala City jobs or donations from local employment are often important in maintaining the family's domestic budget, they do not serve the same purpose as does income from cooperative work in a female productive system. Child labor is much more important to female producers and entrepreneurs than the monetary contributions of children primarily because adequate and available helpers and apprentices guarantee the smooth management of domestic tasks and at the same time give promise of a certain flexibility and continuity in the functioning of female business. The small amount of money sent home is not sufficient to hire women who can effectively replace daughters who help their mothers in domestic and extra-domestic work, nor can it perpetuate traditional women's businesses when daughters enter modern employment. Consequently, as women lose their daughters to job opportunities in the developing economy, they may be forced to abandon their independent businesses and may themselves become employees of more modern and mechanized industries. As this happens in greater numbers it effectively dooms traditional female family businesses.

It should be pointed out that male labor in the family represents an almost completely separate entity, particularly when comparing the contributions of sons and daughters. First of all, men have traditionally been involved in subsistence *milpa* agriculture and only in the last two or three decades have large numbers begun to emphasize income producing activities over farming (Smith 1977). While the male evolution toward wage labor in commer-

cial weaving or investment in trucking and commerce has contributed to a
higher standard of living for the entire family, it has not meant that women
benefit substantially from the work their sons do. There are a number of
considerations. During their childhood, sons, unlike daughters, are not a reliable source of assistance or income. Boys are not socialized to help women
in the home, and therefore do not replace adult female labor that is needed
for extradomestic work. Occasionally, sons do help their mothers in income-
producing activities, but usually as a secondary job, less important than the
work they do helping their fathers. Secondly, in the trend away from agriculture, boys are often regarded as expendable labor that may instead be
permitted to go to school through twelfth grade or even to university, while
daughters are allowed comparatively less schooling, after which they are immediately incorporated into family business. Third, sons who are working
cannot be counted on for support. They may help their mothers, and then
again, they may not. I have talked to families where male children keep their
money to buy things like radios and motorcycles. There are families where
one son regularly contributes and the other one never does, and families
where monetary assistance is more in the form of a gift that is forthcoming
only on birthdays or holidays. Mothers agree to educate their sons partially
in the hope that once they are securely employed, they will send money
home. To manage a budget over the life cycle, a son's remittances become
crucial when the labor of married daughters is no longer available. Unfortunately, this does not always occur. In short, while in some cases sons can be
counted on to divide their income with their mothers, their labor remains
their own.

The Miranda *Tienda*

The following case study focuses on the Miranda female family business.
Many of the descriptive elements discussed earlier are found in this family,
with the curious addition of a spinster aunt who runs an independent and
highly profitable cottage industry without assistance from anyone. What
makes this variation on the theme of cooperation and mutual aid so interesting is that it indicates the costs and benefits of female family business compared to those businesses of single entrepreneurs.

On a relatively busy corner just two blocks from the central market
stands the Miranda home and the family *tienda,* a small shop where the Miranda women transact their businesses. The *tienda* is not only a store, but also
a location where paper goods may be ordered from the mother, Doña Car-

men, sweaters purchased from her two eldest daughters, and where Carmen's sister-in-law, Violeta, may be contacted regarding the purchase or rental of ritual garments. It is difficult to isolate one proprietor for the *tienda* since family members take turns minding the store. During school vacations and weekends, the youngest daughter, Angélica, may be found there off and on as may her sister, Petrona, who is a teacher. When no one is around, Violeta takes over and on slow Sunday afternoons, Don Martín is in charge. Personnel changes during the day depend on what projects are underway and who may be occupied elsewhere. Some evenings schoolwork is done over the counter, and Ana, the second daughter, may often be seen there being courted by her *novio*. It is rare to find one sister alone in the store for long, since Carmen comes back and forth from the house to chat or send someone out on an errand. While caretaking is shared by all the women (aided at times by the men), the responsibilities and businesses transacted in the store are specific to different family members. Each has her specialty and except for Violeta's solitary sewing, all help others meet deadlines where they can. Furthermore, each daughter contributes not only her labor, but a portion of her profits from the store to meet Carmen's family budget.

The Miranda sons are students and professionals. One son lives in Guatemala City with his wife, and the two younger sons are at home. All the young men have jobs, but Chepe, the youngest, is the only son who regularly contributes to household expenses through his connection to the *tienda*. The other boys never help out in the store, nor do they consider it mandatory or appropriate to give their mother part of what they earn. Occasionally a cash gift will be presented from one of them, but Doña Carmen cannot depend upon it.

Ana manages the store's retail business, and profits from the sale of the store's inventory go solely to her. Unfortunately, she has not had enough capital to invest in popular items, but it is hoped that when she marries, her husband's family will upgrade the inventory with goods from their San Marcos store. Presently there are a few things for sale such as cigarettes, candles and Coca Cola, and sometimes the shelves are stacked with noodles or toilet paper or oatmeal bought cheaply by the case for the family's own consumption. Because the refrigerator has not worked in years, no ice cream is sold. Once a year at carnival time children come in for egg shells filled with confetti to break open on each other's heads.

Carmen is in charge of the store's business in *palmas,* in terms of volume the most important item in the *tienda*. The *palma* is a yard-long stick with an elaborately cut white crepe paper zig-zag design attached that is traditionally placed near the casket at funerals. The number of *palmas* surrounding the bier reflects the importance or popularity of the deceased and the family, or the community's sentiment regarding the circumstances of the death. Thus when a 22-year-old *señorita* died suddenly, the Miranda women sensed a demand for *palmas* and worked all day to make about one hundred. Normally, *palma* production meets daily sales of eight or ten, and only one kind is cut. The response to the popular young woman's death called for a variety in quality and type, and consequently in production costs.

Each *palma* costs approximately Qo.06 to make, so the normal Qo.11 *palma* yields a Qo.05 profit. Fifteen centavo *palmas* have a bit of left-over paper wrapped around the stick, with a bit of bridal fern on top, and an even higher profit margin of about Qo.08. The profit on Qo.25 *palmas* with more crepe paper is Qo.12, and the "top of the line" Qo.50 *palma* yields Qo.27 profit. All these *palmas* take as little as two or three minutes to make even with the various extra features, and though the most money is to be made on the more expensive *palmas,* few are ever bought. Normal daily profits are about half a *quetzal,* but on this day of high *palma* demand the total profits were Q7.00. Although all the women work at making *palmas,* the profits go to Carmen since *palma*-making is her business.

One of the consistent best sellers in the store comes from a *piñata*-making business run by the youngest son, Chepe. Originally Carmen began the business, then taught the skill to her son, who has made it his part-time vocation while he attends high school. He splits the profits evenly with his mother. Most of the year Chepe sells only eight or ten *piñatas* each month, but in the holiday months of December and January sales climb to twenty or more. Each *piñata* sells for Q1.75 or Q2.00, and the specially made Mickey Mouse or Superman models run as high as Q5.00. He makes one a day in about three hours' time and nets approximately Qo.75 on each one sold.

All other business in the *tienda* is *encargada* or things ordered. Carmen makes crepe paper flower wreaths (*coronas*) for casket and grave decorations or house-blessing fiestas. She also takes orders for *recuerdos* (favors) to be handed out to the guests at weddings and *quince años* (fifteenth birthday) celebrations. Unfortunately, orders do not come in regularly throughout the year and if she is lucky, perhaps every two or three weeks she will have a project that requires the work of all the daughters. The business is neither steady nor very profitable and its income is minimal, even at All Saints Day when grave decorating and refurbishing proceeds at a frenzied pace. One year when Carmen and her daughters worked thirteen hours a day for a week making elaborate *coronas* on order and for last minute retail sales, she netted only Q20.00.

The two eldest daughters, Petrona and Ana, combine minding the store with knitting sweaters by machine. Their knitting is highly regarded in the town and they often work on the same sweater, one on the sleeves, the other on the front and back. The money earned from the sweater business goes to the sister who agreed upon the price and closed the sale. The volunteer assistance is without monetary recompense but is regularly reciprocated. All the work takes place in the *tienda* where the knitting machine is set up, and work begins with the early morning opening of the store.

Ana also has a reputation locally as a specialty baker and from time to time is called upon to make a cake for a fiesta. One October she contracted to bake and decorate a three-tiered cake for a "*quince años*" for Q40.00. She figured the costs at Q30.00 and the time needed at approximately an hour. Everyone in the family ended up helping, and because the electric beater (borrowed for the occasion) burned out, they took turns stirring the giant bowl of batter by hand. It took six people all afternoon, but the Q10.00 profit paid for Ana's schoolbooks for the coming college semester.

Both Petrona and Ana have worked as teachers, making approximately Q270.00 a month, but both have debts, especially Petrona, who has a history of illness and doctor bills. Both sisters pay their university expenses and personal bills from their salaries and *tienda* earnings, and each contributes regularly to the household budget—Petrona at Q50.00 a month and Ana (now unemployed) at Q20.00. Besides their father's Q250.00 monthly salary, Petrona is the only regularly employed family member. During particularly hard times, all of her salary goes toward paying family bills and she saves nothing toward her schooling costs. Her salary is so critical in the family productive system that during an especially serious illness when she was bedridden for five months, her brother begged the state's permission to replace her in her job so that neither the position nor the salary was lost to the family.

It should be noted that the youngest sister, Angélica (16), assists in all the business ventures discussed above, but has no independent enterprise of her own. She minds the store for Ana, makes *palmas* and *coronas* for her mother, and is learning how to knit on Petrona's machine. She is always willing to be sent on errands and allows everyone to exploit her labor because she has no cash-productive contributions to make as yet. Furthermore, she is the only family member who cannot pay her own private school tuition (Q8.00 a month). She is concerned about this payment as a drain on her mother's budget and tries to compensate her mother by working as much as she can.

In contrast to the cooperation and the selfless nature of the Miranda female family business are the private entrepreneuring efforts of Carmen's sister-in-law, Violeta. Violeta is Don Martín's 48-year-old unmarried sister.

She owns the house the Miranda family lives in, and she trades her brother's family a place to live for the care they provide her, and their company. By renting out two storerooms attached to the house, Violeta makes enough money to be able to contribute Q25.00 a month for food. Carmen and her daughters resent the cash payments, and would rather be recompensed with partnership in her jealously guarded sewing business.

Violeta's business fits in with the funereal theme of the *tienda*. Her basic products are shrouds or dresses for the dead, which sell for Q1.75–Q3.00 for children and Q7.00–18.00 for women, one third of which is Violeta's profit. Making three large items a day is optimum production, and she regularly sells ten a week. When there is a deadline, Violeta sews late by the light of a single bulb so as not to disappoint her customers. Inventory is minimal. She maintains a stock of five or six items with prices depending on the amount of lace, quality of fabric and detail of design. In the case of death of a woman, the customers are usually the husband with his kin or the mother and sister. Often the woman is near death rather than already *muerta,* but in either event, if the customers are even slightly known to Violeta, a ritualized commiseration takes place in the living room accompanied by customary wailing and shrieking, followed by coffee and sweet rolls. The death of a baby is more common. The child is customarily mourned at home without a mass or public grieving. The father purchases the *mortaja* (shroud), and as is the case with women's death clothes, measurements have been taken at home and a length of string is given to Violeta so the size will be correct.

During the weeks before Christmas, Violeta sews about two hundred little dresses or outfits for the doll-like Christ child and other saints in home nativity scenes (*vestiditos de niñitos*). Status-hungry *Sampedranas* often change the *vestiditos* every year, and it is a frantically busy time. Violeta's cost is about Q0.60 for each. Selling them for between Q1.00 and Q1.50, her profit ranges from Q0.40 to Q0.90 a piece, a sizeable net for a few weeks' work.

Wedding dresses which Violeta has made are rented for Q3.00. The most she ever rents are four or five a month, but it is clear profit since she covered her initial cost years ago. All she does now is wash them after each use. First communion dresses are similarly handled although the inventory is greater and all are rented at one time since parishes and *aldeas* celebrate first communions in groups. These dresses rent for Q1.00 to Q1.50, and there are periods when ten to twenty are gone at once. No security deposit is ever asked on the rentals and they are always returned in good condition.

In addition, Violeta—whom people consider "*muy católica*"—has a host of miscellaneous skills associated with church activities or mourning rituals and, aside from some church work, these are all done for a fee. For example, nine days after a death, the family entertains guests at home and has a small mass. Violeta is often called upon to decorate the mourners' home, especially the altar, and she keeps large quantities of lacy pastel curtain fabric on hand for such occasions.

In all, Violeta's businesses earn her about Q1,500 a year. Much of her work is seasonal, so that months go by when she rarely brings out her sewing machine and is idle most of the day. Surprisingly, with so many dressmakers in San Pedro, there is little competition. Only one other *tienda* features *vestiditos* and none sell or rent *mortajas,* and while seamstresses will make wedding and communion dresses to order, few rent them. Thus Violeta holds a tight rein on the availability and prices of her products. Unmarried and childless, she saves all her profits to spend on herself as she pleases. She travels to visit the rest of her family, buys new shoes and a new bed, and recently put a down payment on a new television for the family.

Señorita Violeta is an anomaly in San Pedro in that she does not have to work hard to live. They call her a *paseadora*—a woman who hangs around doing little. She chats with friends, visits all over the town and the country, and passes time in church activities, but this was not always the case. When her mother was alive, the two worked together developing the successful business Violeta now controls. What makes her life comparatively easy is that because of the hard work of both Violeta and her mother, she has security based not only upon her skills as a seamstress, but also from investments in real estate. At her mother's death, she inherited several plots of land in town and on the coast which she sold soon after to reinvest in the modern house where the Miranda family lives. Moreover, she has a consistent monthly income from the rental of two small warehouses in the house and an apartment upstairs which she leases for Q35.00 a month. Thus we can see that Violeta's freedom from *la lucha* is relatively recent and stems not only from her lack of family responsibilities but from her sizeable holdings. A less affluent woman without children or husband would not have the luxury of working only in periodic spurts and spending all her cash at will. As it is, Violeta's ownership of a large home as well as reliable rental property makes it possible for her to be a kind of permanent hostess to the Miranda family and to have the services daughters provide with none of the expense.

Over the past thirteen years, little has changed in the management of the Miranda *tienda.* All the daughters are now teachers who, to different degrees, contribute their free time to the store. The small profits from the female family business enhanced the social and economic mobility of the Miranda women by paying for their education. The skills and worldliness they now apply to retail sales have resulted in the introduction of a few different products and a refrigerator, but the established system of female-based business remains. Meanwhile, the three sons are well-paid professionals who have dedicated themselves as well to commercial investment activities beyond the family's retail efforts. Over the last few years, the brothers have collaborated on a profitable trucking business. Although all the women help in the enterprise, because none of them had the capital to invest in the business, they make no money for their work.

Female Domestic Labor

There are slack seasons and slow periods in most businesses, but housekeeping occupies women's time as a regular daily routine whose rhythm barely abates but only intensifies with holidays, illnesses, or visitors. While in name the duties of the *ama de casa* are strikingly similar to those of a middle class North American housewife, it must be remembered that cleaning, cooking, childcare, and washing clothes are done without benefit of labor-saving appliances or technological aids and as such are time-consuming, labor intensive and difficult.

SHOPPING

Food preparation demands many hours of a town woman's day,[1] but this task is further complicated by the need to shop every day. Refrigerators are expensive and rare, and spoiled food is lost money. So while most women do some marketing on a plaza day, townwomen also run to the market every afternoon when fresh bread is first available, when *tamalitos* are being wrapped in leaves for lunch, or when they need butter or another avocado. Meat and other perishables are also bought daily, and daughters are constantly being sent out for some forgotten item that can only be purchased just before the meal. In a sense, access to the market or to well stocked neighborhood shops is an urban luxury. Distance keeps rural women from this kind of shopping on a daily basis. They attend to their week's shopping in intense spurts of activity on the main market days. If they are also commercial traders on Sundays or Thursdays, they may only bring home enough for those few days in between, but most women come to town once a week. While small *aldea* stores sell a few staples such as eggs, bananas, soda pop and small sweet rolls, most women prefer the prices and variety of the plaza and will patronize local shops only for one or two items needed immediately. Thus, plaza shopping, whether completed in an afternoon or over the entire week, provides the family with its food supply and is a time-consuming fact of everyday life that demands skill, planning and discrimination.

Many national and international contingencies are at work in setting market prices in San Pedro (e.g., fluctuating coffee exports, unstable sugar supplies), but most women are only aware that price may vary by season, day and hour of the market, and the relationship of the buyer and seller. Of course, they can recall the prices of dozens of items from five years before and, despite being outraged by the spiraling costs of food, feel helpless to either understand or affect the inflationary trend. Their efforts to get food at the lowest possible prices are directed instead toward developing skills at bargaining, the careful nurturing of amicable trade relationships whenever possible, and the prudent selection of seasonal items that are plentiful and cheap. As such, shopping for food is a serious, carefully considered activity that women are taught as children, and which they spend years mastering. Mistakes in selection or price may cause serious errors in budgetary management, and normally placid and friendly women have been known to strike their daughters for buying incorrectly.

Women are proud of their skills at selecting the finest and cheapest items in the market. For example, the boasting of one woman that she has bought mangoes at three for Qo.25 will immediately be countered by her neighbor's claim of getting her mangoes for Qo.24. There are many strategies to minimize costs. Some women only patronize vendors from the far *aldeas* whose vegetables are consistently cheaper, if smaller and often bruised. Others do not bother to look around, but instead have long-standing partnerships that are based on always getting the cheapest market prices available. Women can exert their shopping prowess as a group as well. When tomato prices were exceptionally high one day, an informal communication network developed among shoppers searching for that one person who would drop the price a penny or two. No one was found, and all over the market, tomatoes remained twice as high as they had been the week before. As a group, women refused to buy them, and by the afternoon, vendors were forced to drop their prices drastically in order to get rid of their stock before it spoiled.

There is considerable status in being a wise shopper, and in this small town most traders know which women will bargain them down nearly to cost and which will not put much effort into striking a deal. Men do not enter into the bargaining process with as much enthusiasm as women do, nor do they gain any prestige among their peers for developing the skill. Shopping is women's work, and even when men purchase goods for their professional needs, they are not keen to spend as much time comparing and bargaining, preferring to reach a settlement quickly and easily. On the other hand, women love to bargain and will go from vendor to vendor looking for the best deals, often stopping to consult with friends on the prices in the market that day before making major purchases.

The process and strategies of shopping on one market day are illustrated by Doña Emelia, a weaver from San José Caben who brought one of her five daughters to town to help her buy and carry her week's supply of food and inventory for their small *tienda*. When she had finished, their two baskets were so heavy they had to ask help from a man to lift them onto their heads for the trip home.

Emelia arrived at the plaza at 9:30 a.m. and immediately began bargaining for oranges being sold in the doorway of the store where she deposited her baskets with friends. The oranges were too green and too expensive, and she decided not to buy any. Instead, she selected two kinds of sweets for the *tienda* from a lady candymaker at six for Qo.05 to later sell for a penny each. Walking on, she looked at *jocotes* (a small fruit), but did not buy any. Bargaining for string beans, she objected to the weight not being correct and walked away annoyed. A pound of *miltomates* for sauce were cheap at Qo.10 a pound, and Emelia bought some and put them into the *canasta* she had been holding. Easily balancing the basket on her head, she knelt to inspect *ajo* (garlic), but since she did not get her price, she left. Soon she spied *ajo* at Qo.02 each, offered Qo.05 for three, but her price was refused. She finally bought some after bargaining again at two for Qo.05.

Next Emelia inquired into the prices of some string beans but did not like the quality after all and walked by. Again, she stopped to ask the price of string beans without buying. Eggs looked fresh at Qo.08, but she walked on. Without bargaining, a quick purchase of chocolate was made from an old friend. Her tempo began to pick up and she looked at and priced oranges, more *jocotes*, and potatoes. She bought fava beans at Qo.05 a pound, saw bananas for Qo.20 a dozen, offered Qo.15 and got them at her price. Pleased with the low price of oranges, she bought three dozen at four for Qo.05 to sell in the *tienda*. Loaded with fruit, the basket was too heavy for Emelia, and she transferred it to her daughter's head and asked her to return to the store for an empty one. While Clariselma was gone, her mother priced cookies for their store and compared their sizes before buying. She then walked up and down the long row of chile vendors asking about the big black chiles used for *tamales*, but neither the price nor the quality were to her liking, and she walked on. Clariselma and her mother were determined to get good prices in chiles and they split up to deal with various vendors. Finally, Emelia bought two ounces for Qo.10. A fan for the stove's fire appealed to Clariselma. The vendor wanted Qo.10, and in less than a minute, she bought it for Qo.08.

Three kinds of rice are usually for sale in the plaza, and Emelia and Clariselma examined all three, buying a pound of the lowest quality for Qo.21. To pay for the rice, Emelia had to reach into her *huipil* for a Q10.00 bill, and the trader cashed it without flinching, a sign of a good day's business.

She then bought three handmade soaps without asking the price (Qo.21 each), eight beige machine-made soaps, a bag of noodles, and six pounds of sugar, all from one vendor. Again, there was no bargaining on these items. Suddenly, she was reminded of her need of a needle, and she urgently sought a street vendor from whom she bought one. Another street vendor happened by and she bought fifteen stick matches. Time had passed too quickly, and to complete her shopping Emelia had to send Clariselma to the other side of the plaza for vegetables, oil and lime. Meanwhile, she went to collect money owed her by two textile dealers for last week's *huipiles*.

On the way out of the *mercado* she priced a kettle on the sidewalk and ordered a larger one for the following week. Nearby she spied a candle dealer and bought Qo.50 worth of penny candles and Qo.50 worth of two-penny candles. Before she could begin to count the candles, Clariselma returned with her basket filled with onions, potatoes, carrots and candles. Together they counted the candles, and quickly Clariselma was dispatched for forgotten eggs. When she returned with the eggs wrapped up in a cloth, Emelia again sent her for juices and sodas, cigarettes and chewing gum for the store. The shopping seemed nearly over and Emelia helped Clariselma pile the purchases into their two baskets and encircle them with net bags for secure carrying. But Emelia remembered she needed more tomatoes, and rushed out for them while Clariselma sat on the ground to wrap up popcorn in little bags for easy sale in the *tienda*. At the bus, ready to leave for home, Emelia recalled that she had to buy corn and she ran to order it so that the bus driver could drive by and pick it up on the way to San José Caben. By noon they were finally ready to depart, but before the bus pulled out, Clariselma's grandmother needed a few things which the young woman quickly bought and deposited in her own basket.

This seemingly mundane shopping routine shows the importance of personal market interactions which, while they might take less than a minute, are the basis for the success or failure of a sales transaction. The buyer must employ her finest strategies to get through marketing within her budget, a difficult prospect when shopping for a *tienda* as well as for home consumption. The second point to be made is that all techniques are passed on to the attending daughter so that when she is sent off to make independent purchases, she utilizes the same methods of selection and pricing. Women rarely shop alone. Not only is it prudent to instruct an assisting daughter, but her presence significantly reduces the time invested as well as making light the load to be carried home.

COOKING

In terms of time invested in a single domestic activity, the preparation of food for family consumption ranks first. In almost every household women cook and serve three meals a day, devoting two hours or more to the main mid-day *almuerzo* and another hour each to breakfast (*desayuno*) and supper (*cena*). A considerable variety exists in types of foods served and the technology employed for its preparation. The ordinary differences range from an *almuerzo* of *tamalitos* (steamed corn meal buns) and coffee prepared on an open fire and eaten standing up, to soup, meat, vegetables, salad, noodles, *tamalitos* and coffee, all cooked on a new iron stove and served to fourteen people served sitting down at a cloth-covered table. It is axiomatic to say that simpler fare is cooked in simpler kitchens with fewer tools. People's tastes in style of cooking and their budgets for amount and kind of food consumed change with advancing affluence. Although everyone in San Pedro eats simple corn-based foods like *tamalitos* or *tortillas* at every meal, townfolk or wealthier *aldeanos* combine them with other, more nutritious and interesting foods. For the poor they are the mainstays of two meals, spiced with a few chiles and washed down with weak but sugared coffee. The following table illustrates the different diets.[2]

Typical San Pedro Diets

	Civilizada	Gente
Desayuno:	Hot *atol* (cereal based drink) or Incaparina (nutritious cereal) with milk	Cereal or eggs
		Frijoles
	Scrambled eggs	Coffee with sugar
	Cheese	
	Frijoles	
	Bread, *tamalitos*	
	Coffee with sugar	
Almuerzo:	Soup with avocado	*Atol*

	Chicken or meat (six to seven times a week)	Soup of vegetables and potatoes
	Vegetable or potato	Meat (once or twice week)
	Noodles	
	Cheese	
	Tamalitos or *tortillas*	
	Coffee with sugar	
Cena:	*Frijoles*	Sweet roll or *tamalitos*
	Leftover meat from *almuerzo*	Coffee with sugar
	Cheese	
	Bread	
	Tamalitos	
	Coffee with sugar	

The technology employed to produce these two menus is similarly disparate. The *gente* meals may be cooked on an open fire in which three rocks are situated for placement of pots or on a flat-topped stone or cement stove fueled by split wood. Few cooking utensils are used—perhaps two or three wooden spoons and a knife, a few pots for coffee, several casseroles for steaming *tamalitos,* a small kettle for heating *atol,* a corn-based drink. Many *aldeanos* cook over open fires on the floors of dark, unchimneyed kitchens. Firewood must be chopped and the fires tended at varying levels of intensity. Running water is a scarce commodity and rural women often walk a mile or more to fill their water jugs from springs or community faucets and carry them home on their heads. Similarly, *aldeanas* balance heavy buckets of soaked corn on their heads as they make their daily trek to the mill for grinding.

The *civilizada* kitchen centers on an iron wood-burning stove and in a few homes, a propane oven or three burner hot plate. Many kinds and numbers of modern tools are used in preparing and serving food, including pressure-cookers and electric blenders for cooking and liquefying *frijoles*. Urban women can afford to buy their *masa* already ground and moistened, and even those who patronize town mills only walk a block or two.

To illustrate the extremes that *civilizada* women may go to in stocking their kitchens with cooking tools, consider the following list compiled in the home of Doña Juana Teresa, wife of trucker German Orozco. While this vast inventory of the contents of Juana Teresa's cabinets is by no means typical, it reflects a growing fascination with the conspicuous expression of affluence through modern products like kitchen pots and pans. Town women regularly spend money on these *trastos* supplied by traveling salesmen who stop in again and again with new and more modern lines of dishes and pans. It is interesting to note that Juana Teresa was able to list her kitchen possessions without actually counting them, and she was correct in almost every case, although once or twice her teenage daughter re-counted quickly in her head and amended her mother's initial response. Her list:

7 large kettles	1 large pot for pig
4 middle-sized kettles for the table	5 thermoses
4 even smaller kettles	2 pie plates
5 pitchers	7 big spoons
2 coffee makers	8 strainers
4 giant-sized casseroles	5 graters
5 small casseroles	1 colander
10 tiny casseroles	2 ricers
2 giant-sized pots with tops	5 wooden cutting boards
4 big pots	13 baskets
5 large saucepans	1 large tray
14 medium-sized saucepans	7 small trays
3 small pans for eggs	1 refrigerator
2 even smaller pans	3 stoves
5 saucepans with tops	1 blender
3 smaller saucepans with tops	6 sugar pots
1 small saucepan with top	4 tea pots
5 plastic washbasins	3 sets silverware (6 settings each)
7 casseroles with handles	5 dozen plates
4 3-liter milk jugs	3 dozen cake plates
2 2-liter milk jugs	5 dozen cups
2 1-liter milk jugs	104 glasses

Juana Teresa rarely uses this equipment. Her work managing German's business keeps her in the warehouse through lunch six days a week, and she rarely has the energy to make much of a meal at night. On Sundays she makes a big meal and invites friends and family in, but even that effort only means a small fraction of her kitchen utensils are used. Mostly, they are stored away like treasures for her to contemplate and count. Having *trastos* is important to Juana Teresa because their purchase represents the only area where she can legitimately overspend. German tightly controls the family budget in all other matters, but indulges her urge to own these symbols of his affluence.

WASHING

Clothes are washed by hand in cold water sinks (*pilas*) where they must be slapped and rubbed against the sink's ridges to remove the dirt. Women who do not have running water in their homes wash in town sinks or in nearby streams. The latter method is the most arduous, since it requires remaining for hours in an uncomfortable, often painful, kneeling position on the bank or on a rock in the middle of the stream. In the dry season, clothes may be laid out on the grass to dry and are relatively easy to put on the head and carry home, but in the rainy months, everything takes two or three days to dry and must be carried home wet and heavy up the hill from the streams.

Few rural women have more than two or three changes of clothes, but these are washed with great frequency. Even wearing the protecting aprons over *cortes* and *huipiles* does not spare clothes from being stained and soiled. This is particularly true for mothers with infants. Diapers in any form do not exist among Guatemala's peasantry; most mothers merely wrap clothes around the baby's body without a layer between the legs. Consequently, the baby's urine and feces drip down the infant's legs and onto the mother's back and hips as she carries it about papoose-style. Both mother's and baby's clothes must therefore be washed several times a week, which is hard, not only on the washerwoman, but also on the clothing. Cheap and factory-made clothing may fall apart after only a few sessions of being slapped about on the rocks.

THE VALUE OF DAUGHTERS

All these tasks—shopping, cooking, washing—are part of "women's work," but there is no set rule as to which women must do them. As often as not, older daughters of the family shop with their mothers and, like Emelia's daughter, help to carry the loads or to purchase items on the far side of the market where the mother does not have time to go. Likewise, mothers and daughters may cook together, thus cutting preparation time considerably. Washing is usually a one-woman job, but daughters may alternate days or weeks depending on the other household chores assigned to them. In all, daughters—particularly young daughters—are expected to work around the house helping their mothers and grandmothers, and will often be removed from school for the afternoon or permanently for just that purpose. This habit of relegating household work to young girls is borne out in Smith and Wilson's study; when queried as to the work of their children, most said their young daughters "helped their mothers."

The most valuable assistance daughters provide is to free their mothers for income-producing work. Domestic chores like cooking, washing, and shopping can severely hamper female movement outside the home simply due to the time demanded to attend to them properly. Isolation in the domestic work arena means women may only be able to develop very low level income-producing businesses (e.g., raising chickens and pigs), which will not benefit the family in any substantial way. In order to move into trade or business with some income potential, women are first obligated to replace the female labor lost in domestic tasks to assure stability in the home. This means that women must avail themselves of reliable helpers who can carry on at home while they pursue extradomestic labors or concentrate on cottage industry. Daughters are the most logical source of domestic aid, and from an early age they are trained not only to assist, but to take over mother's chores when she is not home. Thus, while she is busy running her husband's trucking business, Doña Juana Teresa sends 14-year-old Gloria to do the daily marketing. When she has a deadline to meet making paper flowers, Doña Carmen asks her two eldest daughters to prepare lunch. And when she runs her bar and *tienda,* Doña Norma Fuentes hands the baby to her 11-year-old daughter to mind. This domestic transfer of work occurs throughout the day in the assigning of daily chores or when something comes up suddenly. The simple fact that the daughter is at home and that she is trained and available means she can be relied upon at any time to assume domestic responsibilities.

Women without daughters[3] attend to all household chores themselves since neither sons nor husbands ever help around the home. Total responsibility for *oficios domésticos* (domestic labor) prohibits such a woman from investing adequate time in the development of business, and without a woman's income, families are forced to depend largely upon male subsistence efforts and unreliable wage labor to satisfy domestic needs. Furthermore, full-time household work not only encroaches on female options for autonomous money-making activities, but isolates women from the companionship and support of other women and girls. Sometimes women without daughters circumvent this female labor shortage by inviting their widowed mothers to live with them. The problem may also be overcome by "borrowing" nieces or cousins, ostensibly to teach them housework, or by apprenticing unrelated teenagers who can help around the house while learning to sew or weave.

A case in point is Doña Tomasina from La Grandeza who had the misfortune to have three sons and no daughters. For years she was forced to do all the food preparation, water-carrying and laundry herself. Opportunities existed for wage labor in town, but she could only extricate herself from household demands on two or three mornings, netting perhaps Q2.00 for the entire week. One of her responsibilities that seemed to recur regularly was the caring for one of her sons or for her husband when he became ill. Chronically malnourished, the family members were constantly falling prey to fevers and colds serious enough to force them to bed. Even when male family members were unemployed and idle, it fell to Doña Tomasina to tend the sick one, further limiting the already minimal earning capacity of the family by relegating the one steadily employable worker to the home. At last, the situation changed when the wife of her eldest son bore a girl who was sickly and fragile. The young mother never cared for the child or for the expenses of her illness and, exasperated by her crying and complaining, gave the baby to the grandmother. The child is now five, and, as Doña Tomasina announced, "she can already wash dishes." Her grandmother's burden has not been significantly lightened yet, but it certainly will be in the very near future. Quite soon the child will be old enough to do simple but critical work like carrying hot lunch to the male family members in the fields, thus freeing her grandmother to earn some money preparing and serving lunch at a house in town.

Town women often overcome daughterlessness with servant girls (*muchachas*) from outlying *aldeas* who usually earn as little as Q15.00 a month plus room and board and, depending on their age and experience, may stay years with one satisfied employer. Recently, this has not been the case and town women bitterly complain of the shortage of good help. *Muchachas* come and go with the market days when their relatives are in town to trade. Many are young and away from home for the first time without any of the skills they need to keep a domestic job. Too often employers promise to teach them but never do because of the pressures and demands of their business lives. Tempers flare, tears flow and servants flee on a predictably regular basis. In some cases, however, if the money and the situation allow for patient development of the tasks, *muchachas* become invaluable in the female domestic system, largely in freeing family members for income-producing labor away from home.

Budgets

When an *aldea* woman gets married, she usually adjusts her market and production connections to work on her own even though before her marriage she may have been working for or with her mother, sisters or another female relative. While husbands are not expected to help the bride begin her trading or home industry, sometimes cash allocations are made soon after the wedding. Most often, however, women begin their businesses with capital saved while working in the family. Sometimes if a woman has the appropriate ties with established traders or businesswomen, she can begin her enterprise on credit. Whatever means are used to set it up, from its inception, a woman's business is regarded as her own and not a joint venture with her husband. She makes the investment and commercial decisions, is responsible for the losses, and singularly controls the profits. From the time she begins, her husband has little to do with the operation of her business, and in the daily management it is clear that she is working on her own behalf and not as a representative of the married couple.

Since a woman's income is usually separate from what her husband produces or earns, there are clear-cut domestic responsibilities for each sex. The husband supplies corn and firewood (the domestic staples) and the wife must meet the remaining household expenses from her business profits. Since land is scarce and poor in the highlands and farming methods are primitive, many men can only grow enough corn for six or seven months. The remainder, and all the firewood, must be purchased. Smith (1977) has documented how, through their exploitation of the thriving San Pedro market, local men have been able to earn enough cash income to fulfill their domestic obligations. In fact, many men have been able to earn much more than they need to meet these expenses. Where a surplus occurs, *gente natural* men invest it in other male enterprises associated with the major upkeep of the family, such as building a new room on the house, buying a small piece of land, or (if enough cash and credit are accumulated) purchasing a radio or motorcycle. The prestige of owning modern appliances or building a new house is sizeable, and men secretly save for years toward these ends.

Where the two incomes overlap is in the education of the children. Both parents share in the cash costs of school tuition and books. The status associated with having a child with a degree is mostly ascribed to the father. Men brag about their educated children, but it is the woman who hopes to benefit materially since employed offspring may send money home to mother for her personal expenses. Remittances from sons are neither predictable nor large, but do occur. One woman saved up her son's monthly checks from Guatemala City only to buy new shoes and earrings, but others sorely need the extra income and educate their children with that in mind.

The budgets of middle-class urban dwellers are not so strictly divided by sex. Because *civilizada* men seek to publicly express their status through the idleness and isolation of their wives, San Pedro's developing economy has created a category of dependent urban women.[4] This domestication of *civilizada* women means that socially mobile women surrender autonomous businesses in exchange for the economic support of their prosperous husbands.[5] Although some urban women spend their time in non-productive activities in the home, most continue to work, but as unpaid employees in their husbands' businesses. The tendency to be incorporated into the husband's commercial enterprise deprives a middle class woman of the control of her personal income. Storeowners' wives who run the retail end of the family trade have household allowances granted them by their husbands. The allocation of a wife's money and all other expenses are the responsibility of the husband. Even where the couple has separate businesses, townfolk tend to pool their incomes and thus share most expenses. Only rarely is a husband's salary turned over to the wife to cover debts, bills and food.

What seems to be a clear pattern is that as they become more affluent, townfolk abandon separate monies and responsibilities and instead adopt the *ladino* habit of male control of domestic resources. It is interesting to note that parallel to this trend runs a pattern of growing consumerism focused on female spending. Women do tend to keep some of their cash allowance aside for extraordinary expenses, and in recent years the habit of gift-giving on special occasions has grown dramatically, as has the purchasing of factory-made furniture and convenience appliances like blenders and typewriters. It is women, more than men, who buy these products, often at the insistence of their teenage children. *Civilizada* women have also been principally involved in the credit-payment purchase of televisions. The television habit tends to accentuate female consumer tendencies even more through constant accessibility to commercial announcements. Intimate contacts with this domestic media experience has also devastated personal communication among family members, who now watch soap operas in the evening instead of talking to one another.

Men also invest in consumer products to some extent, and the habit seems to be most marked among adolescents. The result of teenage buying is that mothers cannot count on their sons turning over all or most of their earnings to them, as was common only one or two generations ago. The availability of motorcycles and stereos on "easy payment plans" has meant that a large percentage of teenage boys' earnings are already committed to the retailer every month. This loss is quite serious, for some male children had been cash contributors to the family productive system.

Female control of the family's domestic budget seems to be dropping with the rising standard of living of the town. At the same time, spending habits are changing as consumer products become more accessible and local credit commonplace. At first glance what this seems to mean for women is that they have less control over their own money but more cash and luxury items in the family as a whole. What emerges after further analysis, however, is that the absorption of women into their husbands' businesses is not so much a choice wives make (to abandon their independent enterprises) but is in part an inevitable consequence of, among other things, the male usurpation of child labor without which female business cannot function. With the energetic expansion of the market economy, many girls have been pulled from their mothers' work to help in their fathers' businesses. This may occur, in a family where, for example, the father's commercial weaving contract requires seamstresses to make clothes from the fabric he and his helpers weave. Because he is plugged into the external market where his goods are in demand, he can generate enough work to pay his daughters to sew for him, while *huipil* weaving for their undercapitalized mother is unpaid labor. This is clearly a tremendous loss for the independent businesswoman who, if she is lucky, may have additional daughters still available to her. But the loss of free labor to male business and the loss of potential teenage cash income to consumer goods is increasingly reason for the wife to have to abandon her own enterprise completely and sign on as another unpaid hired hand in the husband's business.

The fact that San Pedro's children are being educated at increasingly higher rates impacts female budgetary management as well, since the child labor lost to years of schooling is not expected to be repaid in cash donations until the child is grown and "graduated" to employment. While parents anticipate substantial monetary assistance from educated children, the amount remitted is usually small, and in many cases is never paid at all.

To establish the budgetary parameters of *Sampedranas,* I spoke to many women about how they managed their domestic expenses. As might be expected in a large, varied population, there is considerable range in money available and consumer strategies. The following cases span the classes in San

Pedro, and show how women manage the money that comes in to feed, clothe, and educate their families.

DOÑA YOLANDA

In figuring out her budget for a week in 1987, Doña Yolanda, a typical *aldeana* from San José Caben, told me the following. Each week, her husband contributes Q10.00 for firewood and Q10.00 for corn when their own corn runs out, and since he only owns three and a half *cuerdas,* they buy corn for most of the year. In the same week, Yolanda spends about Q35 of her own money on food. This allows them to eat a half pound of meat on Thursdays, two pounds of chicken on Sundays, and occasionally eggs for breakfast. She pays no rent because they own their house. Education for her two school-age children is another expense which she estimates costs about Q1 each week. Over the year, clothes for the children amount to quite a bit; shoes alone are Q70. Although Yolanda keeps no record of her expenses, she remembers to the penny what she spends each week. The reason is that she knows what she earns as seamstress (about Q6/day), and after expenses, she never has any money left over. Yolanda manages her money well by living simply, and the family survives comfortably. From his wages as a commercial weaver, her husband bought a radio for which he made monthly payments for two years, and she is considering buying a TV. To absorb the additional costs, she has the following choices. Either she will have to work longer hours at her sewing machine to increase production, or the family will cut back on their meat and chicken consumption so she can make the payments. When she needed the money for three school uniforms last year, she borrowed from her mother, but a television requires a more serious budget manipulation. Yolanda's day-to-day choices are somewhat limited by her living so close to her income. One day I ran into her on the road to San José. Her eldest daughter was ill with a fever, her glands grotesquely swollen. They were on their way to see a doctor at the hospital where the service was free, but this meant sacrificing a day of work. A private physician was available nearby for a quick visit, but lacking the Q7 fee, Yolanda was unable to go to him.

DOÑA ANTONIA

Doña Antonia, Yolanda's mother, spends considerably more each month than her daughter does. Antonia lives with her husband, her youngest daughter, and two of her grandchildren. Antonia's husband has enough land (twenty *cuerdas*) so that they never have to buy corn or beans, but her daily food expenses for a family of five amount to Q300 each month. This family eats a more varied diet than does Yolanda's family, and they eat meat and chicken more often. Their diet is a habit of many years when four daughters helped their weaver mother produce two or three times as much income, and they were relatively well-off. Now that all her weaving daughters have married and live on the other side of the *aldea,* Doña Antonia's weavings provide only a small cash income, amounting to about Q90 a month. The difference is made up with contributions of money and *quintales* (hundred weights) of staple foods from her two sons who work as accountants in Escuintla.

Antonia and her husband are representative of *Sampedranos* in their fifties who have lived through the boom economy and have taken advantage of it. They have made choices that sustained them when they were young and continue to do so now as they age. They have a radio and a TV, and have educated four of their eight children through high school. They eat well, and have the money for the medicine Antonia needs for her liver. Their standard of living has been maintained first by daughters in the female family business whose labor they counted on. When the daughters left to start their own families, they fell back upon the investment Antonia and her husband had made in educating their sons, who were by then professionals who could and did make monetary contributions.

DOÑA CLARISA

Landless *aldeanos* have a much more difficult time getting enough to eat from what they earn. In 1987 Doña Clarisa's husband was making about Q2.00 a day, but he works only occasionally tending other people's fields. With his salary, Clarisa's husband buys the fifteen pounds of corn they eat each week.[6] Their main source of money is Clarisa's job washing clothes in town four days a week, for which she makes Q1.75 a day, plus food. She eats well on washdays, but her salary is too small to feed her family the rest of the week. With this money, Clarisa buys their food, which is essentially the *masa* for *tamalitos, chiles,* and coffee. About twice a week, they add a half-pound of beans to their lunch. Recently, a kind neighbor who died left Clarisa and her husband a building site where they want to construct a house. Despite the fact that they are now landowners, all their money is used for food, and they have no resources remaining for even starting the project.

Urban *civilizada* families earn and spend quite a bit more each month than do rural *Sampedranos.* They have to pay the telephone bill, refuel their cars, make payments on appliances, ride the bus to and from school in Quezaltenango, purchase ready-made clothing, and cover their monthly cable TV bills, among other expenses. Just adding up their costs for a more varied and nutritional diet, the 1988 total for a family of six was approximately Q400-500 a month. Considering that starting teachers make Q372 a month, it is clear that food alone necessitates at least two salaries, or a combination of salaries and commercial enterprises. Not surprisingly, *civilizadas* are often overextended and worried about money, a situation that their ambition and consumer acquisitiveness only exacerbates.

Female Labor and Schooling

Until quite recently daughters were rarely schooled when they could be used in the productive unit of the family instead. Parents could not rationalize educating female workers to do more than read or write when they were valuable at home. But things are changing in San Pedro. Parents quote a popular radio ad, suggesting it would be a good idea for *Sampedranos* to abandon the old idea of only giving their daughters a few years of school. Rather than training women to be housewives, why not give them the skills available in junior or senior high school? Also, the ad points out, during school vacation, letting children play is a waste of time. If their reading, math, or handwriting needs improvement, they should use their time to practice.

Schools are growing quite rapidly in San Pedro. What follows is a recent list of the town's educational establishments and their longevity:

Párvulos (pre-school)	2 government (old)
	4 private (2 new, 2 five years old)
Primarias (1st–6th grade)	7 government (all older than 10 years)
Colegios (private schools from first grade through high school)	7 private (none is older than 10 years)
Institutos (7th–high school)	2 government (both older than 10 years)
	5 private (three are newer than 5 years)
Universidad de Mariano Gálvez (for secondary school teachers and business administration)	five years old

This list suggests growth in schooling, particularly in the number of private schools. Clearly, parents are choosing to invest in education, and beyond that, quality education.

It is easy to see why economically mobile *Sampedranos* would support private sector learning. Government schools are scandalously underfunded. Students are given a desk and little else. Teachers used to be given at least a few boxes of chalk each year, but no longer.[7] All books, paper, rulers, pencils, and other materials must be paid for by the children or their teachers. At the start of every term, parents have to pay a fee of several *quetzales* to enroll each child. Lists are handed out with the supplies children will need, amounting in most cases to sizeable expense. If they bought all the required materials, families with several school-age children would spend more money on schooling than they make in a month. As such, the education is severely limited, particularly for the less affluent *Sampedranos*. For instance, since only the wealthier students can afford books, teachers must sum up every lesson in a paragraph for the class to copy.

One expense that expresses the pride *Sampedrano* parents take in being able to afford to educate their children is the school uniform. On the Saint's Day celebration in June all the schoolchildren parade from one end of town to the other. It is a major holiday, and families line the streets to wave at their passing children. The parade is even videotaped to be shown on the public access television station. Almost all the children wear uniforms specific to their schools, and although this is not mandatory, it would be an embarrassing admission of the family's poverty not to do so. The cost of buying the fabric and hiring a seamstress to make the uniform is as important as buying books, and many women save their pennies all year to be able to afford it.

In spite of the sizeable expense of education, the sizes of classes are growing as more people seek the status and economic promise of schooling. Approximately five thousand children are currently enrolled, and although there has been considerable growth in the number of school buildings, the size of each class has grown from an average of thirty children each to seventy. Only some of this can be explained by population growth. One important consideration is that *aldeanos* are educating their children with much greater frequency that they did before. They too are choosing a quality education: sixty percent of the students in one urban elementary school are from San José Caben alone. Parents from that *aldea* prefer the teachers at the San Pedro school, and many have made the decision to send their children to town rather than to the local school. Unfortunately, although elementary education is mandatory, the attendance of *aldea* children drops off dramatically after the third grade, and by the sixth year, only half the rural students remain. Many dropouts leave school when they are old enough to be valuable workers at home, or because their family can no longer afford the cost. Teachers recognize the frustration students feel when, after three years of school, they cannot continue, and often will donate from their own salaries to help meet their students' expenses. They understand, however, what many students are up against. One teacher pointed out to me that since many *aldeas* have no electricity, it is nearly impossible to teach the children to read for they cannot study at night.

A review of student enrollments over the last fifteen years shows the percentage of girls in school has not changed significantly. It has been consistently high among urban families, and although their choice of degrees and studies differed, girls go to school with the same frequency that boys do. Where there is a noticeable change is in the number of girls from the *aldeas* who are being educated. The following case is typical.

Doña Emelia relied upon her daughters' help in domestic and extra domestic work. Her oldest daughters had three years of education each, after which they were apprenticed to their mother's loom. As teenagers the girls were full-time workers. They agreed with their parents that educating women was a foolish investment for a family where workers were needed. Not only were they mindful of the value of the labor lost to book learning, but they pointed out that in the end it was a girl's husband and not her natal family who benefitted from the skills a modern education brings. Despite this conviction, it is interesting to note that when the youngest daughter was still in school—the fourth grade—her sisters persuaded Doña Emelia that there was sufficient female labor already available in the family. So, like her three older brothers, Lucinda studied through high school. The results of this investment in their daughter's education are that Lucinda, unlike her sisters, is literate and worldly. In short, she has the potential and the promise the town affords its citizenry. Unfortunately, Lucinda is typical of local high school graduates in that she has already spent two years looking for an elusive teaching job, and while she waits, she works at home doing contract sewing. Nonetheless, she has the tools and the confidence to do a good job, and in fact, I hired her to be my assistant during my last fieldtrip. Meanwhile, she is hesitant to become involved with local boys, many of whom are not as well-educated as she. In that way, she quite consciously avoids the compromises that pregnancy brought to two of her sisters. In all, Lucinda expresses both the promise and the reality of educating rural women: she has been primed intellectually for more than her situation can offer.

At the same time that education is being stressed, the emphasis on familial work obligation has not abated, and has resulted in the founding of schools and the development of programs and schedules which permit students to work while earning diplomas and degrees. Two night schools have been in operation in San Pedro for eighteen years, and half their students are women.

Other ambitious women travel to Quezaltenango on Saturday and Sunday for special college courses, allowing them to work all week long and still receive a university education. Local schools are out by one o'clock and daughters may then work all afternoon and evening. Thus, while there can be no doubt that schooling means productive time lost to classes, many women take advantage of scholastic opportunities that allow them to efficiently manage books with work.

Schooling and work may be complementary in another sense in that girls develop their own small businesses in order to pay their tuition or book costs. This independent entrepreneurship is not discouraged by mothers, since it has been customary for girls and young women to put aside small amounts of money in preparation for marriage. If the mother's business does not earn enough for division, the daughter is urged to branch out on a small scale. In this way, tangents of the original trade grow, allowing daughters a small but significant income for their own use.

This kind of parallel industry or business is, in fact, quite common among educated women. Due to the uncertainty of the modern job market, women with high school degrees are often forced to remain at home for years while they wait for a position. In the meantime, they may continue as members of the female family business but in a relatively industrious way, often juggling familial responsibilities with the management of this small income-producing endeavor.

The easiest and most common sort of diversification takes place in small *tiendas* that dot San Pedro. Young women who have saved some capital purchase new and different products to sell in their mothers' stores, keeping most of the profits from the new items and giving a lump sum or percentage—whatever they can afford—to their mothers. At the same time, they may do work complementary to their mother's business, for example, sewing together *huipiles* from the fabric woven by other women in the family, or embroidering collars to be attached as trim. There is much variation and mothers usually want their offspring to develop new sources of business, as long as they have enough remaining daughters to pick up the slack while the new business is beginning.

Initially, this branching out of the female family business appeared to indicate a keen maximizing of the talents of educated producers. The input of new ideas and energy seemed appropriate to the spirit of the town's developing commercialism, meshing traditional industries with modern savvy. Unfortunately, this model of the combining of schooling and commerce for the benefit of the female family business turned out to be short lived, and in only a few years there has been a precipitous decline in this pattern of parallel businesses. What has replaced it is the commitment of educated young women to alternative industries based upon wage employment or piecework production.

While some high school students continue to parallel their mothers' traditionally independent trades, many more have branched out on their own to become rural proletarians, dependent upon expensive technology, and contracted to *patrones* (bosses) who pay them by the item produced. What is most telling about this transition away from traditional work is that daughters' labor is lost to the female family business. By dedicating themselves to new industries, young women are less available to support their mothers' traditional productive efforts, and because the prohibitive start-up costs of buying the necessary machinery puts off profits for years, daughters cannot offer monetary contributions as a substitute for labor lost to modern jobs. Education, it seems, has combined with the introduction of semi-industrial employment to deprive women of their daughters' labor and monetary gains. Put this together with a declining market for indigenous products and the use of daughters' labor by fathers for their projects, and what seems clear is the demise of the female family business. The following case study illustrates this trend.

THE ITINERANT TEXTILE TRADER

Every Saturday just before dawn, Celestina Velásquez waits by her house for the bus to the Pan American highway. The bus finally appears, the driver pausing only long enough for her to hand her heavy bundles of *típica* (traditional textiles) onto the roof and for Celestina and her 15-year-old daughter Elvia to climb aboard. Celestina sleeps through the two hour ride. At the highway they transfer to an uncomfortably crowded taxi which takes them the additional thirty kilometers to market day in one of the most active Indian markets, Totonicapán. This day, begun so early, most often results in few transactions. Most trading takes place between dealers who keep mental accounts of what is owed to whom. Money changes hands reluctantly. The *huipiles* and *cortes* of Toto are not the same as those of San Pedro, but the women of Toto favor the work of *Sampedrana* weavers and purchase many of their products. The weavers of San Pedro are adept at producing some of the designs popular in Toto, and they are better and cheaper than local weavers. In addition, the hand-made collars embroidered by *Sampedranas* are often sewn onto the floral Toto *huipil* to produce an elegant and colorful blouse. Celestina brings hundreds of these collars, several dozen *huipiles* and the tie-dyed *jaspe* skirt material popular throughout the country. She sells a few collars, a few *huipiles,* and some yardgoods and trades a handful of belts. While she wanders around making her appropriate commercial calls, Elvia minds the stall and shows their goods. Despite the frenzied nature of this huge market, business is slow, the day long, and the profits small.

Toto is not Celestina's only stop for selling her *típica.* Wednesdays, she and another daughter travel to Palestina, a small town where she does a similarly minimal business. On Fridays, Elvia rides the bus to Quezaltenango to do some trading on her own for belts and collars. And on Thursdays, Celestina's stall in San Pedro is visited by *aldea* Indians in town for the important market day. On those days, she and her youngest daughter Beatriz work nonstop showing and bartering *típica.* In terms of profits alone, although earnings are small, it would make sense for Celestina to restrict her business to San Pedro where her *huipiles* and *cortes* are local and therefore more in demand. But Celestina, like other enterprising *Sampedranas,* lives to work, and she has confessed that she is actually unhappy on the days the market is closed. The extra few dollars she makes by traveling hours back and forth to Toto and Palestina are not as important as the maintaining of her trade networks, stalls and reputation. For what matters is to be working, and to be providing her daughters with the flexibility of a reliable business should one market begin to fail.

This dedicated behavior is consistent with that of Celestina's mother — a woman who wove by day, sewed by night, and developed the marketable skills and saleable items now produced by Celestina and her daughters. Every week, Celestina and her mother walked the sixty kilometers to Quezaltenango for market day and then walked back the next morning. They did the same to Palestina: six hours to arrive at the busy market plaza with appropriate *huipiles* and *cortes* and belts and six to walk back. Celestina remembers her widowed mother working as "a man and a woman," taking care of their land, raising four children, maintaining her various businesses. There was, for Celestina, a certain *chispa* (joy) to life when she wove alongside her mother, made candles, crocheted, and became famous for her embroidery. Celestina's mother's dedication to hard work stemmed in part from her husband's legacy of indebtedness after he drank himself to death. A quiet, humble woman, with an immense financial burden, she is always described as a "slave to her work"—the almost saintly image ascribed to the suffering Guatemalan mother.

Then, as now, the profit margin on *típica* was small, the competition stiff. Next to Celestina in the *mercado* are eight other dealers, and prices are kept low despite tacit price-fixing. A fancy *huipil* garners Celestina only a Q3 profit. Common *huipiles* net even less; she makes perhaps Q1.00 on a Q15.00

sale. On a Thursday, the sale of four or five *huipiles* profits less than Q20.00. Her larger earnings lie in machine-made aprons and baby clothes which she carries along with the Indian costumes, but in spite of her expanding into new, non-traditional products, Celestina's sales are flat; she is making about what she did twenty-five years ago when she was first married.

Another concern Celestina has is the role her daughters will play in maintaining the business. Although she taught them all the traditional *artes,* neither one weaves, embroiders, or sews with much interest. They dutifully follow along on her rounds, but lack both the zeal for trade and the appreciation of the handiwork done by her suppliers. Celestina attributes her daughters' disinterest to the middle-class lifestyle her family has attained, the sophistication her daughters developed during their schooling, and their yearning for work more appropriate to their upwardly mobile status. She looks ahead sadly to the disintegration of her family business as the daughters opt for careers outside what she has known to be women's work. Already, her husband has enlisted the youngest to work with him managing his retail store, while the eldest is planning to teach in the *aldeas* when she finishes high school.

Given the small profit-margin and dwindling sales of the *típica* merchant, one is tempted to applaud the move away from this business by Celestina's daughters. Education should provide them with skills and a taste for more modern, lucrative business and employment. At the same time, however, one cannot ignore the fact that the popularity of schooling has been an important factor in the decline of indigenous clothing in San Pedro and the traditional trade network which it sustained for generations. Educated young women eschew *huipiles* and *cortes,* choosing instead the western apparel that is appropriate to the new life-style they have selected. Ironically, their mothers chose to educate their daughters, possibly undermining their own female family businesses in the process.[8]

LA CASA DE LAS MUJERES

Female family businesses exist on the seamier side of San Pedro life as well. There are several local women who learned about drinking, brawling, and swearing as they grew up in *cantinas* owned by their mothers. Many home *tiendas* have a few tables for drinking *fuertes* (hard whiskey) and daughters often attend to the customers as part of their work. Making *cusha,* the local "white lightning," is a female occupation which, like other female family businesses, is shared by mother and daughter, even to the extent of living in the same jail cell when they are caught.

One of the more intriguing of the demimonde female family businesses in San Pedro is remarkable for its "legality" and for the traditionally maternal manner in which it is run. The local house of prostitution, known as *La casa de las mujeres* or *la casa,* is a business owned and operated by a woman and her three daughters. None of these women are prostitutes. They employ four women from out of town for that work. The owners are from San Pedro, but had been living on a coastal plantation where Doña Tila's husband ran the office. Apparently, there was a robbery and the husband was accused and sent to jail. Without any financial support, the women moved back to San Pedro where they got a job cooking for the previous owners of *la casa.* When the owners wanted to leave, Doña Tila, at the suggestion of her son, sold her refrigerator and bought them out with the proceeds. Since that time the family has regretted this decision. They barely make a cent on the business, and have been thinking of closing.

There are several reasons for the failure of the business. Being women and inexperienced as employers, the family extends normal female business practices to the running of a bordello, seriously undermining profits. They see that not having a man around is a definite drawback only in that they and the prostitutes sometimes need protection from drunks and physically abusive customers, but not having a male involved has other more direct implications for the businesses's potential success or failure.

In the first place, the women owners have no control over the prostitutes, who only work when they want to. If the employees leave for the coast for a few days, the owners cannot open and thus lose money. They complain quietly, but have neither the leverage nor the powers of persuasion normally attributed to a male owner, madam, or pimp. This lack of authority is not simply a matter of physical strength, nor of sexual exploitation, but is as well a result of the absence of female experience as employers. Women have traditionally worked with relatives alone. As minimally capitalized corporate enterprises made up of the labor of female family members, by their very nature these businesses make employment of outsiders difficult. Where *muchachas* or apprentices *are* hired, authority may be expressed almost as an option of status or class. With a group of independent, strong-willed prostitutes, however, this is an improbable response for *Sampedranas* who do not have the experience of men as employers. Rather than being bosses and strong authority figures, *la casa* owners are as kind and considerate to the prostitutes as they would be to any houseguests. They are not coercive. To the contrary, Doña Tila tries to take good care of them by feeding them lunch and dinner, with sizeable portions of meat as often as she can. She pities the prostitutes for their way of life and in small ways attempts to ease their situation by doing things like caring for the son of one of them while his mother works. In another sense, their being women is fiscally limiting as they have little access to capital to invest in the business. They have only debts.

Prostitution is legal in Guatemala. This means that above the normal costs of running a business, taxes and fees must be paid in cash every month to the local and federal governments. These expenses include Q25.00 a month as a business tax on houses of prostitution and Q30.00 for the liquor license. Each week, prostitutes must by law be examined by a doctor, costing the family Q2.00 for each. Normal business expenses further deplete their slim profits, Q25.00 rent and Q15.00 for electricity to run the jukebox, plus the high costs of food for the family and the prostitutes. To meet these expenses, the family offers the services of the women at Q3.00 each; Q1.00 goes to the house and Q2.00 to each prostitute. On most nights the four prostitutes have perhaps two customers each for an Q8.00 house gross. When the rare X-rated movie plays in town, they have up to five customers each and the house grosses Q20.00. Many men come just to dance and drink, but beer and liquor offer slim profit margins because of the tax and the bottle deposit. Other houses of prostitution can meet their high overhead because they have capital, own their own house, or have partners, but the family of Doña Tila has none of these.

The daughters of Doña Tila do not want to invest in the business, preferring to direct all their capital gains toward their educations. Clearly, none of the daughters sees a future for herself in running a whorehouse. It is not traditional in their family, it is not profitable, and even if it is legal, its social status is marginal. Sharing their table with prostitutes means they too are social outcasts. While this may not bother Doña Tila, who prefers to stay at home anyway, her three daughters are ambitious and have conventional social aspirations. They are all in school, and the eldest daughter, who runs the cash register at night, will soon be an auxiliary nurse and her mother will lose her services. The others are too young to be licensed for that job and Doña Tila does not seem inclined to take her place. She refuses to be part of the evening's activities, even to take the money at the cash register, and feigns ignorance of what is going on.

La casa is both like other female family businesses and different from them. It does contain many of the common elements of female business systems such as minimal capitalization, donated labor of educated and uneducated women, reciprocal responsibilities. On the other hand, it was begun a year ago as a desperate investment by a group of inexperienced women. It has no history in their family nor do any of the members express loyalty or dedication to it. It has been a difficult and unsatisfying business experience which has barely sustained them financially. Interestingly, the pending disappearance of the eldest daughter from *la casa* is typical of the trend away from female family businesses and toward modern employment among *Sampedranas,* as is the closing of the business that will doubtless accompany her resignation.

FEMALE LABOR IN THE FUTURE

Female family businesses can be characterized as labor intensive, often financially marginal businesses which nonetheless may persist for years as the typical work of female family members. The routine and the economic connections of the enterprise are passed on from mothers to daughters in the hope that the business which sustained one family will continue to support another. Integral to the system is a domestic division of labor that assures the mother the household is being maintained so that she can invest in her business, and thereby earn a living.

The family productive system I have described is changing in San Pedro. It still forms the backbone of the town's positive economic profile, but not in the same way it has for decades. Despite the tradition and the perseverance of female businesses and industries, indications are that cooperative female enterprises are on the wane. Independent female entrepreneurs are losing the labor of their daughters to modern employment, education and male business. Some of these options allow women to continue helping one another in specific money-making activities, and provide female labor for domestic tasks as well, but many pull women from the home so that they are largely useless in managing the family. In all, the female family business that focuses female labor around mothers' work—both domestic and extra-domestic—is being replaced by isolated income-earners. As productive activities make female mutual support less valuable, and as education becomes an important investment for girls, the role of child labor will by necessity be diminished, effectively destroying the mother's management system. If mothers lose the benefit of their daughters' free labor, the costs of running their own businesses will rise so that they will have to abandon them. The process is quite direct. Without daughters, they will either forfeit income-producing hours to domestic tasks like cooking, shopping, and washing clothes, or they will have to hire a *muchacha* to do it for them. In the next ten years as girls move away from contributing their labor to the family productive system, other strategies will emerge as well. As the next chapter suggests, if trends continue, it is certainly possible that in a decade's time, the autonomous female family business will be gone. Once they have lost their market share as well as their labor supply, what choice will women have but to abandon independent business and go to work for someone else?

Notes

1. Quantification of the time women spend in food preparation is complicated by the variety in family size, diets, stoves, budgets, and number of kitchen helpers a woman may have. On the low end of the range is a wealthy woman with a cook, or a middle-class family where the *muchacha* takes the corn to the mill, cleans the vegetables, and washes up afterward. In the first case, the woman spends no time cooking, but in the second, more common instance, the mother and her daughters probably devote two hours to the main one o'clock meal and perhaps an hour to breakfast and supper. In a rural home far more time is spent preparing food. Corn must be taken to the mill for grinding twice a day. Depending upon where the family lives in the *aldea,* that could take an hour or two. Water needs to be drawn, and again, the time involved depends upon the water source and its relation to the home. The actual cooking of food can take quite a bit of time as well. For instance, it takes over an hour just to pat out and grill tortillas for a family of seven. Overall, there are probably five or six womanhours of work devoted to rural food preparation. Urban women, due to their modern stoves and access to mills and pre-ground tortilla *masa,* spend less time cooking, perhaps three or four hours a day.

2. The more time I spend in San Pedro, the more I realize how difficult it is to isolate so-called "typical" behavior. Like any town, in spite of obvious class distinctions, this large population does not break down into neat categories. This is true in diet as it is in work, ethnicity, religion, or social interaction. And, of course, no behavior is written in stone; things change over time. Thus, any attempt to identify typical menus for a *civilizada* family compared with that of a *gente* family has many pitfalls. Looking at this list today, I would make these modifications: 1) Almost no one is eating as well in 1988 as they did in 1977. Among the landless *aldeanos,* few people have the money for beans at breakfast, much less meat once or twice a week. Hardly any rural *Sampedranos,* urban or rural, can afford to eat meat anymore; for most people, chicken has taken its place. Even so, chicken is not eaten everyday. For the ordinary *aldeano,* meals tend to be entirely meatless until Sunday, when a pound or two of chicken will be made into a soup. 2) The variety in diets is greater than this list would suggest. The poorest families eat *tamalitos* and coffee three times a day, with perhaps a weak broth and beans at the main meal. Better off *aldeanos* have more complete meals, such as that listed above. Only the urban middle class can afford the extensive menu I have suggested; less affluent townfolk eat more along the lines of the better off *aldeano.*

3. Although women most often tell me they want their first child to be a boy, they confess that daughters are equally valued, if not more important for their labor, and for their company.

4. See the discussion of a similar phenomenon in the American Industrial Revolution (Sennett 1970).

5. I am indebted to Fran Rothstein (personal commun.) for helping me to understand the domestication of *civilizada* women.

6. Note that fifteen pounds a week for three people averages out to a little more than half a pound of corn a day each. If you think about the more than forty pounds Yolanda buys each week for her family of four, it is clear that this landless family, dependent upon corn as the mainstay of their meals, has a comparably poor diet.

7. Teachers say the only things they get from the government are the room, the desks, and the parents' criticism. Since teachers are the only representatives of the school system that parents ever meet, they receive a lot of complaints in the form of personal accusations of being layabouts, thieves, gossips, and whores.

8. Perhaps women like Miranda understood that the upper limits of their businesses had been reached and, like American parents after World War II, directed their children toward new and different lifestyles without appreciating the possible consequences.

Woman from San José Caben.

Huipil *weaver at her loom.*

*Mother and daughter in costumes
typical of their generations.*

Aldea *extended family*.

Civilizada *couple at daughter's baptism*.

San Pedro shopowner.

Plaza trader.

Preparing thread for the loom.

Using a treadle machine to sew maxi-skirts.

Typical near-aldea house.

Girls practice for domestic work.

Mercado *textile shop.*

Canasta *traders.*

4

𝒴

Female Traders

EDULINA OCHOA SELLS SUGAR, salt, soap, and plastic bags in San Pedro's Thursday and Sunday markets. Edulina and I often chat about her life, market activity and San Pedro while she sells. I buy warm Cokes from a neighbor's stall for us to drink as we talk, and she gives me helpful tasks to do, like filling up small plastic bags with sugar from a hundred pound sack. As each bag is filled, she weighs it, closes it with a tiny knot, and it is ready for the next customer. Sitting with Edulina gives me a handy perch for observing market activities. Moreover, her stall is a fine starting point for visiting other women, especially the dozen or so members of Edulina's family selling elsewhere in the market that sprawls over the central park and down dozens of small streets. In a sense, by associating with a plaza woman of long standing who has a wide network of kin and acquaintances, I also legitimate my presence there. And it gives other traders something to laugh at as they watch the *gringa* anthropologist struggling to do things they consider mundane, like eye-balling a pound of sugar scooped into a little bag. People greet me, smile, and comment kindly on my apprenticeship. After a moment of conversation, even strangers open up and unhesitatingly answer my questions. Many shoppers recognize my fondness for taking pictures, and they return with their children for a free family portrait. In all, market day is for me both a chance for social interaction and for work. In that sense, it is quite similar to the experience of the market women. They, too, look forward to Thursdays and Sundays not merely to make a dollar, but to visit, gossip, laugh and commiserate with other traders or shoppers whom they see only in this environment.

On this day, I have set out to count and categorize the people who pur-chase something from Edulina—almost everyone who stops at her stall buys something—and asking them where they have come from. It is about 10 a.m. and the market is very busy, so it is not surprising that in two hours Edulina has had fifty customers. Almost all of them are from the *aldeas,* some from as far away as Chim or Sacuchum, a four-hour walk. When I ask them why they came on foot instead of taking the twenty-five *centavo* bus, the an-swer is always the same: this day they did not have the twenty-five *centavos.* What draws this population of poor rural *Sampedranos* to Edulina's stall is *panela,* the cheap sugar by-product she sells. *Aldeanos* put *panela* in their cof-fee, their hot cereal, in their *atolito,* and some use it to make *cusha,* the lo-cal "white-lightning" whiskey. *Panela* is a common item in coastal towns near the sugar cane fields, and is very affordable in San Pedro. In one market day she sells all the half-balls of *panela* her husband has purchased in San Juan Ostancalco. She figures her business in sugar is good because a family— her own included—goes through about a pound of sugar or *panela* in only one day.[1]

Edulina has traded from this same stall in the plaza for fifteen years, and never has had a day off. She works "eight days"—the Guatemalan week— preparing for the markets and then attending to her stall. Yet she says, "Life for us isn't that hard, because one thing I always have is work." She allows herself an hour for mass before the Sunday market, but that is the only non-productive activity she enjoys. Her tattered clothes are evidence of her fiscal prudence; beyond business costs, the only expenses she permits herself are for food for her family of five. But Edulina's thrift has paid off. After fifteen years of trade, she and her husband Rosario have been able to build a new house in town with the Q5,000 they saved. From the small warehouse (*de-pósito*) they are building as a storefront, Rosario will be able to sell grains to local merchants, thus increasing their market share by managing both a re-tail and a wholesale outlet.

Edulina attributes her market success to the home production of soap, a skill she learned from her mother-in-law, Maria Luz. Over the years, Edulina has doubled her output and her profits by maintaining her low prices against the rising cost of factory-made soap. Few other products have afforded trad-ers an income as reliable as this. When female-run cottage industries are hav-ing trouble competing with new industrial products, and are fast becoming obsolete, it seems ironic that one woman's achievements should be based upon a hand-made item. In fact, when I added up Edulina's profits from her stall, I realized soap was only part of the explanation for her success.

The figures from June 1988 illustrate. From Thursday and Sunday sales,

Edulina makes a weekly Q24 profit. Half—about Q12—comes not from a traditional cottage industry, but from being a middleman for the plastic and cloth bags traders use to package their wares. Sugar sales amount to only a Q2.50 profit; salt a little more, and soap Q5. Because her profit on every sale is tiny, Edulina banks upon the volume of plaza sales to make any money. She figures that she earns less than a half *centavo* profit on every pound of sugar she sells. So she counts on selling 150 pounds on Thursdays, and 100 pounds on Sunday in order to pocket even the small profit she does make.[2]

Although Edulina has been counting pennies for more than a decade, with four children and a husband to feed, it would have been nearly impossible for her to save Q5,000 on her tiny market income alone. To accomplish this goal, she had to combine her market strategy with other income-producing schemes. To begin with, she and Rosario are in a favorable position because they have land enough that they never have to buy corn or beans. In fact, each year they sell one *quintal* of beans. Furthermore, Edulina supplements her commercial income by contract sewing of clothing which she does at night while keeping an eye on the soap caldron. Although she only makes six or eight *quetzales* a week at her sewing machine, it adds up over the years. Lastly, when Rosario travels to San Juan Ostancalco twice a week to buy *panela* and the animal fat for soap, he makes a few *quetzales* selling Edulina's soap balls in the market. In all, Edulina and Rosario built their house by combining a sufficient land base with a profitable home industry, contract artisanship, and commerce in two regional markets. It might appear that saving such a large sum of money from only a few cents profit is a monumental and un-usual task, but this degree of ingenuity and hard work are not rare in San Pe-dro. Indeed, most market women attack their work with equal vigor, jug-gling plaza time with one or two other productive activities. As we shall see, Edulina is different from other women only in how she chooses to invest her carefully accumulated savings.

Trade in San Pedro Sacatepéquez involves almost every *Sampedrana*.[3] There are very few women who do not make a *quetzal*—directly or indi-rectly—from a sale in the plaza, the *mercado,* or the stores. The population is big enough, and the level of their consumerism such that sales are con-stant. While the volume of retail trade fluctuates year by year and season by season, on the whole it is substantial enough that San Pedro is considered economically prosperous by Guatemalan highlands standards. People have to work extremely hard to achieve economic security. The norm seems to be long days, little rest, and the integrating of several kinds of home production with schooling, travel, and trade. Different economic niches and class position allow some people to exploit San Pedro's economic potential to a greater degree than others. This is certainly true in the market where one woman's daily profits from her vegetable stall can amount to less than a store-owner's monthly electric bill. A woman's approach to her work varies according to class and thus her access—or lack of it—to capital resources, but there are other considerations as well, in particular, management of domestic responsibilities and a woman's skill in running a trade enterprise on her own.

Many of San Pedro's female vendors are involved in commercial endeavors which are entirely autonomous from their husbands' work or business. While women may include their husbands in their petty trade relations, it is usually only as a pair of extra hands. This high degree of economic separation means women have a certain freedom from the rigid constraints of male control over their productive efforts or their money. Men recognize that they cannot support their families by themselves, so once a woman embarks upon a career as a trader, she is free to face the risks and demands of business herself.[4] Strategies depend upon her history—and before her, her family's history—in the market; her ability to organize children and spouse as workers; her skills in managing money, suppliers, and customers; and lastly, how her personality and devotion to trade meshes with the demands of the marketplace.

This chapter describes the personal and cultural context that envelops women like Edulina who are so tightly connected to commerce, and includes a discussion of the contingencies of the marketplace and the strategies women of different classes use to make a dollar. Their stories explain the life of the market, its nature as a central source of cash, and the demands it makes upon the people it supports.

The *Comerciante*

San Pedro's market women vary from the *aldeana* who periodically sells a basket of radishes to obtain cash for needed commodities to the large-scale, full-time retailer who handles a variety of merchandise and large amounts of money and credit. The *municipio* is large and diverse enough that the multiplicity of commercial options extends beyond the open air market plaza to the large indoor *mercado,* and then to *depósitos, tiendas,* and stores up and down the main streets of the town.[5] The character of the *Sampedrano* economy is such that some businesses can operate on a regular daily basis while others depend solely upon the swelled traffic of the Thursday market and to a lesser extent the Sunday market. To illustrate just how this works, let us examine the movement of fresh flowers in the market.

No flowers are available on non-market days because the diminished volume of buyers militates against the secure sale of the entire lot of this perishable product.[6] Flower sellers recognize that their customers behave as they do, i.e., they rarely make a special trip to town for small items like flowers, but will buy as they pass through the plaza doing their weekly shopping. So, like other small traders, flower sellers bring their products to market on the day they come to town to buy other goods, Thursdays and Sundays. For flower-sellers to consistently attempt to buy and sell on another day would be counter-productive.

Clearly, there are always daily sales to be made of necessities that will not wilt and die if they linger on the shelves. Thus, stores that line the main streets selling cement, shoes, medicines, flour, etc., are open every day, as are nearly two hundred *mercado* shops and thirty plaza stalls. In addition, about two dozen *canasta* women carrying on sporadic trade on non-market day sell enough everyday goods like avocados, tomatoes, peanuts, and mangoes, to make it worth their trip to town.

Female traders maintain control of the internal market through trade connections based on wholesale products supplied by men. The most common strategy is for female traders to bring small amounts of product from home and their *aldea,* and once they arrive to purchase a few additional *canastas* of tomatoes or onions or pineapples off the trucks of male wholesalers. The morning of the market, trucks arrive from the coast or Guatemala City to supply these small female plaza dealers. But this is only one pattern of local trade handled by *Sampedranas.* Some of them buy cases of produce in other markets or from farmers in coastal *aldeas* on the way to market. Others buy from local warehouse *depósitos* or in smaller quantities from women traders in the plaza for later resale, either in San Pedro or in their home *aldeas.* When their trucks are empty, male wholesalers on their way to distant markets buy from women selling products grown or processed at home. Whatever is left over after all these transactions will be bought up by a late arrival to be sold at inflated rates in the afternoon or at reduced rates for the next day's sales.

A few women are mainly involved in trade networks outside the town. Their activities involve travel to periodic markets located hours away in the highlands and on the coast. Some travel to the daily markets in Quezaltenango, sixty kilometers from the town, or to more distant places, selling local products or purchasing goods in these markets for sale elsewhere. Many women travel to Guatemala City solely to stock their San Pedro stalls at lower wholesale prices. As we shall see, a single trader may combine more than one of these modes of operation to maximize her earnings from trade.

THE TRAVELING BREADMAKERS

Doña Rosalinda and her family are bakers. Four days a week, from 5 a.m. to 10 p.m., Rosalinda, her children, and her mother work together preparing and baking bread in huge woodburning ovens. Rosalinda's husband helps too when there is a slow period in his work as a tailor. Once the bread is baked, Rosalinda and her mother, who started the business fifty years ago, supervise the loading of between five hundred and a thousand pounds onto a hired truck. The next three days are devoted to making two trips to the markets in Tumbador and Mazatenango where they sell the *pan francés* and whole-wheat *shecas* for which *Sampedrano* bakers are known. The two women, or sometimes Rosalinda's husband, travel by bus for three or more hours to meet the truck at the market. Costs are high. They have to pay for firewood, ingredients, trucking, and travel expenses, but the profits are good. Over-all, they make approximately Q250 a month, a net income nearly equal to a teacher's salary. I asked Doña Rosalinda if it was worth all that traveling. She and her mother pointed out that the route had been developed in response to growing competition from local bakers who were better capitalized, had good locations, and a regular clientele. If they had stayed in the local bakers' market, they would be out of business. As it stands, being traveling bread-makers has afforded them enough of a living to send all six children to school; the eldest is now attending the national university in Guatemala City.

The commercial orbit a woman selects is mainly based on the products she trades, her available capital, and the energy and enthusiasm she devotes to the business. Covering a route requires a keen assessment of the costs and benefits of travel, as well as a sixth sense for market predictability. Women need to have remarkable entrepreneurial energy to pack up and move their goods every week. Some women are eager to get on the bus to their Friday market, but many do it only because the route has been in their families for generations, and they have no alternative marketing plan. I know of several educated women who are maintaining a family trade orbit while they wait for teaching jobs, meanwhile displaying little initiative or interest in what they have come to see as an old-fashioned business. Unfortunately, when tradition and family history are the only incentives, women like these some-times are at a loss when their complacency is challenged by new competition or decreased market activity. For example, one long-standing trade route was abandoned when interest in San Pedro's hand-embroidered *huipil* collars waned in Chichicastenango and the young trader immediately saw this as a sign that she was better off staying at home.

The devaluation of plaza trade is becoming more common among economically mobile girls from town and the near *aldeas*. For generations, *Sampedranas* have depended upon their daughters for help in preparing goods for market and as willing assistants in the plaza or *mercado*. As daughters matured, they worked side-by-side with their mothers, doing more and more of the work until eventually they took over the business. Since the 1960s, the town's emphasis on education has made this kind of mutual support and generational continuity hard to come by. Not only are daughters in school until the afternoon, but the higher the grade completed, the less likely girls are to want to continue in trade, and the more they prefer modern employment. It is difficult to predict how this trend will eventually impact female participation in the market economy. I have spoken to many women who want their daughters to be educated, but because jobs are hard to find, are teaching them the business as well. It remains to be seen whether employment opportunities will expand to include a growing number of educated girls. Perhaps modern daughters will be forced to follow through in their mothers' traditional trade when no jobs materialize. For now, it seems clear that mothers are encouraging their daughters to utilize both strategies just to be sure. As tiny as the profits from trade may be, it has been a reliable productive activity, one that mothers say their educated daughters can always "fall back on."

While development may eventually cause a shrinkage in the number of female traders from the town or its near *aldeas,* the number of men in trade is growing. The active, extensive wholesale trade sector, involving well-capitalized export crops such as coffee or other goods in national demand has historically been dominated by males.[7] The virtual exclusion of women from wholesale or export trade may be due to the male monopoly of trucking, an industry begun in San Pedro in the late 1950s when new roads increased the efficacy of modern modes of transportation. Men were able to buy trucks because they were in a better position to take advantage of the availability of financing due to their historical role as commercial mule trainers and because through trade they developed urban connections to dealers of new and used trucks. Because women in San Pedro bear the major responsibility for feeding the family, men have been able to accumulate the cash reserves to capitalize the wholesale trucking of agricultural products. A handful of women have owned large trucks that are driven by their sons or husbands to the coast for fruit or vegetable purchases. The town looks askance at female truck drivers, and the only one I have ever heard about was, in fact, murdered in her truck in the 1970s.

The inability of women to enter the wider, more profitable trade and transport sectors severely limits their growth as entrepreneurs. The majority of *Sampedranas* remain small-scale intermediaries whose stalls redistribute goods and artisanal products much as their grandmothers and great grandmothers did years ago. While such maintenance of family and local tradition is certainly seemly, it is also problematic. Smith showed that the share men control of the *Sampedrano* economy continues to be fruitful as their investments in local, regional, and national level commerce expand. Yet while men are taking advantage of ever wider and more profitable trade circles, women are active in markets with more limited potential.

Although some women vendors may accumulate quite a bit of money, even they are unable to find investment opportunities beyond the expansion of internal trade symbolized by perhaps the ownership of a bigger permanent stall. Unable to move into long-term, well-capitalized commercialism dominated by men, women invest their trade profits elsewhere. Where substantial amounts of capital do accumulate over time, women utilize their savings to raise their level of consumption (e.g., more meat, a radio, new clothes), to purchase the machinery for modern industrialized cottage industry or, more important, to educate their children. Historically, women reinvested their slender capital and the labor of their children in order to expand their trade, however limited this expansion might have been. They now appear to be turning away from such investments, utilizing their savings for school instead.

Plaza Traders

In 1988, about two thousand people regularly traded in the Thursday market, and nearly ninety percent were women. Each paid for the privilege. The town has a system of collection of market fees which nets approximately Q600.00 on Thursdays, Q100.00 on Sundays, and Q50.00 on each of the non-market days. Traders are assessed an amount based upon the size of their space and the type of product they sell. *Canasta* women who sit beside their goods pay from Qo.10 to Qo.15 according to product: beans and rice are by the *quintal* (hundred weight), Qo.05 for the sale of cheeses, Qo.15 for each *red* of herbs or greens, Qo.15 for each *red* of avocados, etc. Covered stall space in the plaza for the sale of a larger variety of goods is charged at Qo.20 a square yard. A ten percent tax is levied on each small pig or lamb sold. In-

side the *mercado,* permanent clothing and *típica* stores rent by two-year contracts amounting to between Q9.00 and Q50.00 a month. The ten meat and
twenty pork butchers occupying half the upper floor pay between Q5.00 and
Q20.00 apiece; the eight *comedores* (food stands or restaurants) Q20.00 each.
Approximately one hundred smaller stalls and *canasta* women trading in the
mercado pay lesser fees from Q0.05 to Q0.15 a day. The store-front businesses ringing the outside of the *mercado* and accorded the highest prestige
and most consistent business pay from Q20.00 to Q65.00 a month, electricity not included. Men with trucks backed up to the plaza for retail sales on
market days pay Q0.75, and an additional Q1.50 for a loudspeaker.

In the plaza, sections are set aside for the sale of animals, but the majority
of the spaces are accorded certain products and vendors only by custom.
Thus, for example, the brick street below the park is where cheaper vegetables — especially avocados — can be found; cauliflowers from Almolonga
or onions from Sololá are in the far buildings; the flower dealers front on the
old basketball court. Shoes and modern fabrics are sold across from the may-
or's office, and the *chiles* are on the second set of stairs near the bus terminal.
The order of arrival determines priority for fringe sellers to some extent,
but regular vendors know their spots and the town has rarely had to monitor the market, except for whatever health problems may have arisen.

The variety of products available at competitive prices in San Pedro's
plaza market is due in part to the town's location near the coastal plain and
the Mexican border, yet surrounded by highland villages, and with rapid
modern transportation to major cities. Vegetables and fruits grown only in
the tropical coastal climate arrive for every market day, enabling *Sampedrana*
trade intermediaries to then disperse them through their market networks.
After the market, truckers stock up with locally grown goods and products
or produce brought in from other parts of Guatemala for their return trip to
ladino coastal towns. Trade items from Mexico, legal and illegal, have been
a market mainstay for decades.

The variety demanded by the thousands of plaza customers encourages
women to develop a multiplicity of product strategies. Women produce
items at home to sell in the market, and they act as trade intermediaries for
agricultural, industrial, and artisanal items as well. The following examples
are but a few of the hundreds of different approaches to plaza trade.

THE SOAP SELLER

Maria Luz used to be one of dozens of soap makers and dealers in the market on Thursdays and Sundays. Today she is one of only ten — most from her

aldea of Chamac—who still make soap at home. Maria Luz's tenure is due to the fact that over her forty-five years in this trade, she has developed trade partnerships with regular customers who buy large numbers of soaps to sell as far away as Coatepeque, Mazatenango, or Tapachula, Mexico. To meet the wholesale and retail demand for her product, Maria Luz works every non-market day preparing her soap. She is assisted in various aspects of production by her *campesino* husband and unmarried sons and daughter, but it is clear both in the soap production and selling that Maria Luz is in charge and that she accepts help only in areas demanding the strength she no longer has or in time-consuming repetitive tasks. After a few weeks, home-made soap becomes bug infested and as a result, Maria Luz has no inventory. She sells her week's work immediately. She begins the process every Friday after the main market day to ready her supply of soap for Sunday. It takes twelve hours to cook the animal fat–based soap and this is Maria Luz's primary responsibility: stirring the soap mixture and keeping the fire going all night. When the mixture has cooked and cooled, she and her children work together measuring and shaping the soap into hundreds of individually priced balls. For each twelve-hour batch it takes another hour or two to complete this final preparation. In the three days' time between Sunday and Thursday, Maria Luz readies six huge *canastas* filled with soap. Her sons tie them in large *redes* and all travel the three kilometers from Chamac in a taxi early Thursday morning. Maria Luz sits in her customary spot in the market plaza until about two or until her two hundred soaps are sold. She grosses approximately Q30.00 on an average market day, and even after subtracting the cost of fat and firewood, she has earned enough to explain her persistence in soap-making to the exclusion of any other trade or wage earning activity.

THE VEGETABLE LADY

Hilma Orozco is thirty years old, and cannot remember when she did not work in the market. Her large vegetable stall is busy everyday, and it was in search of that kind of traffic that she decided to move out of the *mercado* three years ago. Like other traders, she realized that her competition was growing daily. So now she sits in the plaza everyday, selling tomatoes, potatoes, onions, beans, rice, and sugar. In the twelve years I have known her, Hilma's business has not really changed. Like most plaza women, she has no capital, and very short term credit with her suppliers from Quezaltenango. She must pay each Thursday for the previous week's goods, and often in the slower rainy season has had to borrow from Doña Juana, the hardware dealer. Because she buys quality produce, Hilma's regular customers are better-heeled urban women who can afford her slightly higher prices, but regardless of the good volume of her trade, Hilma's profits are small—often less than Q0.75 for each hundred pounds (*quintal*) and Q0.50 per case of vegetables sold. In a week she usually sells three *quintales* of beans, three of rice, four of sugar, and five to ten cases of tomatoes. Her total weekly net earnings amount to about Q12.00, a figure that has remained about the same for the last decade.

What is telling about Hilma's business is that in spite of the small profit margin, her work (and that of her elderly mother with whom she shares the stall) has produced enough money to pay for the university educations of her three brothers. To repay the women for their sacrifice and to help them meet expenses, each month Hilma's mother receives Q30 from her sons who are now successful businessmen in Guatemala City. The two women, who have always toiled without vacation or even the time to watch the television set they bought last year, continue to invest in schooling, but for a new generation. Since Hilma's husband left her three years ago, she has been solely responsible for her two children, and it is for their future that she now labors. As she did for her brothers, at night Hilma makes sweaters on a knitting machine to pay for her children's clothes and cost of their schooling.

THE TIN MERCHANT

Doña Marta has had a tin business in a plaza stall for eight years. She sells only on Thursdays after buying her Salvadoran tins from a wholesaler who arrives Wednesday nights. She makes a Q1.00 profit on every dozen pots she sells. On the *comales* (flat plates for grilling tortillas) she would like to make more, but she rarely gets her Q1.50 asking price. In the dry season when the market is busy, Marta can turn a straight Q10.00–15.00 profit in one day. She has an extremely low overhead in her stall and sales are brisk. However, in winter her profits drop to Q3.00; because of the rain, people do not come and she leaves at one. To supplement her disappointing average income, Marta and her husband run a small store-*cantina* in the front of their house. While the store is comparatively well-stocked, she complains of the taxes and deposit fees which lower her profits to about Q7.00 a week. As she sees it, she has to live off the two businesses; when one is bad, hopefully the other is good.

THE YOUNG TRADER

Not all traders are as concerned about business as is Marta; some are more relaxed about their day in the plaza, seeing it more as a comfortable social occasion than an economic strategy. These women are most often young brides without pressing domestic expenses who are just starting up in business. For example, Olga sells potatoes and rice in the plaza next to her Aunt Anita, who also sells these products. Olga has relatives all over the market, but her heart is not in commerce; she rarely pays much attention to the bargaining, preferring to nurse her infant, talk to Anita, or play with her two-year-old niece. Olga comes to market on both Thursdays and Sundays to make a few purchases, and figures she might as well take advantage of her family's trade relations in order to buy a few cases of potatoes for resale. She only makes a few cents on each case, and since sales are in small amounts, the entire day passes and only Q1.00 is earned. Just before leaving, this money is entirely spent in the rapid purchase of the tomatoes, chile, fat, rice and squash necessary for the three days' meals before the next market day. In certain months the intervening time will be filled with work as a sweatermaker, a cottage industry paying her Q0.20 per sweater, or half a *quetzal* a day.

Each of these women is engaged in market transactions outside her home, but the actual time spent trading varies from one to seven days. Their trade orbits are restricted to the plaza itself where they sell in six hours all they have brought or produced. Generally speaking, local plaza *vendedoras* (sellers) are sedentary traders, in that they rarely diversify their efforts to other marketplaces. More often they augment their market income with other work at home, a topic discussed in the next chapter, on the demise of cottage industry.

Mercado Merchants

Compared to the thousand or so plaza traders in a Thursday market, there are far fewer women in the stalls and shops inside the *mercado*. These women are permanent full-time *vendedoras* usually open for business every day from eight to six. Permanent stalls are in great demand. At the time of the construction of the *mercado* in 1973, hundreds of plaza traders clamored for the relatively few spaces available. Now fifteen years later, a second indoor market is planned to open in 1990, and all of the two hundred spaces were taken one month after construction was announced in 1987. Why is this strategy so eagerly coveted by *Sampedranas* when, as the following discussion shows, *mercado* sales require more labor and often result in similarly minimal profits? My assessment is that the lure of credit, a permanent stall, and the status of having moved inside the *mercado* make up for the disappointing net income.

The layout of the *mercado,* familiar to anyone who has been in a Guatemalan market, is as follows. On the first floor is *ladino*-style clothing, women's sweaters, and Indian *típica* (traditional textiles and clothing), with soap, combs, mirrors, and other small articles sold near the door. Up a stone ramp are the butchers of cattle and pork, informal eateries, and piles of *shecas,* vegetables and fruits, packaged noodles, cereals, and provisions. Across the ramp are several dozen small-time *típica* stalls featuring aprons, napkins, shawls and fabric. Outside are male-run hat and basket stalls where one can also purchase plastic items and heavy net bags for packaging cargo.

Many of the larger *mercado* traders buy their stock in Quezaltenango or Guatemala City. Some buy directly from wholesalers whose trucks arrive on Wednesday nights. The butchers, however, raise and slaughter their own beef and pork at home. Here we find a distinctive division of labor between male beef butchers and female pork butchers. It is interesting that men, rarely with their wives, own and operate the one business, and women, usually accompanied by their daughters, the other. The female monopolization of pork and sausage trade is further enhanced by the large number of stalls owned by sisters and cousins from the same *aldea,* which partially explains the fact that pork traders cooperate while beef butchers (who are by and large neither related nor neighbors) are fiercely competitive.

All the stalls are organized in the typical Latin American fashion with the same products being found together, what Tax (1953) refers to as "atomistic" organization. Since the prices are almost always the same at first request, buyers make satisfactory deals by developing a pattern of purchasing from individual *vendedoras* based on friendship or recommendation. In the plaza, buyers go from *canasta* to *canasta* pursuing a good potato at a low price, but *mercado* sales of food involve only brief bargaining. Rather, the buyer assumes she is getting a fair price since she shops in the stall often and considers herself a favored customer. *Sampedranas* know all the fluctuating market and non-market prices extremely well, and if not treated properly in a sale, will simply develop a trade pattern with the *vendedora* next door.

Mercado stall owners cannot compete with plaza bargaining partly because of their location on the second floor of a crowded building on the edge of the plaza. In addition, the overhead that accompanies permanency in a market precludes matching the bargained-for prices set by a plaza trader with but a day's supply of oranges in her *canasta.* While *mercado* dealers benefit from the volume of market-day trade and customer traffic, their potential earnings are limited on those days by their location. This problem is commonly circumvented on market days by asking a family member to set up a second stall in a plaza location.

Market *vendedoras* have the flexibility to cover both markets because unlike plaza traders they carry an inventory of goods. And because of the variety and volume of products sold, *mercado* traders are involved in more elaborate networks of trade. Some of their trade agreements are based on credit, thus they have some liquid capital to exploit various market opportunities not available to more limited plaza traders. These examples illustrate the nature of such extended *mercado* trade.

THE *TÍPICA* DEALER

Doña Rosaria was one of ten textile traders in the *mercado,* and she knew every weaver or embroiderer in town. She loved her work, and devoted long hours to her stall and to maintaining good relations with the many rural suppliers whose work she sold. Doña Rosaria died in 1986, and since then the stall has been run in absentia by her daughter Norma, who is a nurse. During the day, an employee, Rita, handles the dwindling number of transactions. Like all *típica* stands selling traditional handwoven textiles, this business is barely holding on. When Rosaria was alive, the sale of *huipiles, cortes,* belts and shawls from the stall netted about Q40 a week, a figure she considered sufficient. Today, Norma says the earnings do not approach that figure, low as it is. As mentioned earlier, the cost of imported thread has priced *típica* out of the clothing market. Accordingly, the profit margins on most traditional textiles have been forced down as consumer interest dips. For example, ordinary cotton *cortes* which used to cost Rosaria Q10 and sold for Q15, now cost Q20 and sell for Q22. Moreover, Norma and Rita have had to adjust their inventory to changing consumer tastes in order to make any sales. Far fewer items are handmade; most sales are of factory goods produced elsewhere. Even women in *traje* buy ready-made clothes for their families. One morning in June, just before the *feria,* the festival celebrating the town's saint's day when people normally buy new clothes for the celebration, Rita sold one knit shirt for Q4.50 and a small wool blanket for a baby at Q1.50. She had no expectation that her sales would pick up at any time soon. With her salary (it includes meals at Norma's home), the rent, electricity, and what they already owed to weavers whose work was languishing on the shelves, she was despondent about ever being able to meet their overhead.

THE WHOLESALER/RETAILER

Maria Ramirez works with her grandmother and mother in a vegetable stall in the *mercado.* She is the fourth generation of women in her family to sell vegetables. On a typical day in May, she displays for sale carrots, tomatoes, peaches, apples, plums, onions, oranges, spices, chiles, limes and cabbage. Because it is the rainy season, vegetables are abundant around San Pedro, and Maria and her mother buy many from local farmers, most only on short-term credit agreements. In summer, when it is dry, prices are higher and, based on who irrigates and who does not, trade agreements change. When the produce they want is hard to find locally, or when it is too expensive, they buy in Guatemala City. Maria's mother rides with ten other *vendedoras* in the back of a large truck to the capital. They leave at 9 p.m. to be at the Guatemala City terminal market for the 4 a.m. delivery of fresh produce. Finished by 2 p.m., they ride back slowly in the loaded truck and are home by 3 a.m. Maria's mother then becomes the weekly supplier for many traders, almost paying for her own vegetables with the profits. And while Maria's suppliers extend credit to their regular customers, her mother sells all her products to small-scale *canasta* ladies who pay cash.

Like Maria and her mother, *mercado* traders need to take advantage of any opportunity to cover costs or increase sales volume because their profits from the stall alone are small. On a weekly basis, Maria's largest profits are Q4.00 for selling eight cases of tomatoes, based on a margin of Q0.01 per pound. All other products together approximate tomato profits, for a rough weekly profit of Q15.00.

To augment stall sales beyond wholesaling certain vegetables and fruits, Maria milks two of their four cows and delivers the milk to customers near her home. For the daily sale of eight liters, she makes Q2.00. In addition, in some months she works eighteen hours a week at her knitting machine, earning about Q3.00 more each week.

In many ways, full-time vegetable traders like Maria are involved in considerable risk-taking behavior that can mitigate against the success of expanded trade. For example, rotting leftover vegetables and fruits present a real problem in terms of lost income which at first glance appear solvable by the investment in pigs. But the economics of raising pigs confounds this opportunity because pigs cannot live on leftover vegetables alone. Growing pigs eat five pounds of grain every day, so that during the five month maturation period, pigs eat more than $60.00 worth of feed. Add to that the Q8.00 originally paid for the piglet plus the cost of five months of rotting vegetables and the owner will actually lose money when the pig is finally sold for the prevailing Q80.00 price.

Moreover, unlike plaza sales, which involve perhaps six or eight hours of selling once or twice a week, *mercado* businesses demand constant coverage. Few women have the space or inclination to engage in another productive activity during market hours; most sit idly and chat with their neighbors until a customer arrives. Corresponding to these lost production hours, time away from home means having to rely on female family members or a *muchacha* to prepare meals and take care of children. Since these are two activities which have a high social value for a woman, *mercado* traders are never at ease with their economic situations and seem to be forever planning to be home more.

In all, while the actual volume of sales is greater inside the *mercado* than on the plaza, the profit margin remains so small that *vendedoras* must either take advantage of their minimal cash flow to trade in distant markets or cut their cash expenses by manipulating credit relations, or both. Risk-taking behavior increases markedly and the permanent location away from home disrupts domestic patterns. Furthermore, while market *vendedoras* have gained a certain status and a base of operations as full-time traders, like plaza women, they too must supplement their market income by cottage industry.

Canasta Women

Many other women—called *canasta* women for the baskets of produce they carry on their heads—are attached to the market in less fruitful ways than either plaza traders or *mercado* merchants. These traders travel into the market to make fifty *centavos* or a *quetzal* in order to buy the food their families will eat that day or that week. *Canasta* women utilize a variety of market strategies. Some sell their baskets of fruits and vegetables on the fringes of the market where other *aldeanos* shop for bargains. Others walk from house to house hawking prepared foods like *atol, chuchitos* (little pork-filled *tamales*), or cheeses for twenty-five cents a piece. Those with specialty items like herbs, candies, and fish crowed into the *mercado* to sell to local *civilizadas* who are loath to enter the chaotic plaza. *Canasta* women are usually *de corte* or partially so, have to keep their eyes on their young children around them, and while they love to bargain, they cannot allow customers to walk away from a sale. For many this is the only opportunity they have all week to make a few cents.

The *canasta* women found throughout the *mercado* experience the daily trading on many different levels based on their products and the regularity with which they visit the market. Those from the far *aldeas* trade only once or twice a week. But poor urban women are likely to trade as often as possible in order to generate income. Generally speaking, *canasta* women represent the poorest element in the market, women who are unskilled and illiterate; they have no access to cottage industry and survive on one meager income. The following account of the work of a well-known *canasta* woman illustrates the constraints of such a life.

THE *MASA* MAKER

Every morning for the last nine years, Petronilia Fuentes Orozco has stationed herself at a busy upstairs corner in the *mercado* to sell *masa,* a ground corn dough or paste used for making *tortillas* and *tomalitos.* Greeting her customers by name, she works rapidly, wrapping up and selling different sizes and types of *masa* for the noon meal. This was her mother's business; forty years ago she became a useful assistant and so it is with her own daughters. None has more than three years of schooling. As it was with her own mother, so it is with Petronilia; she cannot allow her children to learn other work because she needs their help *en este santo negocio*—in this blessed business. The more *masa* Petronilia and her daughters prepare to sell each morning, the better her sales. She must compete with other *vendedoras* (including her sister), and only by being reliable has she built up a steady clientele.

Her work begins when her daily *quintal* of corn is delivered to her house near the cemetery each evening. She cooks the corn with water and lime in order to peel it, then lets it cool overnight. At dawn, she washes the corn, fills up her largest tin, and carries it on her head to the *molino* to be ground. She and her daughters make many trips, and by 7 a.m., they are finally ready to prepare the different corn products to sell. Petronilia adds water to the *masa* for *tamalitos* and divides up the drier, better-ground *masa* to be used for *tortillas.* A special hand grinding is necessary for the *zapote* pits and ginger which are added to toasted *masa* for *atol,* the popular creamy drink. By nine o'clock everything is prepared. After quickly eating a breakfast of *tamalitos* and coffee, Petronilia and her daughters pack up their *masa* into huge *canastas* and, carrying them on their heads, walk the half mile to the market. Morning business is slow, so they wrap up hundreds of individual *tamalitos* in leaves grown for that purpose or deftly divide and wrap the *tortilla masa* into the round *bolito* shapes. Early *atolito* business is customary. Petronilia combines the *atol masa* with hot milk or water for a morning drink that shoppers drink quickly on their way past. As the morning grows late, wrapping and sales speed up almost to a frenzy and then at 12:30 or 1 p.m. abruptly stop. All *masa* is usually gone by then, but any remainder goes cheaply to another *vendedora* for the slower dinner business. The women carry their empty baskets home and eat a meal of vegetables, noodles and (occasionally) meat. A little later the next day's corn is delivered and work begins again.

Petronilia figures that for her preparation and sale of *masa* she nets Q0.50–0.75 a day and on Thursdays when she prepares an additional supply, Q1.00. Her expenses are a demanding but necessary burden: she pays Q7.00 for a hundred weight of corn every day. Firewood to fuel her cookstove is Q16.00 a month. She needs Q2.00 worth of leaves on a daily basis to wrap the masa and since she has no wholesale supplier of large amounts, she can only buy them at the retail market price. To this she adds the expense of Q1.00 of lime every week and the Q0.10 market fee, which averages Q10.00 a day overhead. Before her mother died fifteen years ago, she sold three *tamalitos* for a *centavo* and *bolitos* for Q0.04. Today's prices are not that much higher in spite of the currently inflated cost of corn grown on the coastal plantations. Traders are concerned that the market could not sustain a price hike, and as a result the profit margin in this traditional food has actually shrunk. Today each tamalito sells for a half-cent, *masa* for ten *tortillas* is Q0.05 and the *atolito* balls Q0.01. Based on these figures, to make her Q0.50–0.75 profit, Petronilia then would have to sell a thousand *tamalitos* and one hundred *bolitos* of *masa de tortilla* to cover expenses; leaving her with a profit from the sale of fifty to seventy-five *atolitos*.

This income, based on a seven day work week is considerably less than the average Q1.50 daily average wage for laborers. What brings the critical nature of the daily regimen into sharper focus is that apart from the two productive daughters living with Petronilia, she has two smaller children in school and four grandchildren. Her husband shows up occasionally on weekends, home from his job as a mason in Quezaltenango, and contributes Q3.50 for half a *quintal* of corn and "not one cent more." Nine people survive on this corn, the meager profits from the *masa* business, and the Q5.00 a month sent to Petronilia's daughter by the father of her child. In spite of the acknowledged meagerness of their income, over seven years Petronilia managed to save a few cents a day to build a new kitchen. The "new" nature of the room comes from the four cement walls and cement floor. It is bare except for a small wooden table and the utensils of her trade. Because she could not afford Q40.00 for a *plancha* (a flat cement stove three feet high with controllable fire and grates) she does all her cooking for work and family on a *pollito rústico* or open fire on the floor enclosed by a small cement border. Petronilia is proud of the new additions to her house although she bitterly complains about the lack of toilet facilities and drains in this part of town which means one constantly has to contend with streets and porches covered with mud.

But she manages. The trade her mother taught her sustains her family, and although she complains that her back and arms constantly ache, she brags that "we women are more valuable than men because we work so much harder."

Storekeepers

Appraisal of stores and storefronts around the *mercado* and down the main streets of town leaves the impression that there too women are engaged in trade, but on a much more powerful level. Eight out of ten street businesses are run by women selling groceries, shoes, fabric, hardware, paper goods, grains, clothing, beds, paints, building supplies, whisky and beer, drugs, bread, plastic products and *típica*. Most of these women are urban *civilizadas*. Compared to merchants in the plaza or *mercado*, female storeowners are more extensively attached to trade through their large inventories, high overhead and long-term indebtedness. Their commitment requires considerable capitalization and an understanding of market trends on a local, regional and national level. On this scale of trade, women develop extremely intricate and well-honed business skills as literally thousands of dollars change hands each week.

There are dozens of women running large stores by themselves, and an equal number of female shop owners working alongside their husbands. Women in the latter category commonly manage retail shops while their husbands control the wholesale side of business, transporting goods or filling their trucks with merchandise for waiting customers. Although men and women have complementary roles in the plaza or the *mercado*, among storeowners the system of mutual support is quite different. Among poor *Sampedranos*, the independent productive activities of the sexes overlap in the home or in the market, but the spouses tend to maintain control of their own spheres of influence. Thus, when Rosario, a farmer, buys animal fat in San Juan Ostancalco for Edulina to make into soap, he is making an important contribution to Edulina's business. In the same vein, if Rosalinda's husband, the tailor, travels to the coast to sell bread, the money he makes is turned over to her upon his return. While men and women at this level of trade help and depend upon one another, and in doing so raise their probability for success both in business and in terms of household income, in the final analysis, plaza and *mercado* businesses are normally controlled by females. Men are involved peripherally. They juggle their regular work outside the market with the help they give their wives. Among storeowning couples, however, women can play a less important role, particularly where the business depends upon trucking as part of its strategy.

The ownership of trucks is clearly a key to commercial power. Trucks leaving daily for Guatemala City or the coast are rarely empty. They haul cargo both ways, providing commercial and private service for businesses and residents of San Pedro and San Marcos. Not only do they carry merchandise and produce, they will deliver a refrigerator or a motorcycle or forty-five migrant coffee pickers. A few truckers even have terminals and offices in Guatemala City with employees in both places to schedule and load the shipments. The truck traffic is so heavy that downtown San Pedro has begun to sound, look and smell exactly like Hoboken, New Jersey, the western portal of the Holland Tunnel into New York City. Day or night, one cannot go outside without running into a constant stream of laborers shouldering bags of flour, or cement or lime from trucks to small warehouses.

With transport being an important key to success in San Pedro, it is quite telling that so few women own trucks. Unlike independent storeowners, women married to wholesalers and transporters often find themselves minding the store, rather than making business decisions. They are only employees or in terms of San Pedro's characteristic entrepreneurism, members of a family productive system controlled solely by men. Although the business bank account may swell, these women recognize that the money belongs to their husband and not to them. Certainly a woman's standard of living improves with commercial success, but she rarely directs the business fiscal policy or manages the family's financial affairs. She may be wealthy, but she spends money only as it is allotted to her by her husband. Often women are the acknowledged "brains" behind the enterprise, yet however high a woman's commercial acumen or prestige may be, if she is working with her husband, she may be excluded from control and ownership, and occupy a secondary status. However, as mentioned earlier, a significant percentage of storeowners are women who, due to widowhood, because their husbands are occupied elsewhere, or through force of personality, entrepreneurship, and ambition, operate independently. The following case studies illustrate both the commercial success and sexual segregation characteristic of women storeowners.

TERESA FUENTES

Along one border of the *mercado* are a series of small open-front stores offering a variety of products from blankets to boots to pencils. In the middle of the block are two tiny grocery stores specializing in canned, packaged, and frozen food—the processed foods which are now growing in popularity and which were previously purchased raw or live from small traders. There is a regular stream of traffic past these stores as they are just down from the entrance to the *mercado* and many women have been introduced to such modern products as yogurt or freeze-dried beans by a passing glance. One of the stores is owned by Teresa Fuentes, who with her husband has been responsible for making available pasteurized milk in cartons, cottage cheese, and sliced processed ham. The demand for these and other industrialized food products has risen dramatically in the three years they have owned the store. They now distribute to a half dozen stores in San Marcos, San Rafael and Tumbador. In fact, the *"depósito distribudora Fuentes"* is also a major supplier of eggs and frozen chickens to local stores. Each week Francisco Fuentes drives his eight-ton truck to Guatemala City to buy the quantity he needs for his store and his wholesale customers. The wholesale business extends also to walk-in purchases from owners of small *tiendas*. Teresa is regularly visited by sales representatives of large grocery suppliers who keep her stocked enough to handle walk-in retail and wholesale trade. She is billed by these companies on a monthly basis, but herself extends no credit through the store. Wholesale customers differ from retail only in the volume they buy. Teresa charges them the same prices, thus passing on the price hike to their consumers who buy closer to home. For example, she pays Qo.50 for a pound of margarine and her customers pay Qo.55. The wholesale clients then sell each of the four bars for Qo.15 and like Teresa, make a profit of a nickel on the pound. Owners who pass by can buy large amounts of chicken or eggs at a somewhat reduced price since Francisco Fuentes is himself the middleman of those products.

The success of this business is based in part on the determination Teresa and her husband made to earn a living by exploiting the commercial "boom" economy of the town. Both came from poor families and like most Guatemalan children, grew up with little schooling because they comprised the family work force, she in the family bakery and he in fresh vegetables. When they first married, Teresa and Francisco failed dismally at running their own bakery, and he went to work for a prosperous immigrant German who owned a large mill. This man helped them to get started with good advice and a loan, and so they began their first small store. Now, eighteen years later they have few debts, own their own house, and have a very prosperous business. The only obstacle to saving some money is the Q200.00 a month they pay on their truck, but they do not begrudge that debt, for without the truck, their business would be of an entirely different nature.

Since he is always out buying and selling wholesale goods in his truck, Francisco never works in the store. Teresa works there every day, but she has a very competent assistant who knows more about the store than she does. He works eight hours a day, six and a half days a week, which allows her an occasional few hours off. No more than two people can efficiently work the store since it is so small, but those two people are constantly busy. No one comes in to browse; every customer buys something, and sales figures reflect this. Sundays are the best days when they sell Q100.00 – 200.00. On other days this figure drops to Q50 – 60.00, still a sizeable sum.

Trying to work out the business's profitability with Teresa was difficult. Besides these rough sales figures, Teresa only knows about the Q16.00 a month they must pay for rent on the store and the Q18.00 electricity bill. All financial matters are handled by her husband and her grown sons, two of whom are accountants. Every day they give her a bag of silver and bills to make change and every night she gives back the bag filled with the starting cash and her sales. She never counts up the sales herself, nor does she care to. Teresa is content with her role and eschews more responsibility. In her mind, by overseeing their store, she is getting just what she wants—the recognition and respect she deserves as the wife of a rich man. In addition, the public nature of a busy retail business satisfies her need for company, attention, and for keeping up on the latest gossip. In all, Teresa basks in her middle class life, happy to be protected by the men around her, free of the business obligations and worries of independent female merchants.

MARGA MÉNDEZ

Marga, a widow, is one of the best known merchants in San Pedro. For the last twenty years, she and her sister have run an elite downtown store that is famous for having fine chocolates, imported sardines, or just the right spice for a special stew. Her customers are clearly *civilizada,* allowing her business to grow as the middle class expanded. Currently, she is worried that she will have to close her doors. In fact, on the day she told me her problems with competitors, inflation, and corruption in the export sector, she was very upset. She had found old copies of the national newspaper, and caught a glimpse of the prices from ten years before. As she recounted, she nearly died laughing. Chicken had been one sixth the price it was in 1988. Tomato paste was now five times as much. Shrimp and clams were eight times higher. The price of food had literally skyrocketed. Her customers—whose salaries had *not* gone up—were buying less from her, and shopping elsewhere to boot. Years of loyal service meant nothing when plaza traders in cheap stalls were able to sell her products for less than what she had always needed to charge to stay in business.

Marga's fiscal woes extended beyond her shop to her milk business that

supplemented her commercial trade earnings. Over twenty-five years, she
had built her herd up to eleven cows, but feed concentrate had become so
expensive, she could no longer make any money from their milk. She had
narrowed the blame down to the high price of the U.S. soy in the feed, but
the Guatemalan corn and molasses that made up the other ingredients were
also expensive. The two businesses together did not afford this sophisticated
trader the ten percent profit margin she needed to pay her rent and the electricity bill. Marga had decided that she could do just as well—or just as
poorly—by closing her business and putting her money in the bank instead.

JUANA OROZCO

In his chapter on "A Developing Indian Town," Smith (1977:108–109) re-
counts the story of the Orozco brothers, German and Anselmo, as an example of dramatic entrepreneurship in San Pedro:

> The brothers have prospered as truckers. At present, each owns a ten-
> ton diesel, a pickup truck for local deliveries, and a house and ware-
> house in downtown San Pedro from which they run their wholesale
> businesses. Their children will all receive higher education, and each
> brother has one son about to graduate from the local military academy.
> In two generations this aldean family has become wealthy and modern.

But there is also the neglected role played by German's commonlaw wife,
Juana, in his continuing business achievements.

While German travels twice weekly to Guatemala City hauling cargo,
Juana manages a three-room warehouse which is both truck terminal and
store. Out of this cramped storehouse comes cement, tin roofing, paint, and
other hardware to supply the growing construction industry in town and the
aldeas.[8] The business often grosses Q3,000 on a Thursday when groups of
men and women must wait their turn to order and buy. Juana sits behind her
metal desk and deals. She bargains with hundreds of people over quantities
of cement, from a hundred-pound bag carried on the back of a *campesino* to
the truckloads needed for new government buildings in San Marcos. Known
as a shrewd, sly trader, Juana's prices vary person to person for every product she sells. In each case she weighs the amount bought, the history of trading, and the relationship she and German have with the buyer, against her cost
that week. Then, depending upon her mood, she comes up with either an
appropriate price, the brush-off, or a steal. Men love to bargain with her and
she, too, revels in the process. Often a small purchase will take over an hour

as Juana holds court, recounting a choice bit of gossip or giving advice in a personal matter.

But her power in making deals brings little pleasure to Juana. Despite her playful banter, her sad eyes are a constant reminder of the unfaithfulness of her husband and her much-begrudged obligation to remain with him for the sake of their children. Months pass when German has moved out of their house to be with a second wife who lives around the corner, and the only contact Juana and German have is in the office. The constant flaunting of his independence and his sexual dalliances only serves to further cement Juana's role in the business. While she longs to move to Guatemala City and open a business making and selling bedspreads, she is convinced that her husband would not only deny an education to their children, but that he would exercise his legal rights to prosecute her for abandoning their home.

The disruption of Juana's home life extends beyond a wandering husband. Working the long hours she does, she must rely on a *muchacha* to prepare meals, do the washing and ironing, and supervise their daughters. She is critical of her *muchachas*, never appreciative of the capabilities of the woman she hires. The result is a long string of dismissed housekeepers. For a while she tried cooking the noon meal at the shop, a plan that quickly went awry when heavy business traffic kept her at her desk past lunch. The solution has been for the children to eat in restaurants, an alternative Juana despises but must accept. In addition, the absence of a mother to supervise her and her access to street life have been partially responsible for the unfavorable reputation now attached to Juana's eldest daughter just going through puberty. In all, Juana's obligation to manage German's business has significantly alienated her from fulfilling her domestic role, a situation of which she is fully cognizant and indeed, resentful, but incapable of changing to any great degree.

I first met Juana when she was running German's business six days a week, throwing the profits into a desk drawer *quetzal* after *quetzal*. I noticed that she was dipping into the money drawer when she needed a few dollars for lunch or to buy some cheeses from a passing *canasta* lady. She justified her action by saying German spent more on cards and women each week than she did in six months. Aside from those household expenses, she did not steal what was, after all, her husband's money. At night she added up the stacks of bills, and the next day, took them to the bank where she deposited them into German's account. But Juana is no fool. She was biding her time with German, just waiting for him to be drunk enough, unfaithful enough, and away enough for her to get up the courage to pounce. Eventually, she did. By 1987, through crafty legal maneuvering, she had managed to wrest fiscal control away from her husband, and was depositing the daily receipts into her own account. She now owns both the business and the house, and has just purchased a larger site to build a new store. Meanwhile, German spends most of his time gambling, or in Guatemala City, stopping into the store only occasionally when he dips into the sales drawer to put a few *quetzales* into his pocket.

Female Traders and the Internal Market

Female traders in San Pedro approach the market with a variety of strategies, capital, time, and entrepreneurial skills. Like female traders all over the world, *Sampedranas* sell what they produce themselves. But they are also non-producing intermediaries who purchase commodities from farmers, artisans, manufacturers, and distributors to be re-sold in towns or in plaza marketplaces elsewhere. The elaborate systems of transport developed in the region over the last three decades make accessible the large, concentrated population of San Pedro and its hinterland. In order to reach this population, traders must combine the ingenuity, mobility, and entrepreneurship long associated with the town. They do this with varying degrees of success.

What San Pedro's female traders do have in common is that few of them can make a living from the market alone. Regardless of a woman's adeptness at her craft or her good business sense, only the wealthiest *Sampedrana* can depend upon commerce as a full-time livelihood. Because profits are small and competition strong, women have to couple their market earnings with other income-producing activities. Those who can—urban women and women from near *aldeas*—invest in cottage industries. The emphasis on home production is so strong that many women exploit the market mainly as an outlet for their home-made bread, soap, cheese, or textiles. Others work at home as piecework laborers, sewing or machine knitting for contractors who sell in larger urban markets.

As San Pedro continues to develop economically, women will shift the emphasis of their income-producing efforts and move away from traditional home-based artisanship. As the shrinking sales at Doña Rosaria's *típica* stall illustrate, the trend has already begun. Meanwhile, in the last decade, the size of the market has doubled. This is a result not only of population growth, but of the inability of cottage producers to maintain their standard of living by selling traditional products. In order to generate income, more and more women (and men) are entering the market as traders of goods they purchase from distributors. Unfortunately, the rising number of retailers, while providing a better deal for the consumer, severely cuts profits for the entire market. While the San Pedro market is among the busiest in the highlands, it can absorb increasing numbers of traders only up to a point.

For generations, successful female traders have been able to rely upon San Pedro's strong family productive system. Trade necessitates cooperation among adult family members, and when a woman has historically depended upon assistance and cooperation from her mother, sisters, and children, she may maintain her business apart from her spouse's control or input. But, while autonomous female businesses are a source of female status, in this case they have drawbacks as well. Within the normally female internal market, a woman can advance only so far. For example, in terms of reinvestment of the money earned in trade, solitary *Sampedranas* have little opportunity outside the market itself. One crucial reason for the limited nature of the woman's trading sphere is the difficulty women have obtaining the credit necessary for expansion. Because autonomous female traders are seriously undercapitalized, few women have access to the more lucrative external market where export crops are traded, or to the transportation of goods. Both these areas remain almost exclusively male domains.

In concert with a male partner, however, women's opportunities improve. With their wholesaler husbands, women might expand their trade in the San Pedro market or other plazas in large towns on the coast. As wealth increases, this complementarity often diminishes as wealthier male traders' dependent, powerless wives merely "mind the store." On the other hand, the frequency of independent female storeowners suggest that the secondary status characteristic of some wealthy women merchants is not necessary the norm.

Because women's potential for entrepreneurial growth is limited, many traders instead raise their levels of consumption with the purchase of TV's or other modern goods. The most common investment strategy, however, is to educate their children, particularly daughters. Female traders—mostly illiterate—overwhelmingly opt to send their children to school. Hilma Orozco pointed out to me that her daughters would get more out of life than she: "There are days when I have no business, but my children will always have their education." Because many female traders are disadvantaged by comparatively fewer years of education than their male counterparts, they are stimulated to educate their daughters partly to overcome this handicap in the next generation. By sending their daughters to school, women lose helpers and the heirs to their businesses because educated children prefer employment in the modern sector to selling tomatoes and chiles in the plaza.

In a number of ways, the trend away from trade and toward education and employment, while indicative of decreasing productive control for mothers, demonstrates the increase in options and mobility for their daughters. Trade is a difficult and demanding way of life with limited income opportunity for women. For a long time, *Sampedranas* have invested in trade to support their families, but it is not surprising that when they can offer their daughters education and the chance for a better life, they take it.

Notes

1. Sugar provides the only source of energy in a diet deficient in important nutrients. Thus malnourished working people need to get themselves going with coffee and sugar at every meal.

2. These figures, compiled over two years of afternoons in June and July may be somewhat misleading. In fact, they are characteristic of Edulina's profits for only part of the year. After November, business picks up considerably. There are two reasons why. First of all, traffic is heavier in the dry season. Trading takes place well past one o'clock when from May to November rains signal the departure of customers. Secondly, after the fall harvest, when they can count on their own corn and do not have to buy it, people have more money to spend. Traders look forward to the change of seasons when they say people buy three pounds instead of two.

3. There is a considerable literature on Third World female traders that outlines the requirements for successful commerce and the constraints on their status and social power. See, in particular, Boserup (1970), Sudarkasa (1973), Mintz (1971), Chiñas (1976), Chaney and Schmink (1976), Bossen (1984), and Ottenberg (1959). Similarly, analysis of Guatemalan highland markets has occupied such writers as C. Smith (1972, 1977), Goldin (1986), Tax (1953), McBryde (1933), McDowell (1976), Swetnam (1975).

4. For an examination of cultures with a far greater degree of female commercial autonomy, see Boserup (1970), Mintz (1971), and Sudarkasa (1973).

5. According to a recent study done by City Planners from the University of San Carlos (Rivera B. and Yoc Pérez 1987), there are 765 commercial businesses in San Pedro.

6. The cheap and abundant flowers in the San Pedro market always amazed me, and I regularly bought armsful to cheer up my apartment. Unfortunately, it was through these flowers that I made my first cultural blunder. Being an educated and polite American, the first two or three people asked me to come for dinner, I thought it appropriate to arrive with flowers in my hand. My hosts always seemed surprised when they saw the flowers which were summarily banished, never to appear on the table. I wondered about this, but did not fully understand it until I went with a friend to visit her father's grave. Looking around at all the daisies, irises, and lilies carefully placed on hundreds of tombs, I realized that flowers were plentiful in the market because people used them to remember their dead. When I offered them as a housegift, it was a macabre and clearly inappropriate gesture.

7. See Mintz (1971) on Haiti and Ottenberg (1959) on the Afikpo Ibo for further analysis of male circumvention of female traders in the marketing of profitable export goods, as well as the alternative routes women vendors use for economic mobility.

8. While normal population growth accounts for some new houses every year, the dramatically increased demand for new and better "modern" houses seems to reflect the growing patterns of conspicuous consumption evident in other consumer habits.

5

♌

Cottage Industry

HARDLY A HOUSE IN TOWN or near *aldea* is without a woman (mother or daughter) who weaves, embroiders, sews, makes soap or cheese, bakes bread, fattens pigs, picks eggs, or is otherwise involved in cottage industry.[1] The home production of saleable items is a mainstay of the female productive strategy, and it is a sensible, convenient system. Involvement in work in the home allows women to attend to their regular domestic duties while causing minimal disruption of the normal household routine. Daughters who literally grow up with the traditional skills of their mothers are apprenticed to the family business early enough to be valuable workers at ten or eleven years of age. The location of cottage industry in the home permits women to further augment their incomes by investment in small *tiendas* in the front room or window of their houses; stores are left unattended until a customer enters and calls a woman away from her work to buy a cigarette or a soda. Often, if she does not market her goods in town, these small stores serve as an outlet for a woman's products. In brief, investment in cottage industry affords women a working situation that maximizes their utility in the family productive unit by allowing for the production of cash items, maintenance of domestic routine and the mobilization of additional labor from among the children. Furthermore, traditional cottage industry has allowed women to control their time and the earnings and expenses of production, to contract their labor or goods if they wish, and have the freedom to trade where they please.

This situation is rapidly changing for women, many of whom are losing their roles as independent producers and becoming part of a rural proletariat. For years, women's domestic work has centered around the production of traditional textiles and trade goods. Women could rely upon home businesses handed down to them by their mothers and grandmothers because *Sampedranos* had no access to or appetite for industrial or modern alternatives. With the town's post-war economic take-off, its new orientation toward national and international values, and its emphatic investment in education, consumer preferences and market conditions are changing. While homemade goods are still important in the town's commercial profile, in many cases they are being edged out by mass-produced or factory-made items. In some areas the erosion is gradual though persistent. For example, well-equipped bakeries are flourishing, but *canasta* women with two hundred home-made breads in their baskets can also make a small profit. Similarly, while today there are fewer soapmakers or women who deliver fresh milk, those who remain still do business largely because their low profit margin means they can be competitive with higher-priced powdered soap or milk in cartons. In these cases, modern, factory-made goods have reduced the home producers' market share, especially among urban consumers, but there is still room for the small-time, under-capitalized producer as well.

Elsewhere, however, the market for traditional goods is evaporating far more rapidly. This is particularly true of the textile industry where untoward economic circumstances and a changing expression of ethnic identity combine to make the wearing of *traje* less popular. Weaving has long been the most important female cottage industry, but I have watched it disappear over the last decade, first gradually, and then quite precipitously since 1985. Each year fewer and fewer women choose to spend their money on the relatively expensive traditional costume, opting instead to wear cheap conventional dresses and to spend their disposable income on radios, televisions and other modern things.

In this chapter I examine the world of female domestic production in light of the town's development. I do this by contrasting women's traditional autonomous production with the new kinds of cottage industry that have replaced it in the 1980s. Let me begin with a few important considerations that surround this discussion.

First, it must be remembered that women's reproductive and domestic responsibilities somewhat constrain their productive mobility, making them a particularly available home work force. As the earlier examination of female traders showed, women feel guilty when the demands of their work remove them from the house. Cottage industry is perfectly adapted to the fulfillment of culturally derived expectations for maintaining the family and earning a living at the same time. The town's reliance on this system is evidenced by its persistence even when manufactured products make traditional goods obsolete. Over the last twenty-five years, a variety of modern technologies has undermined traditional household production, depriving women of reliable businesses they and their mothers had developed. However, since women are still expected to be both income earners and primary caretakers, they continue to work at home, but now in a variety of new productive enterprises over which they have little control.

Second, this new pattern of household production is based in part on an aggressive system of debt-removal contract labor, which since 1975 has embroiled unskilled or poor women in the promise of easy wages for different types of piecework by coming into the homes to hire. Women who have not developed reliable cottage industries of their own eagerly accept this exploitative work because it is easy and requires little organization or business acumen.

Third, as years of schooling increase for girls, many educated women are unable to find jobs that meet their new expectations. Not as mobile as their male counterparts, most wait at home for the promised position. Meanwhile, shunning the old-fashioned occupations of their mothers, girls with schooling look eagerly to maintaining their new "civilized" status through the time-payment purchase of a sewing or knitting machine. As we shall see, sewing and machine knitting fit the profile of the modern home industries that now typify San Pedro. It is true that, like traditional cottage industry, this new work complements female domestic responsibilities. But it is fundamentally different because it ties home industry to the demands of mechanized factories and contract laborers, thus depriving women of their status as autonomous producers.

Lastly, as a result of the previous three considerations, the disappearance of traditional systems of production deprives women of the cooperative work of their daughters. In modern home work, skills are transmitted neither through socialization nor the standard family apprenticeship system. Because machine production is relatively new, girls must rely on women outside the family for instruction, sometimes at great expense.[2] The best example of this method is the system at any of the local sweater factories where girls work at no pay until they learn to knit. Since the determination of "learning" is at the discretion of the owners, it often takes up to two years of free labor before they are skilled.

In contrast to the changes women are confronting in cottage industry, male household production has not been significantly disrupted by the developing economy. Men have also dedicated their energies to cottage industry as artisan producers, e.g., brickmakers, carpenters, tanners, etc. What differentiates male household labor from that of their wives is that men are better capitalized, more mobile, and less occupationally segregated. Together these conditions mean male homeworkers are more flexible and can quickly and successfully adjust to market fluctuations while women cannot. Women in cottage industry tend to be confined to a narrow band of productive efforts based upon skills they need for domestic tasks. By commercializing skills like textile and clothing production, soapmaking, breadmaking, and candlemaking, women carved a market niche for themselves, but one that in its emphasis on traditional production methods has become highly susceptible to replacement by modern factory goods. When women lose their marketshare, they have limited household productive options available to them. Although plaza trade is always a possibility, many women rely upon cottage industry for part of their income and as a stable way to manage the home. In contrast, male artisanal trades include dozens of relatively profitable occupations and skills, most of which are still locally viable. If their work becomes obsolete or loses money, men have more opportunities for alternative employment partially because they are free from domestic responsibilities and can move to locations outside the home. Take the case of the shoemakers who recently lost their market when manufactured shoes were introduced on a large scale. Several of the shoemakers joined the vanguard of entrepreneurs opening shoe stores on the main streets; others took advantage of commercial opportunities in the plaza; one went into partnership with relatives in transport. The town's business climate afforded these male artisan producers ready solutions to a decline in their industry, but such avenues are not as easily accessible to women who have neither the capital nor the mobility their husbands do.

In short, one consequence of San Pedro's economic development has been to remove ultimate control of production from individual women in cottage industry and place it outside the domestic sphere into the hands of labor contractors and factory bosses. While the relocation of labor in the public sphere affects male as well as female employment, the historical emphasis on cottage industry as women's work means that its decline alters female occupations to a much greater extent than it does those of men. As the modern external market has grown, bringing a modicum of affluence and "civilization" to the town, so the traditional market shrinks, forcing women into alternative—and less influential—modes of cottage industry and employment. More and more women are obliged to search for new work to replace "old-fashioned" businesses that are dying out. Since they retain responsibility for the home and children, but need to bring in an income as well, women have been targeted as an available and easily exploitable work force.

Weaving as a Cottage Industry

Weaving, the largest cottage industry, lies at the heart of this process, and its demise is particularly problematic. The production and wearing of the local costume has been emblematic of the *Sampedrano* ethnic identity, and until recently, a secure cottage industry for women. Obviously, at one time all *Sampedranas* wore the indigenous costume. I know of one woman whose mother dressed her in western clothes as early as the 1930s, but that was rare. The move away from universal *traje* began slowly in the 1950s among urban *civilizadas* until today only a handful of middle class women wear *huipil* and *corte*. In contrast, rural women and poorer urbanites do wear *traje*, but in varying degrees. Generally speaking, the habit of donning western dress is distributed along a continuum beginning with the almost universal wearing of *traje* in the remote *aldeas* while among the more prosperous near *aldeas* one finds many women in dresses as well as *de corte* women dressing their baby daughters in modern garb.

The direction of the trend is reflected in my 1988 study of 80 households in San José Caben showing 90% of grandmothers still wear *traje típica*, while 64% of their daughters maintain the costume as do only 28% of their granddaughters. When fewer women buy *traje* each generation, it is clear that weavers will eventually be out of business. Whether this tendency will reverse itself and salvage the art remains to be seen. Normally, once a girl is dressed in western clothes, she never goes back to *huipiles*. I have found a few deviations from that model among *aldea* women who purposefully returned to their costume after years in dresses, but so far this has not become a trend, and the increasingly expensive price tag attached to *traje* suggests that it probably never will be.

I am emphasizing traditional weaving both because of its historical preeminence as work women do, and because the fate of this cottage industry strongly reflects the direction the community has taken with development, i.e., greater involvement in and identification with the national culture as shown in new clothing and consumer preferences. The cost of the materials aside, opting to spend money on consumer goods rather than the traditional costume certainly says something important about how *Sampedranos* see themselves in relation to the world outside the town. Economically, what this discussion shows is that although on the whole, the population may benefit from the increased commercial activity brought by a new modern orientation, some businesswomen—in this case, weavers—suffer a considerable loss in control of production. To better understand this process, let

us examine an *aldea* family where weaving has been basic to the family production system.

THE OCHOA FAMILY WEAVERS

Doña Angélica and Don Carlos live with their six children on the main road
of San José Caben. As in most of the other houses in this weaving village, five
huge footlooms fill up the three front rooms. All five of these looms are constantly busy. Three are worked by Angélica and her daughters in the weaving
of *huipiles*. The other two looms are strung for the weaving of yardgoods, but
Carlos, like other entrepreneurial men in San José, has enough business that
he can hire two young men to weave for him. The profits from commercial
weaving belongs to Carlos, and unless called upon in an emergency, he contributes little to the daily support of his family. He has saved what he could,
and invested some money in a men's weaving cooperative. The family relies
only upon the women's work to meet daily cash expenses, and with eight
mouths to feed, these are considerable. Carlos' land provides beans, corn
and a few vegetables, but the women pay cash for everything else.

Angélica and her three teenage daughters have developed a schedule for
the production and sale of one *huipil* every week although three are always
in process. They alternate weaving with domestic and sewing chores, two
working together at one loom while the others wash clothes and cook, make
the necessary preparations to string a new loom, or sew the collar on a
finished *huipil*. Angélica has learned that two girls working a total of eight
hours a day for a week can make one *huipil*. Their production schedule is designed around that goal, and even though there are four of them, with all
their household responsibilities, it is not unusual to see someone working
her loom by candlelight.[3] These women take great pride in their work, enjoy weaving together, yet do not take it all that seriously. They never work
on Sundays when the girls sing in the church choir or Thursdays when Angélica markets. Some mornings it will be 11 a.m. before anyone begins work.
It is evident that there being four of them allows them a certain flexibility.
They are confident of meeting their production schedule and making enough
to cover expenses. The fact that the eldest son attends high school full-time,
doing no work at all, is evidence of the success of their system.

Every Thursday Angélica brings that week's *huipil* to San Pedro where she
has had a long trade partnership with Doña Celestina, the *típica* dealer. In the
mercado, she exchanges the *huipil* for Celestina's payment on the previous
week's work. Although these women are of different social classes and dress,

they treat each other and their partnership with great respect. Should Celestina balk at a payment or refuse to meet a price, it is understood that Angélica could easily strike up a new trade relationship with any one of the eight or ten other dealers in stalls nearby.

Because of the rising cost of thread and the relatively stable price of traditional goods, Angélica's profits are not high. For enough *lustrina* or silk-like thread for one *huipil,* she pays Q21.00. A week later, she sells the woven product for Q35.00; a Q14.00 gross profit or Q2.80 a day for less than five days' work.[4] This money goes into Doña Angélica's pocket, and is spent promptly on the food the family will eat that week. As we will see later, there is no redistribution of this small profit as the girls' labor is entirely contributed. They do not expect to be paid for their labors, as they are only fulfilling the duties of a daughter to help the family make ends meet.

If it is indeed true that traditional weavers like Angélica have a relatively reliable and personally satisfying home industry, then it seems problematic that it is a disappearing art. Earlier it was mentioned that the closing up of external *huipil* trade due to urban competition and the concurrent opening of new markets for more commercial yardgoods were contributing factors in the decline of this cottage industry. These variables are just two of a myriad of events fueled by economic and cultural changes which are a part of the process of development in San Pedro. The following discussion examines one of these factors, the evolution of clothing preference in light of the growing awareness of the tastes and symbols of the national and international culture of which *Sampedranos* are now a part.

Traditional and Modern Clothing in San Pedro

Visitors to San Pedro on market day are often awestruck by the throngs of Indian women wearing the elegant and colorful costume typical of the region. Women in yellow silk-like *cortes* and brocaded *huipiles,* carrying their babies on their backs and their baskets on their heads, fill the streets and plaza. These are the *gente natural* made up of the largely rural agrarian population living outside the town in *aldeas,* and the poorer urban women. Because many are traders or commercial home producers, few of these women weave their own clothes. Instead, when they have the money, they purchase their traditional clothes in the *mercado.*

Most town women have abandoned the indigenous costume common in *aldeas* in favor of Western dress.[5] They carry their children in their arms like *ladinas,* and while *aldea* women and urban *gente* are likely to be selling in the market, *civilizada* town women buy. These middle class women are not only better educated and more affluent than *de corte* women, but they are in constant contact with national and even international culture through their television sets and their educated children who may live in Guatemala City, Miami or Los Angeles.[6] They think of themselves as living at a social level above the common *aldeanos* where their material needs and aspirations are much greater, and they reject *traje* as a symbol of poverty, illiteracy, and a life they left behind a generation ago.

Among these middle class *Sampedranas*, the abandonment of *traje* is considered an appropriate step toward civilized status. As such, there is a certain amount of scorn for *de corte* women as backward *campesinas*, even if they are urban. For example, one woman was at first disturbed and hurt to hear of yet another of her husband's lovers, but she had to laugh when she saw that the woman wore *huipil* and *corte*. Oddly enough, while town women often snicker about *aldea* women, their own honored mothers often wore *huipiles*, something they mention with pride. But while they venerate the customs and clothing of the past, there seems to be a demarcation in time after which the prevalent attitudes changed toward the demonstration of those traditional behaviors. What has occurred is that the impact of rapid economic development and the access to the world outside San Pedro and Guatemala caused the expression of traditional values to be denigrated, and with them the value of traditional symbols. This means that in terms of status, while being successful and rich have long been important factors in this trade town, the two are now being expressed in modern, consumer-oriented behavior and by donning western clothes.

In the process of evolving toward the western trappings of class, the device of deeming traditional female apparel a relatively precise index of ethnic and socioeconomic differentiation has been rendered useless. Until fifteen or twenty years ago, wealth and power among Indian women were demarcated by the distinctive cloth and pattern of their *traje*. Osborne (1965:126) refers to the Quezaltenango *huipil* of the 1930s with this in mind, and strong parallels may be drawn to San Pedro:

> The huipil known as "pishiquin," bearing pine trees and birds in red, purple and yellow silk and usually made on hip-strap looms in San Pedro Sacatepéquez (San Marcos) is deemed suitable for high-class Indians. The "ranciado sencillo" worn by the lower classes has no embroidery at the neck and scanty "jaspes," and is now often woven on footlooms. The "ranciado de palito," woven on hip-strap looms and worn by the middle class has silk threads throughout the fundamental design.

While it is still true that among *de corte* women, character and condition of *traje* reflects social status, the growing numbers of all classes of women wearing cheap Western dress considerably obscures class distinctions. Even more confusing is the fact that many *Sampedranas* are in a state of transition away from *traje,* keeping some symbols and discarding others. The following examples illustrate the point:

- Women who persist in wearing their yellow *cortes* are often garbed in cheap cotton blouses instead of *huipiles.*
- Cotton towels are sometimes used to cover the head in place of *perajes* or folded wraps.
- All but the most westernized women continue to carry their *canastas* on their heads.
- The most common hair style among *Sampedranas, de corte* or not, is the single braid tied without string or elastic bands on the end, the traditional Indian mode.
- The sweater has replaced the wool *serape* which *de corte* women now only use to cover their heads in church.

The paradoxes of vanishing ethnic symbolism can be seen every year when the upper class literate elite of the town (doctors, teachers, civil servants) sponsor a highly competitive contest for *Reina Indígena* or Indian Queen of San Pedro. One by one, selected teenage girls from the town and *aldeas* enter the townhall wearing traditional costumes and jewelry, some—the *huipil de misa* or wedding costume, for example—no longer made or worn on other occasions. They dance the traditional harvest *son* and are lauded by the master of ceremonies as examples of "our beautiful Mam race." Meanwhile, none of the *reina* contestants can speak one word of Mam, some had to borrow or rent their costumes from relatives and neighbors, and they are surrounded by hundreds of people in every stage of transition away from the culture being touted in song and poetry from the stage.

THE VALUE OF *TRAJE*

In trying to explain the movement away from *traje,* it is generally agreed that the inherent value of the costume itself is not at issue. *Sampedranas* are aware of the intrinsic beauty of San Pedro's *huipiles,* their protection against the cold and the damp, and the elegance of the yellow striped *corte* and pastel hair ribbons. Yet they no longer buy or wear them. When women are asked why they prefer dresses over *traje,* the response—urban or rural—is always the same: the cost. Women consistently note that the purchase of a new *huipil* or *corte* involves spending quite a sum of money while skirts and blouses are cheap. To see if this was indeed the case, in 1977 I made a list of the clothes a traditional woman would wear—not necessarily all at once—and compared them to the wardrobe of a western dresser.

Item	1977 Price
Huipil	Q10−40
Corte	Q6−20
Faja (belt)	Q1−2
Camisón (slip)	Q3
Delantal (Half-apron)	Q3−8
Gabacha (full apron)	Q4−10
Peraje (shawl with tassels)	Q12
Tapada (plain shawl)	Q2.50−4
Listón (hair ribbon)	Q0.75−2
Pañuelo (scarf)	Q1.25

Típica dealers agree that most women own two or three of each of these items. There is some regional variation, e.g. near *aldeanas* use sweaters instead of *perajes,* but overall, the items are fairly standard. Typically, the outfit will last for ten years. Most women hold in reserve their best *huipil* and *corte* for fiestas, but the other sets of clothing are worn every day or every other day. The aprons, introduced in the 1930s, protect the costume from getting dirty, further lengthening its longevity. In the market is a huge variety of quality, design and price, but taking a rough average, in 1977 the initial cost of *traje* to the retail buyer was between fifty and one hundred dollars. Over the ten-year-life of a garment that works out to one or two cents a day for clothes.

The western-style clothes common to more and more women are another matter entirely. Most modern dresses worn by *Sampedranas* are made by seamstresses who copy the design from magazines and books. Only the wealthiest professionals and civil servants can afford the ready-made dresses and pants at the jeans store. The rest buy Q3.00−5.00 worth of fabric and take it to a seamstress who, for a few *quetzales,* then makes it into a dress. Many of the dressmakers are new to their work and not very creative or skilled. Accordingly, one or two styles of dress are made in widely differing fabrics, and often not very well. For approximately Q6.00, a woman has a relatively ordinary, poorly-made dress that after being pounded on a cement sink or river stones with each wash, will wear out in only a few months unless she can regularly alternate several dresses. In addition to the dress, she buys an apron for Q3.00–8.00 and a sweater for Q1.50–4.00 for a total (with shoes) of Q20.00. She can purchase several pairs of shoes and several dresses together or simply replace them when they are worn out, but in either case she is spending up to Q20.00 or more every four months on clothes, or almost ten times what *de corte* women spend.

What this analysis suggests is that while the immediate purchase price of a traditional garment might be greater, its absolute value clearly makes it the wiser investment. But given the emphasis on modern behavior and looking *civilizada,* the conclusion must be that despite the acknowledged beauty and intrinsic value of *traja, Sampedranas* prefer to spend their money on consumer items that satisfy new-felt needs and bring with their ownership a modicum of modern status.

This trend, aside from what it reveals about consumer preferences and style, also reflects a change in the pattern of saving and actual allocation of funds from the family budget. While women previously saved their *centavos* over a long period for the future purchase of a *huipil,* they can now save enough for a polyester dress relatively quickly. Furthermore, instant credit is available in most stores to encourage people to buy appliances and furniture "on time." For a monthly payment of Q20, people take home their first television, bicycle, or radio-tape deck.[7] I asked a woman why she had bought a radio with the money she might have used for a new *huipil,* her response was, *"Es fácil. Por estar alegre!,"* i.e., life was fun now that she could listen to music and news as she worked, an attribute quite distinct from what *traje* offers.

What about men and the ladinoization of clothing? Even among *aldeanos,* the traditional male costume has not been in evidence for years. Men wear modern *ladino* garb and no one remembers any costume other than the already westernized clothes their grandfathers wore. O'Neale describes the 1930s outfit as "Shirt: White, mill-made material cut European style with collar, cuffs and pocket. . . . Trousers: Usual long white trousers cut European style" (1945:266). The persistence of female *traje* despite the absence of a men's costume is a recognized phenomenon in Latin America (Tax 1952). One reason is that male control of external trade has brought men into contact with national *ladino* culture for centuries. Locally economic and civil connections to the neighboring *ladino* capital of San Marcos have also been part of the pressures on males to loosen their Indian symbolic identities. Traditional women, on the other hand, rarely leave the town even to go to San Marcos, five minutes away. While they are aware of the fact that other women do not necessarily wear *traje,* only in the last twenty years, when communication and education have grown so dramatically, has the ladinoization of women's clothing trickled down to traditional women. The process, begun in Guatemala City, is brought to San Pedro by students travelling back and forth to the capital for schooling, and by the popularity of television. While it has taken some time for even town women to abandon their *traje,* now that friends and relatives are wearing dresses, the idea has quickly spread. Housing nearly one-third of the *municipio*'s population, the town has considerable influence on its hinterland. This should soon prove devastating to the tradition of hand-woven, locally-made Indian costumes.

Modern Cottage Industry

As traditional weaving's predominance among female occupation fades, two mechanized modern trades have risen to take its place in home industry. These two industries—knitting and sewing—have filled an employment gap which, left open, might have been extremely detrimental to the local economic and domestic infrastructure, relying as it does upon female cottage industry for its contribution to the family's cash income. These new trades afford women the opportunity to continue to earn money through labor-intensive processes that like weaving can be efficiently exploited at home. Women have been quick to adopt the new skills which have spread throughout the *municipio* to places where even footloom weaving never developed. To many rural women, modern home industry is a completely new economic option since distance or lack of capital or other responsibilities previously excluded entrance into any type of weaving enterprise. Distant *aldeanas* are now being actively recruited to sew or knit by *patrones* who take care of all the production and business details. Since the jobs, materials and money are thus contracted to come to *them,* women are no longer materially hindered either by their inability to get to market regularly to sell their product or by their ignorance of the business world.

Thus, in one sense, modern cottage industry—in the form of treadle sewing and machine knitting—has performed a service for San Pedro as a ready replacement for a disappearing trade and by incorporating many more women into profitable cottage industry. This last effect is a positive characteristic of development (i.e., expanding boundaries of home work) that cannot be ignored. But even so, it is impossible to evaluate the contribution of either enterprise without noticing that compared to their predecessor, neither one affords women the economic autonomy, control of production, or the job satisfaction that weaving does. Rather, they incorporate women as an essentially docile and exploitable workforce in a home industry system based on the efficient management and manipulation of large numbers of cheap laborers for the benefit of a few bosses or factory owners.

THE KNITTING MACHINE

The knitting machine was introduced in San Pedro in the 1950s, and while it had a slow start, knitting eventually became one of the most common female occupations in town and in some *aldeas*. Most knitting centers (either physically or fiscally) around one of the sweater factories that began twenty-five years ago when enterprising *Sampedranas* recognized the potential market for machine-made knitted goods. (Sweaters are now so common in San Pedro that, like aprons, they seem to be part of the native costume.) The original incentive for investment centered on a growing interest in knitted baby caps in Quezaltenango and the inability of Luisa Orozco, the owner of the only knitting machine in San Pedro, to meet this demand. Interest in learning to knit by machine quickly spread and women began sending their daughters to study with Luisa, a woman who has now achieved some local fame as the legendary founder of the industry who, because she never charged for lessons nor had capital to invest, reaped none of the later profits.

Soon several women owned new or used machines. At this early stage, the markets for knitted products were rapidly developing; materials were inexpensive and the profits were high. A Q50.00 investment quickly yielded a Q50.00 net profit. For five years earnings remained at that level and a few enterprising *Sampedranas* capitalized on the interest in the product and on the desire of local women to learn the skill. Sheny Miranda, the daughter of weavers, had purchased Luisa's original machine and had taught others to knit. Quickly, she and her husband bought a new Singer sewing machine to sew sweaters together, apprenticed dozens of young *Sampedranas,* sold their products in Quezaltenango and eventually used the enormously high profits to build the *Fábrica* Suzi. Every year or two they invested in another Q2,000 industrial machine, apprenticed more young women as operators, and opened new trade networks in Guatemala City, an as yet untapped market.

By 1980, the owners of *Fábrica* Suzi had twenty-five employees and were *patrones* to hundreds of cottage industry knitters. While the profit margin had narrowed considerably as competition stiffened and the market became saturated, *Fábrica* Suzi thrived. Sales of Q4,000 a month afforded a net profit of more than ten percent, and they had a substantial line of credit. Witness the Q30,000 machine in a ten-room house built also for cash; they have three cars and children in universities and private schools. Much of this luxury is at the price of the town's respect, because it is widely acknowledged that the *Fábrica* exploits its workers. The agreed upon apprenticeship period of six months is twice or three times the time required to master various machines. This free labor is often extended to years, and such blatant exploitation once resulted in a thousand dollar settlement when the irate father of an unpaid knitter finally sued. Few families have enough nerve or money to take the factory owners to court so that the predominant response is to first quit, but to then extend the indenturedness by the factory-backed purchase of a knitting machine for home use with the products contracted to Suzi.[8]

Much of the sweater factory profit is based on labor extracted from adolescent girls who are moving away from traditional skills. Better educated than their parents and wearing western dress, these girls do not move easily into their mothers' traditional businesses or trades. While many may have high school degrees, most often they cannot find work in town as teachers or bookkeepers and are waiting for the elusive opportunity on the coast or in an *aldea*. (While the over-saturated labor market in the town—and in the state capital, San Marcos—is a major stumbling block to securing a salaried job, a more critical variable is the lack of *cuello* ["pull"] or a sufficient *mordida* ["pay-off"] necessary to secure civil service jobs.) In the meantime, sweater-making is a socially valued "modern" skill for a woman and many take it up through the *Fábrica* apprenticeship system, being the first in their families to knit. Forming a stable labor supply, *Fábrica* women were the first *Sampedrana* proletariat, a group destined to grow at first with the predictable increase in capitalization and diversification of the factory business, but then to solidify as the town's reserve labor force.

Despite the "umbilical" tie to a *fábrica,* knitting is so well established that women have developed a variety of relations to the production of sweaters, developing the capital potential of the knitting machine in markedly different ways: indenturing themselves to a *patrón,* trading with distant retailers, or specializing in order to capture a particular market. The manner of exploitation is largely class-specific, a complement of the means a woman has for supplementing her income in other ways.[9] The following cases sample the different strategies.

Floridalma is an unmarried 26-year-old teacher who knits during her school vacations. Living at home in a family of seven women, she has few domestic responsibilities other than an occasional stint in their *tienda*. As soon as school ends, she immediately sets up her knitting machine behind the store counter to take advantage of the short sweater-making season. Compulsive and nervous by nature, Floridalma works rapidly, knitting intricate patterns one day and sewing the pieces together the next. She knits "on order" from women who stop by the store and also maintains a small inventory. Occasionally, someone will indicate a preference for a hand-knit sweater which she then produces within a week by working day and night. This woman's frenzied dedication to work as a way of life stems partly from her family's traditional pride in its female labor and from the mountain of debts they have accumulated in the maintenance of their middle-class life-style. Even with her teacher's salary of Q340 a month, for the last ten years, she has been compelled to supplement the family income by knitting. For a three dollar investment in *lana* (*lana* translates as wool, but actually it is 100% acrylic) this knitter nets Q6 for four half-days of work, a profit she considers satisfactory. Floridalma is intelligent and creative enough to invest her time well. Her knitting meets the needs of a market for sweaters created for the relatively affluent town women with whom she was educated. Enterprising and independent, in meeting this special demand, she carved out a satisfying niche in the knitting business that allows her to pay off her debts in a manner befitting her status as a teacher and middle-class woman.

A very different, and more typical approach to the knitting machine is that of Ofelia, who lives a traditional Indian existence in Chamac with her peasant-weaver husband and his extended family. Twenty-one, she has two small daughters to care for, a few years of school, and not enough money to live on. Like so many *aldea* women plagued by ill health, her extra *centavos* go into an unending series of pharmaceutical "cures" prescribed by the local druggists. Her clothes are old and badly worn, her cheap shoes useless. Unskilled and desperate, Ofelia took up knitting in the vain hope that she might get ahead of her expenses. Indentured to the *Fábrica* Suzi at Q0.50 a sweater, she earns only a few dollars a week because she is self-taught and makes mistakes. Her income is further compromised because she has been paying off her machine for the last three years and has another two years to go before she can keep any of her profits.

Another strategy is to invest in sweater-making at home by having a regular buyer. Hortensia, an urban *de corte* woman, worked at the factory for three years, first as a fifteen-year-old apprentice, and then for the standard ten *centavos* a sweater. When she realized that she could make more at home, she left to work on her own schedule. She bought a Q375 knitting machine, and took the next four years paying it off by selling sweaters back to the factory.[10] While she was paying off her machine at Q20 a month, Hortensia had to knit full-time. She made five or six dozen simple sweaters a week for a profit of Q2.40 a dozen. Today, she uses the eighteen or so hours she has free from her market stall each week to knit, but although the price she makes for each sweater has increased, inflation has made her 1988 earnings about the same as what she made ten years before.

Women who travel to Guatemala City to sell their sweaters fare somewhat better economically, but their incipient entrepreneurship involves an eight hour, third-class bus ride. Ilsa Sanchez knits five *corriente* (ordinary) sweaters a day and every Monday sells two dozen to retailers in the capital for Q60.00 a dozen. Subtracting the cost of yarn, buttons, and thread to sew the pieces together, as well as the bus fare and meals in the capital, her profits are about Q15 or Q20 each week. Buying uncontracted sweaters from friends and neighbors allows her to maximize her trip potential to afford her a relatively decent profit. Ilsa is a quick-witted woman who seizes any opportunity to earn money. For example, when new Peace Corpsmen came to town she was the first at their doorsteps to take in wash, although she had never been a professional washerwoman before. Any odd job is to Ilsa's liking. She will even clean house and cook, an occupation normally relegated to poor *aldea* adolescents. The reason Ilsa is so ready to discomfort herself for a job is that she and her husband are landless urbanites who must pay cash for everything. Apart from the corn and other food they must buy all year round, they have monthly expenses for the house they rent, their modern furniture and their television. To meet their unusually high overhead, Ilsa had been hopeful that through stamina and perseverance, she could develop her knitting trade into a reliable business venture. Unfortunately, the rapid industrialization and successful capitalization of the sweater factories meant their sales force was always hungry for new markets and could underprice her with her best customers.

There are several inescapable "givens" in knitting as a home industry. First, there is the reality of the seasonal nature of the business: only from November to Easter are there guaranteed sales. (There are two reasons for the sweater business cycle. The end of the rainy season in November means the beginning of the summer months which bring dry but cold weather when sweaters are practical apparel. This coincides with the October harvest when people have money to spend on clothes. Later in the year, when their own corn has run out, all available funds will go to purchase staples.) When market activity subsides, women put away their machines and, if they can, do something else. Second, the functioning of this industry is based on an expensive knitting machine imported from Italy. Rarely are used machines available any more; they are almost all bought new. Since most women cannot pay cash for their machines, if they are not affiliated with a factory, they are caught up in the process of securing credit and then making high-interest payments which eat up the profits of their first three or four years of knitting.[11] Third, the technology for repairing a broken machine is only found in Quezaltenango, an hour's ride away. Shipment and parts involve time and considerable expense, so a damaged machine is often put aside for years of lost income. Fourth, even after overcoming the initial expense of the machine or the lost labor of extensive apprenticeship, most knitters cannot look forward to earning more than Q2–3 a day during the season. The sweater factory pays very little for each sweater produced. An experienced knitter can turn out about six or seven in a 12-hour day, but women rarely have that much time away from their domestic responsibilities. Independent knitters make more, but they face an unreliable market and competition from the better capitalized factories. Thus, although the potential is there for earning a decent living from sweater-making, its structural drawbacks severely limit the profitability of the work (see Table 5.1).

Finally, most sweater-makers have no access to an external market for their product and must rely upon middlemen. Except for the work of a few private specialists, the local sweater market is almost entirely monopolized by the *fábricas*. Even the incipient entrepreneurship among the middle-class women who buy in their neighborhoods to sell in Guatemala City is not cause for optimistic reappraisal of this situation because inevitably the growth-oriented factories in San Pedro or Quezaltenango will force them out of the market. Even worse, since 1985, San Pedro's five largest sweater factories have moved away from *mano de obra* or piece-work systems to heavily mechanized, efficient industrial machines requiring a minimal labor force. For example, the well-capitalized *Fábrica Patricia*'s eight machines only require six employees (five are men) who monitor the technologically sophisticated knitting, ironing, sewing, and production of buttonholes. Although they still purchase from local sweater producers, it is clearly a buyer's market. The factory itself produces cheaply, and the great numbers of knitters competing with each other gives it additional rationale for not having raised their piece-work price in ten years.[12]

In all, the dynamics of the knitting industry are such that earnings and growth potential are extremely limited. With the enormous material demands necessary for entrance into the industry, income possibilities are circumscribed for years. Furthermore, over the entire year, this modern cottage industry, while appealing to the upwardly mobile aspirations of many *Sampedranas* as well as to the need for cash, barely matches the already minimal income of traditional weaving. It is a deceptive business, especially for rural women who are just entering home industry, since work is available

Table 5.1 *Income of Weavers vs. Knitters*

Occupation	Costs	Price/ Salary	Weekly Net	Weekly Hours	Weeks of Work/Yr	Hourly Wage	Total Income/ 1 year	Deductions	Total Income/ 5 years
Weaver	Thread for 1 huipil = Q21	Q35/ huipil	Q14	40	52	Q.35	Q728	loom/ Q100	Q3540
Factory Knitter	o	Paid Q.10/ sweater	Q12	48	24	Q.25	Q288	18 months free labor	Q1008
Home Knitter	Wool, buttons, misc. = Q3/ea. sweater	Q3.20/ sweater	Q14.40	54	24	Q.26	Q345.60	Knitting machine/ Q960	Q768

during the season, but then disappears until the following year. Like all artisanal industries in San Pedro, competition is stiff and few can survive on what they make knitting. Finally, machine knitting is a solitary endeavor, antithetical to the supportive female family business of weaving. Most knitters are the only ones in their family dedicated to making sweaters, and consequently this new cottage industry dramatically realigns the relations women have had with production and with the control of their children's labor.

COMMERCIAL WEAVING

Since World War II and more intensely in the last ten years, contact with tourist and export markets has developed and diversified the San Pedro commercial weaving industry. Town and *aldea* men are abandoning full-time agriculture in larger and larger numbers, preferring instead to weave. Many now hire full-time *mozos* or day laborers to work their fields while they sit at the loom. Utilizing their facility as traders, *Sampedranos* distribute their commercial textiles in urban, regional, and to some extent, international markets, regularly modifying their design and product emphasis to the market demands. In keeping with the traditional sexual division of labor, men produce the cloth and women then process it into widely marketable consumer items, largely clothing. The system of male weaving and female sewing operates within families, but one also finds men and their wives contracting to different bosses. The latter is usually the case either when a man weaves tablecloths or yard goods that are sold without needing further processing or when he does not weave and his wife seeks sewing work on her own.

The development of reliable trade networks has been an incentive for diversification in the textile industry, especially in the near *aldea* of San José Caben. Enterprising Caben weavers combine the production of yardgoods and clothing and sell them in separate markets. One might find San José Caben maxi-dresses in the textile cooperative in Quezaltenango, skirts in a *típica* stall in Chichicastenango and yardgoods in a downtown market in Guatemala City. Walking through the small *aldea* one hears the constant clack-clack of looms and the whirring of foot-pedaled sewing machines. While traditional weaving is still common in many families, the decline in that industry has turned women instead toward the carding and spinning of thread for commercial weaving and then the processing of cloth woven by men into clothing and novelty items.

A typical division of labor in San José Caben is that of Don Antonio and his wife Doña Mariselma. In their home, as in most others in the *aldea,* the two main rooms are devoted only to weaving. Four large, bulky Spanish footlooms and cumbersome boxes of thread take up nearly all the space in the dark rooms. Doña Mariselma sits outside on the patio handwinding cards of different color threads onto spools. Her daughter's treadle sewing machine sits in the sun awaiting yardage so she may begin production of maxi-dresses. Antonio employs four young male weavers at home and, like many other men of the *aldea,* owns looms in other parts of town as well. Each week he gathers up the yardgoods and clothing he ordered the week before and sells them in various markets. After paying the weavers and the overhead, the profits from these sales usually amount to Q14.00 a week. But neither Doña Mariselma nor her daughter directly receive any of that money. With her husband as trade intermediary, Mariselma has no real power in the external market. Rather, she is part of a production process that is removed from trade interaction altogether. The trade network in commercial textiles is controlled by men, relegating all women to subordinate "processor" roles, without benefit of income. All monies accrue to the male, who, while he relies on his wife's participation in production, is not obligated to remunerate her in any way. She is helping him with *his* business.

Because men control external trade, women who receive little or no compensation for sewing or carding further supplement their household incomes in other ways. For example, Doña Mariselma has always been a specialty baker in addition to her carding; she also sells chickens and pigs although they have become quite costly to raise. The more affluent men of San José Caben allot their wives Q10 a week additional food allowance, but this has no relation to the female role in production. Rather, it is a contribution to household maintenance aimed at minimizing female labor outside the home and maximizing her time at home in non-productive domestic activities that service men.

In town and in many *aldeas,* sewing is also done on a contract piece-work basis usually by young mothers who either have no other skills or cannot make enough money as weavers. *Patrones* bring them the fabric, then pay them Q0.20 a piece for long dresses, skirts, and blouses. A fast seamstress can make about Q10 a week doing this work, but it is unpredictable and tedious. Moreover, it requires six months' apprenticeship and the purchase of a Q240 sewing machine that might take two or three years to pay off. Other rural women without the capital for a machine do handwork such as putting fringe on capes for about fifty cents a day.

In 1988, I found a new version of "*corte confeccionando*" or sewing hand woven fabric into clothes. A *patrón* from San José Caben had moved from his small home business to a mini-factory in town where he and his wife employ five full-time sewers and ten people on a piece-work basis. In addition, they purchase clothes from outside piece-workers who bring them dozens of pairs of shorts and blouses for the U.S. market. The owner supervises the many weavers who supply the cloth, and carries the finished product to Guatemala City for shipment. Meanwhile, his wife manages the factory. Sewers in this small *fábrica* make about Q6 a day for turning out ten or twelve items. As small as this income seems, it rivals the profits of both knitting and weaving, and the owner notes that people are constantly coming by to ask for jobs, but they only hire the fastest, neatest seamstresses and must refuse the rest.

In all, it appears that in San José Caben, as well as in town, the transition from traditional weaving by women to commercial weaving by men relegates females to secondary roles as unsalaried rural producers or factory workers. Instead of controlling their own local partnerships as weavers, women are now exploited for the labor they provide in readying products for male external trade networks. Furthermore, wives and daughters of commercial weavers are not being encouraged to develop independent business enterprises that amount to much beyond small animal sales or a storefront. They are preferred at home supported by male-controlled endeavors. In comparison, the weaving women of the Ochoa household have each other's company and help while weaving intricate creative designs that take relatively few hours of their day. Moreover, while the sewing together of yardgoods is almost always externally determined contract work, traditional female weaving is an independent enterprise where a woman can commit herself to weaving whatever complexity of design she is skilled to do and where she may have a choice of buyers for her work.

DRESSMAKERS

Another kind of sewing, mentioned earlier, is the *costurera,* the woman who makes clothes for western-dressed women. This trade has grown rapidly as women abandon hand-woven garments, and the town is currently overrun with seamstresses. For decades male *sastres* have made clothing for men, the result being that treadle sewing has a solid reputation as a cottage industry, and in the last ten years, married couples have developed tailoring businesses together where each specialized in clothes for their respective sexes. Although girls can study sewing in any number of schools, most have little craft or sense of style, but since many women buy all their clothes—even slips—from seamstresses, what they do have is a lot of options. Besides the women who sew to order, there are those who make up dozens of cheap dresses to sell to poor highland women on their way to coastal plantations and others who specialize in making aprons, both half and full, for *de corte* women. Each of these groups sells their work in small lots to *mercado* stalls, or sometimes their families own the stalls themselves. Some of their business is seasonal, especially before holidays and school pageants, when busy *costureras* must stay up for nights to whip out dozens of costumes or school uniforms.

Some independent dressmakers, if they are fast and skillful, make a good living from sewing. Doña Nedia, who once played the marimba in an all-girls' band and is a very canny, creative woman, figures she profits Q36 for six days' work making two pairs of pants and a dress daily. For the October costume *baile,* in addition to her regular work, she turned out ten butterflies, ten bees, and ten birds, netting Q1.50 each. Most *costureras* do not do nearly this well. For example, independent slipmakers sell about a dozen a day, for a Q1.50 profit, while women who make simple aprons net Q2.00. Piece-work slip and apron-makers whose unskilled work is contracted to *patrones,* make far less than independent producers because they have no control over orders. One Chamac woman, desperate for an income-producing cottage industry but inexperienced and slow, could only get two days' work, for a total of seventy-five cents a week.

The question remains, how does the occupation of *costurera* fare in the developing economy? Is it the cottage industry that will replace weaving and still offer women the autonomy and potential they lack in *corte confecionando* or knitting? In a word, no. For the last fifteen years sewing has afforded dozens of skillful seamstresses a livable income, but as more and more women entered the occupation, competition forced many independent dressmakers to charge less and less for their labor in order to stay in business. Moreover, the occupation does not seem to have a bright future. Since 1980, dozens of ready-to-wear clothing stores have opened in town, offering casual sportswear like jeans, blouses, and jackets. In addition, cheap factory-made dresses are now available in the *mercado,* mostly to sell to a plantation-bound customer, but plans are afoot to expand this trade to local *gente.* Middle-class women looking for finely made clothes or all-leather factory-made shoes grumble about having to travel to Tapachula where the array of stores is quite extensive, so the demand seems to be there. My assessment is that soon women will be able to buy all the clothing they need over-the-counter, from simple, inexpensive pants and blouses to fancier holiday dresses. Dressmakers will be occupationally marginalized, called upon to make school uniforms and butterfly costumes, but little else.

The Demise of the *Huipil*

If westernization severely weakened the *huipil* industry in San Pedro, the 1985 drop in the value of the *quetzal* certainly dealt the coup de grace. San Pedro's weaving business was one of the areas hardest hit by the falling value of the Guatemalan monetary unit because of its long history of utilizing finely made threads produced abroad. For decades, San Pedro's *huipiles* have been made with high quality mercerized cotton called *lustrina*, a silk-like thread imported from China, Japan, France, and Mexico. Only the warp is Guatemalan cotton. As the value of the *quetzal* dropped internationally, the cost of importing these raw materials has skyrocketed. In 1977, the thread for an excellent *huipil* cost Q25 or Q30; today it costs five times as much.[13] The consequences of this unexpected upturn in the price of materials are far-reaching for the weaver, the *traje* dealer, the woman who wears *traje,* and the town.

For the last three years it has become increasingly difficult for urban women or women from the near *aldeas* to purchase good quality *huipiles.* Even the simplest cotton *huipil* costs three months' salary. Rather than feel embarrassed wearing an undecorated or *corriente* garment that is all they can now afford, many elegant *de corte* women prefer to maintain an upwardly mobile appearance by switching to Western dress. This trend, begun a decade or more before, has now accelerated and spread beyond the town to even the most remote *aldeas.* Poorer women who choose to wear *traje* either purchase far fewer pieces of hand-woven clothing or combine cheaper polyester or cotton-blend blouse-like *huipiles,* called *blusas,* with their traditional *cortes.* Almost none of these women buy *huipiles* for their daughters.

Due to the lower volume of sales and resultant competition for business, the weavers have had to accept a lower profit margin on the work they sell to dealers. One woman showed a drop over five years from a Q15 profit to only half that for five days' work. Her despondency was typical of all the weavers I talked to. When I visited the Ochoas in 1987 and again in 1988, the house was practically empty and the mood depressed. Business was slow. The price of thread had increased so dramatically that Doña Angélica was afraid women would soon stop buying *huipiles* altogether. The same *huipil* she and her daughters had produced ten years before for Q21 now costs her nearly six times as much just for materials! For her efforts, the profit Angélica earns is almost exactly what she profited ten years before. But slow retail sales mean she is only selling one *huipil* every two weeks instead of one every week, and is netting half.

Storeowners have had to pay less to their trading partners—many of whom have been weaving for them for decades—because traditional costumes no longer sell. One shopkeeper had displayed the same *huipiles* on her shelf for more than two years! The only way that San Pedro's *traje típica* dealers can stay in business is either by having capital to invest in the different *huipiles* and *cortes* from distant rural areas where women still favor traditional dress, or by stocking the machine-embroidered *blusas* that are now quickly replacing San Pedro's *huipiles*. Storekeepers like the new cotton-blend *blusas* because they sell for only Q10 each, allowing a quick profit of at least Q18 per dozen. While the *típica* dealers might favor this product, in the long run, this new costume style can only contribute to the undermining of the town's weaving industry, since the *blusas* are not produced locally but are brought in from factories in Quezaltenango or from cottage industries in Sololá.

How does all this affect the value of *traje*? When the 1987 buyer of *traje* needed to replace the worn out clothes she had purchased a decade before, she would find that the price of a complete costume had more than tripled. Previously she paid between Q50–100; now the price is Q150–425. The cost was more largely because the price of a *huipil* was up to seven times as expensive. Given this dramatic escalation, can we say that over the long run *traje* still compares favorably to western clothing? Like everything, the price of fabric has gone up. Two yards of cotton or polyester for a dress now costs Q14–30. Seamstresses are still relatively affordable since there is a lot of competition. They charge Q7–10 for a simple dress. Blouses run Q12–35 finished, pants Q35–50. The apron is now Q12, the sweater Q10–40, and her shoes Q20–40. The total for the same outfit she purchased ten years before is now approximately Q90, more than four times the 1977 price. What remains stable is the wear factor. Even at the inflated prices today's traditional woman pays, over ten years' time, she still spends about Q0.08 a day on clothes. Meanwhile, the modern woman who buys clothes more frequently to replace worn out skirts or shoes pays Q0.74 a day, almost ten times as much. The differential between the two types of clothing has stayed the same over time. The analysis stands; over the long run, hand-woven clothes are still a better investment for the money. Remember, however, that a traditional woman still has to save for a long time to buy her costume. Since neither wages nor income have increased with inflation, the buyer can probably afford to put aside the standard one *quetzal* each week, which means she would have to save for almost three years to buy a change of clothes!

After more than ten years observing the decline of weaving as a cottage industry, I am aware that analysis of its long-term value has little to do with the decision to maintain or abandon *traje*. Clearly, women who are spending money on radios, televisions, and their children's education are committed to sending the next generation along a more modern path than the one they trod. The trend away from *huipiles* and *cortes* is only one symptom of the waning of traditional ways and the birth of new cultural patterns. One consequence of this process is the decline of female-based cottage industries which permit women to control not only their own labor, but the labor of their daughters as well. While today women are making money as piece-workers, the structure of the new cottage industries means women forfeit control of production on many counts. It remains to be seen whether a new home-based industry will arise that will maintain intact the female family business that has been a cornerstone of the town's commercialism. For now, it appears that traditional cottage industry can neither muster the laborers it needs nor compete with coveted factory-made goods, and as such, has closed up shop.

Notes

1. In this chapter, I use the term "cottage industry" to mean both the "putting out" industries of the British Industrial Revolution, as well as domestic business characterized by self-employment and worker control of the means of production.

2. Hawkins (1984) reports that he encountered homes where up to six knitting machines were employed by mothers and daughters in a quasi-factory atmosphere, but I never found evidence of this strategy.

3. This changed in 1984 when the *aldea,* after years of wrangling with the government, finally was wired for electricity.

4. Notice that the women's time invested in weaving is not a consideration when figuring their profits. This is consistent with the identification of female productive activities with housework, i.e., what a woman must do to take care of her family.

5. The ladinoization of Indian *traje* in Guatemala is a subject of much notice and speculation, but few satisfactory studies or explanations of the process have emerged in the anthropological literature. There is, of course, general agreement that increasing contact with the outside world is changing the costumes of the country as machine-made textiles are replacing hand-loomed materials (Wood and Osborne 1966, Whetten 1961, Tax 1952, Gillen 1951, Hinshaw 1975). While some monographs (e.g., Gillen, Hinshaw) do include descriptions of the acculturative loss of symbolic dress, i.e., how the change to western clothing takes place, there is little discussion of why it should be happening in that particular place. One notable exception to the dearth of material on loss of costume is Annis' *God and Production in a Guatemalan Town,* which emphasizes religious preference and its relation to ethnic identification to explain why Catholic women in San Antonio Aguas Calientes retain their *traje* and Protestant women do not.

6. Although the tendency of educated women is to remain in San Pedro, this is not necessarily the rule. A few high school graduates have moved to Guatemala City or even to cities in Mexico, Costa Rica, or the U.S. in order to find work, and remained there to marry and raise a family. However, these women were from the wealthiest families that had well-established ties outside the town. Often they migrated to join their siblings while their parents stayed in San Pedro.

7. The interest rates on consumer items in San Pedro are extremely high. Radio-tape decks, for example, sell for Q199.00 cash or Q240.00 in twelve Q20 monthly pay-

ments, for an annual interest rate of thirty-six percent! Nor surprisingly, the usurious interest rates of the *enganche* payment system do not hinder unwary buyers who have never before had any familiarity with the process or the products they now have the opportunity to buy for as little as Q5.00 a month.

8. San Pedro has long relied upon an apprenticeship system to train its young artisans and craftspeople. Knitting is distinguished from this revered and well-established training system in two main ways. Rather than a carpenter or a weaver taking a young apprentice—usually a relative—under his/her wing to train them, the factory owners apprentice dozens of young women at once, most of whom they do not know. Secondly, although there have been abuses in the traditional system, they are usually minor and settled within the family. In researching the knitting industry, however, I encountered frequent and virulent complaints from parents that their daughters worked far longer than they needed to without being paid.

9. The diversification of sweatermaking options may be interpreted as potentially weakening the *fábricas* because it draws workers away from the factory and establishes local competition. In the ten years I have been following the growth of the sweater industry, I have noticed just the opposite. The number and volume of sweater factories has grown from 1977 to 1988, and local producers have found that they must work even harder to secure different buyers for their sweaters because the rapid industrialization of the factories means they need fewer home or on-site knitters. Although only five of the more than twenty factories now utilize only industrial machines, it seems an obvious trend for all of them in order to cut labor costs.

10. Customers I spoke to rarely considered the percentages of their interest payments on purchases. Instead, they told me how much it cost and how many years it took to pay off. Amazingly, the discrepancy between the stated price and the total price did not shock anyone but me. For example, this knitter reported she bought a Q375 machine from the appliance dealer and paid it off at Q20 a month for four years. What she did not realize was that this capital investment was costing her fifty-seven percent interest! During the four years, she was making five or six dozen sweaters a week from which she netted about Q56 a month. That left her, after the payment for her machine, Q36 profit for a month's work.

11. It has been pointed out to me that all businesspeople secure credit and pay off equipment as a normal requirement in today's economy. While I understand that capital investment is a wise step to take for developing a successful business, in light of the decreasing share of the sweater market controlled by home knitters, I am not sure that forfeiting up to three years of income to insure later earnings pays off.

12. The rapid success of the sweater factories and the enrichment of their owners became clear to me a few years ago when the young daughter of the founders of the four-year-old *Fábrica Patricia* became *La Florecita de Retama*. Named for a local flower, this office is celebrated during the town's saint's day festivities when the *Florecita* is elected through the casting of votes—at two *centavos* apiece. It is a well-accepted fact that because they can afford to buy and cast more votes, the town's richest families control the outcome of the contest, which they use as a public expression of their wealth. In 1987, Patricia de Leon's parents spent more than Q1500 to make their daughter *Florecita,* an unprecedented sum that will most likely set the standard for all the *florecitas* to come.

13. In doing a study of a community over a decade, the value of money changes along with everything else. The dollar to *quetzal* ratio has vacillated over the years, changing what had been a simple one-to-one relationship into something more complicated and unreliable. In addition, inflation has caused prices to rise domestically, so that what cost Q3 ten years ago costs Q10 or more today. While inflationary matters clearly affect the existing price structure of most things, where *huipiles* are concerned, they are particularly nettlesome. The reason is that two-thirds of the thread used in the San Pedro costume is imported from Europe and the Orient. A falling exchange rate inflates the cost of raw materials so that what had been a considerable expense requiring months of savings now is a big-ticket item far beyond most people's budgets. Where analysis of this becomes problematic is in the translation from *quetzales* to dollars, i.e., what the prices look like to *Sampedranos* and how a dollar-based audience views them. For example, if a 1977 *huipil* costs the consumer Q40, this would be $40. The 1977 Q40 could buy a radio, five hundred pounds of sugar (enough for as many days), or the 800 pounds of corn a six-member family would eat over a period of nineteen weeks. However, given the 1988 exchange rate of $1 : Q2.70, and the rising price of imported thread, the same *huipil* now costs about Q110 or $41. While this increase seems small in dollars, it means quite a lot to the local *quetzal*-based consumer who purchases clothing after providing for subsistence needs. This is especially true since the prices of staples have risen even more in response to inflation, sometimes to five or six times what they were a decade before. For example, corn has gone up locally to more than four times its 1977 value to Q0.22/lb, and the price of sugar has risen to Q.32/lb. In terms of corn, the price of the *huipil* equals a lesser, but still considerable 500 pounds, or eleven and a half weeks of corn, and the amount of sugar the family can buy with a *huipil* has dropped to 344 pounds. In all, *traje* is expensive, staples are even more expensive, and wages have not kept pace with inflation, making it doubly hard for consumers to set aside extra money for the purchase of handmade clothes. Bear in mind, however, that the radio which could have been purchased at the cost of one Q40 *huipil* in 1977, can still be bought for the price of one *huipil,* but at the new price of Q110. What is pertinent here is that juggling the domestic and international value of the Guatemalan *quetzal* could muddy the water in a discussion of the value of wearing *traje*. Given this already complicated international financial situation, translating from *quetzales* to dollars can be somewhat deceiving, particularly since domestic inflation has seriously reduced the buying power of the *quetzal* variably, depending upon the product. To avoid confusion, I have, as I said in the introductory chapter, kept pre-1985 prices as I originally wrote them down at the one dollar to one *quetzal* rate. After that, all prices are dated so the reader will keep in mind the rate of inflation and, where necessary, alterations in the foreign value of the *quetzal*. The main thing to remember is that consumer values, subsistence needs, and ethnic identity are all involved in the decision to buy *traje* or to buy western clothing. While expense is certainly a consideration, it alone does not explain this behavior.

6

🌿

Women and Men

> How is an avocado like a husband?
> A good one is hard to find.
>
> —Guatemalan riddle

The Game of Love

Sampedranas love to gossip. While they are cleaning onions in market stalls, patting out tortillas for lunch or lingering over afternoon coffee, women predictably put their heads together to sort out the melodrama of everyday life. After quickly dismissing the latest *chismes* (tales) about the neighbors and the *ladinos,* they get down to the topic they relish most, men. Grousing about male vices and mocking their puerile vanities is popular, but more often than not, discussion focuses on tales of the *novios* (boyfriends) each woman has had, amounting in many cases to a dozen or more. Even among *viejitas* (old women) much joking and exaggerating takes place about past romances and present prospects. While the sexual act itself is a taboo topic, each memorably romantic moment is rehashed and savored by the group. Oddly enough, sometimes a *Sampedrana* raises her status in one of these conversations by going to the opposite extreme of saying that she had had many *amigos* with whom she danced at fiestas, but that she had never been romantically allied. The truthfulness of these assertions is not in question here. Real or imaginary, the fascination with such talk suggests that *Sampedranas* actively participate in the "game of love," valuing it as a good and normal pastime that women are encouraged to enter from an early age. Emphasis on the game is so pervasive that middle-aged *señoritas* are extremely rare in the town. Adult women are either married, abandoned, divorced or widowed.

As an inevitable consequence of the game of love, girls become inextricably involved in the serious relationship of marriage. What is curious about this phenomenon is that, in spite of the attachment they have to flirting, courting, and romance, at one time or another, most *patojas* (teenage girls) swear they will never marry. However momentary such adolescent affirmations may be, on the whole, hesitancy to wed reflects a clear vision of what the marital role implies. Local women are aware of the realities of marriage and are skeptical of their chances for happy unions. Stable marriages are rare, women believe, due to the inevitable failings of men whom they consider to be hopelessly unreliable. For their part, many men do their best to live up to their reputation as insensitive *macho* scoundrels who owe women no explanation for their intemperate behavior. Spoiled and pampered as children, men grow up to expect servitude and obedience from their wives.[1]

Women are socialized to fulfill their subordinate, long-suffering roles passively, accepting male irresponsibility, wickedness, and foolishness as their destiny. This they do with fatalistic consent, buoyed in their martyrdom by the firm conviction of the supremacy of their sex in matters both mundane and spiritual. Thus, women enter into a marital union expecting the worst from their spouses. They anticipate his drunkenness, brutality, and betrayal with equanimity, spending years of schooling and work preparing themselves for the eventuality of having to support themselves and their children.

This pattern of female passivity has been dubbed "*marianismo*" (Stevens 1973a, 1973b). *Marianismo* depicts a religious and morally superior woman who engenders abnegation and an infinite capacity for humility and sacrifice. No self-denial is too great, no limit exists to her vast store of patience. While women seem to be submissive, beneath the surface lies the strength of conviction that men must be humored because they are *como niños* (like children) and cannot help being intemperate, foolish, and obstinate. Stevens argues that Latin women welcome this martyrdom as the spiritual verification of their true womanhood. Men's wickedness, she claims, is the necessary precondition for women's superior status as semidivine figures without whose intercession men would have little chance of obtaining forgiveness for their transgressions. As evidence for the existence of this pattern, Stevens cites the editor of a fashionable woman's magazine in Chile who was asked to identify a Chilena whom she particularly admired. Her answer: the humble woman from the slums who did her laundry. She had ten children and a drunken, out-of-work husband, but she struggled valiantly herself by taking in wash.

Marianismo is a fascinating and compelling concept for which there is ample evidence. But even in combination with classic historical analyses of its complement *machismo* (Paz 1961), it is not entirely satisfying as an explanation of the social domination of women in Latin America. Rather, it is only a descriptive overview of a behavior pattern. Researchers have tended to accept *marianismo* as described, without interpretation or explanation of its origins. That work still needs to be done. For now, I suggest that exaggerated femininity is based initially upon the relegation of women to the private domestic domain where females support male production and bear and raise children. There they are socialized to avoid men and public visibility while valuing female kin within a mutually supportive cooperative household, outside the public realm. Not too long ago, this agrarian model of the sexual division of labor applied in general to Latin American peasantry. It is a cultural framework that still has enormous influence on male-female interaction even where it is obsolete. However, the model of female isolation in the home breaks down quickly when economic demands draw female labor out of the "women's sphere" and into competition with men. The existence of a working wife or mother challenges male domination in the home, and may result in the culturally sanctioned callousness toward women commonly called *machismo*.

While women may hate and resent *macho* behavior, they accept it with the same resignation that they accept other hardships in their lives, as God's will. On another level, it appears that while female tolerance of abusive behavior acts to reinforce continued male irresponsibility and female suffering, it is a rational response or adaptive strategy for women whose only economic and emotional security continues to be based on the family, namely children. Furthermore, the reinforcement of the mythology and the reality of feminine identification with the domestic role as their only source of power means women act to bear and nurture a large and exploitable labor force (an action which, by the way, ironically perpetuates male powerlessness in the larger economy).

The balance of *machismo-marianismo* power that Stevens finds stable and symbiotic seems to me clearly tipped in favor of male dominance. I often wonder whether the idealized behavior of *marianismo* may have been popularized as a patriarchal fantasy. After all, it sanctions male independence and irresponsibility by salving potentially disruptive female resentment through the identification of women with the silently suffering figure of the Virgin Mary. This mystification of passive female pain that is worshipped and glorified in the Virgin thus takes something very real and mundane (humiliation and brutalization) and defuses it by making it holy (martyrdom). While women may gain status as long-suffering and semi-divine, it is clear that in the long run, they are the losers.

To this problematic coupling, add the culturally patterned silence among women on the subjects of menstruation, sex and childbirth, and a difficult personal situation is made worse through ignorance. The promised revelation of "male mysteries" terrifies many *patojas,* who, despite their amorous teenage flirtations, are utterly unprepared for the marital bed.

The normal practice of patrilocal residence is also a source of apprehension. Girls who have been socialized to live and work among a corporate group of female relatives most often leave the security of their natal homes when first married, moving in with the groom's parents for a few years until the young couple has the money to build a house of their own. While being a wife and then a mother fully legitimizes a woman's position in the community, the initial separation from her female kin—if only by a few kilometers—is an immediate source of personal pain and in a more material sense, a loss of productive power and status. Wrenched away from the female family business, the bride is obliged to either start her own cottage industry or to assist her husband in an enterprise he has fashioned. Furthermore, she carries the major responsibility for providing the family's food, and as a bride she must gather her wits together to manage by herself, not having assistance in most of her tasks until her daughters are eight or nine.

It is clear that romance ends—and adulthood begins—when the bride crosses her husband's threshold. Nevertheless, she retains her status as a dependent female, for power over the *patoja* is transferred from her father to the more restricting reins of her husband. Expected to succumb to his domination, she is both defenseless and immobilized. The freedom to stroll with girlfriends, for example, is no longer sanctioned. A married woman properly remains at home anticipating the return of her husband, venturing out only to work or church, and then only with his permission.

Marriage means abandoning the security of work and kin in a girl's natal home and taking on the lonely *santa carga* (blessed burden) of a grown woman. In some ways the *patojas* are prepared for their new role because of their experience doing housework with their mothers. Where they are shocked and dismayed is in the physical and personal contact with their new husbands and in the isolation from the lives and work they knew. But women quickly realize that passive acceptance of male behavior—however abusive—guarantees the presence of a husband and, more important, his participation in creating children, thus transforming a wife—a non-prestigious, almost transitory status—into a beloved, respected, and sanctified mother.

Female Seclusion in Class Perspective

At all class levels, the Latin American family is marked by a patriarchal structure maintaining that a woman's proper sphere is inside the home and that she must defer to her husband in all public matters. Though there are notable variations in class and racially differentiated groups, both men and women subscribe to rigid definitions of sex roles, accepting them as "natural" (Nash and Safa 1976). Women are socialized to prefer the sanctity and protection of the family to the competitive hostile world outside—a world that is described as essentially dangerous because it is the realm of men and as such is hostile to women.

The ability to remain within the safe confines of the home has always been a matter decided by the constraints of class. Research has shown that despite a certain commonalty among Latin females under male hegemony, class plays a primary role in defining the relationship women have to the domestic and public domains (Safa 1976). Both elites and non-elites suffer considerable restrictions, but for different purposes. For example, the personal mobility of wealthy women is severely constrained in order to control sexual access and thus insure patrimony. In contrast, lower class Indian women cannot be isolated in the home, since their participation in the public labor of the market or working class sector is necessary for survival.[2]

This pattern of class-specific adherence to the male-female domains persists to this day in Latin America, and this section examines its implications for women in San Pedro in terms of social and economic constraints placed upon female behavior by the ruling patriarchy. Regardless of class, the San Pedro ideal ascribed to by men and women alike is that women's income-producing labors and social interactions should include and center on the family where childcare and housekeeping can be managed along with other productive chores. In one sense, the restricted visibility should also serve to isolate women from non-family males who represent a potential disruption to the tranquility of the family and danger to the purity of its female members. But as will become clear, the control of women of different classes may have a variable expression, one that is intensified with development.

A few wealthy women in San Pedro have traditionally been able to maintain themselves at home, fairly close to the ideal of total seclusion from public life. Money buys their privacy with servants, private schools for the children, and automobiles to take them to the homes of their friends and family. They would never consider venturing out alone, and public visibility is practically limited to appearances at mass where they are always accompanied by their children. Their primary concerns are household management, involving the supervision of servants, governesses, and cooks, for the pleasure and satisfaction of the man of the house. These wealthy *Sampedranas* commonly subscribe to a nuclear family pattern that further isolates elite women in the home. Sometimes the only female company they have is an illiterate teenage maid, and when entering an upper class home one often sees the servants and their mistress watching cartoons together on television.

Middle class women aspire to this epitome of domestic isolation, but being economically unable to achieve it, they adhere to a modified *purdah* in which they venture out, but rarely alone; trips to the market are done in pairs or a child is sent; movies and fiestas are attended in groups. Young women who cannot resist the urge to stroll on a nice evening literally hang onto each other as they walk, giggling and whispering, but never stopping to talk to the groups of boys watching them nearby. A woman alone is immediately suspect, especially late at night.[3] A middle class woman's reputation is often based on how often she is seen in the street. "Good" women are not supposed to be interested in the world outside their doors.[4] In fact, houses in town have traditionally been designed to face inward onto the family patio rather than out toward the public streets. Women with small *tiendas* attached to their homes may stand watching the passing crowds during a slow afternoon, but only from the safety of the shadowy doorway. Even inside the houses females work, chat and relax in groups. No one sleeps alone even if rooms are available. It is not unusual to find four teenage girls sleeping in two single beds, a situation they prefer to the lonely and troubled sleep of an isolated bedroom.

Poor women or rural *aldeanas,* by dint of economic necessity, are in public more often than either of the other two groups. Many live outside of town, and they walk great distances, baskets of goods on their heads, to reach the market and the shops. Their economic connection to the town is structured mostly around open plaza trade or door-to-door services. They may sit for hours in the market selling to friends and strangers alike. They walk back and forth to customers or market alone, travel on buses to wholesale suppliers or in open trucks to coastal trade centers as well as into the mountains, to Quezaltenango, Guatemala City and Totonicapán. Poor women have developed public strategies for hawking their goods, haggling over prices, effecting beneficial credit arrangements with suppliers. Economic necessity forces them to disregard the implicit admonition that good women should stay at home, and they are freer to transact business and to travel, independent of prescribed domestic identification. Nevertheless, in spite of their personal visibility and mobility, they, like more affluent women in town, maintain a strict regimen for their daughters whose non-domestic movements are regulated by *permiso* (permission) meted out only for church or family social obligations.

Yet this entire model of class-specific female isolation is fast disappearing with development. As avenues for retail and wholesale trade open in San Pedro, women are far less intimidated by the public domain. This is particularly true for upwardly mobile women. Opportunities now exist for women who had managed small businesses only as supplemental income, to expand into the retail sector full-time. They do this readily despite the attendant disruption to household management when the mother is absent six or seven days a week. In addition to commercial development, the town's emphatic support of co-educational high schools and colleges nearby brings young women into constant contact with males. Mothers who are overly concerned with the *abusivo* (abusive, fresh) nature of *patojos* may send daughters to Catholic girls' schools in Guatemala City, but in either case, young women of the growing middle class are not as secluded and domestic as they once were.

Male Authority and the Family

In spite of the rise in female visibility that comes with investment in commercial and educational opportunities, male members of San Pedro households continue to try to exercise authority regarding the contacts that females of the family have with non-related men outside the home. To a certain degree the restraint placed upon female accessibility succeeds in that it keeps women within the family productive unit until their late teens, at which point it breaks down entirely. At that time in the life-cycle, the authority and power of the *novio* (boyfriend) supersedes that of the father or brother, and a young woman becomes highly susceptible to the romantic and sexual advances of her male peers. With pregnancy and/or marriage, women come under the less resilient authority of husbands whose demands and proscriptions are not flaunted as easily as were their fathers' rules, largely because of the young wife's isolation in her new patrilocal residence, and the dependence of a bride upon her husband. These young women who, being between statuses as well as between one male authority (father/brother) and another (husband) are noticeably insecure. Such emotions might seem predictable given the knowledge of how most male-female alliances turn out. Yet at the same time, a certain optimistic flirtatiousness exists that suggests an eagerness to get on with the game of love and the business of becoming a woman.

As a girl matures, paternal control of her sexual behavior may first be expressed with reference to all public contact such as the refusal to grant permission to attend a dance or fiesta even with the company of older female relatives. Particular constraint will be exercised over a daughter's affiliation with a new *novio* when she will again be denied permission to meet him at the movies or to stroll quietly in the square. Sometimes a brother will exercise priority as authority figure over his sister in matters that do not directly concern their father or come to his attention, as the following story illustrates.

Carla, a middle-class teenager, loved to play basketball in high school and was on the school team until the evening her older brothers stopped by after their classes to watch a game. From that night on, she was not allowed to play basketball because the team members wore shorts. But the matter did not end there. Spurred on by the "shorts" issue, the brothers decided that the boys in their school were *abusivos* and that Carla should instead receive a private Catholic education more appropriate to her innocent status. Despite her protests, she was immediately transferred, with the brothers taking upon themselves the added financial burden of private school tuition.

Generally speaking, a girl's mother would have some input into decisions concerning the visibility of her daughter; males neither mete out nor refuse *permiso* to daughters or sisters without the indirect approval of the mother. Until the time that a girl leaves the natal home for good, she is under the supervision of her mother in domestic and extradomestic activities, and while the final say may be expressed by male family members, the mother is always considered, consulted and respected regarding household decisions on *permiso*. It is expected that mothers, having been through the process themselves, will be somewhat more indulgent with teenage daughters and often they will knowingly turn their heads long enough for a daughter to sneak out with her sisters for an evening's *paseo* despite the assertions of their father to the contrary.

Once the benevolent supervision of a girl's family has lapsed, the unilateral authority to completely restrict female mobility is only available to husbands, who can take advantage of a wife's singular isolation and dependence. A husband's control over his wife is particularly facilitated in the middle class when a woman has no productive activity of her own, or when, for example, she works with her husband. Financial dependence in these situations is a powerful weapon, especially when the wife's family lives at some distance. Outside kin groupings, female cooperation and support is rare. To the contrary, women mistrust friendships almost as a matter of course. "Good friend today, tomorrow is an enemy" is an often heard saying. While groups of females gather for religious meetings and fiestas, women are suspicious of the intentions of so-called "friends," assuming that they will become the source of gossip about the family or about oneself, a constant fear in a town where everyone knows and keeps an eye on everyone else.

Even more fervent is the belief that friendship between a man and a woman is impossible in San Pedro. It is a common assumption that men will take advantage of women in compromising situations, so to avoid uncomfortable interactions, an etiquette is set for the informal meeting of men and women. Usually a woman will know how to manipulate a chance encounter when alone on the street or at home, but husbands sometimes reinforce the limits of their wives' casual interactions with their own rules. This is especially true for the wealthy. For example, one affluent husband said his wife was not permitted to dance with any men who were not close relatives, that she could never seek out a man—even a close friend of the family—to speak to him, but if the friend came to visit and the husband were not at home, that was different because the servant and children were present. If a woman were to violate any of these rules, her motivations would be construed as sexual. Thus an unmarried couple alone in a car are always suspect, as is a woman out late at night. Sometimes a woman's whole life will be circumscribed by a husband's preference for her to remain apart from public contact, but as was mentioned, this is possible only among the relatively wealthy as the following case illustrates.

Maria del Carmen Portillo wanted to start a small store selling cheeses and other delicacies previously available only in the capital. The family did not need the extra income and her designs on starting her own business were clearly expressions of her bored isolation and complete economic dependence. When she proposed the venture to her husband, he off-handedly rejected the idea because "people would talk," and she was forced to comply for the sake of marital peace.

In this case, the authority of male family members can be seen as social control by means of gossip. The fear of gossip is constantly cited as reason for not acting in a certain way, for not breaking established rules of social conduct, for not taking chances. Inevitably, its effect is only felt by straying women since male reputations are only enhanced by gossip. Nevertheless, the model of proper female behavior—reinforced by fear of public disapproval—is constantly challenged and, while individual transgressions may forebode personal tragedy, they fit into a historical pattern of rule breaking that is in itself a set of parallel or hidden rules of behavior. Local statistics show, for example, that while virginity is highly touted before marriage, the norm among *Sampedranas* is to marry *after* the initial sexual encounter, usually after the first child is conceived. Courtship etiquette is another form of social control imposed upon women, but like the loss of virginity, through the intervention of determined males, its norms are constantly challenged. The following discussion contrasts the ideal with several cases of real-life courtship and real-life seduction.

AUTHORITY AND COURTSHIP

Courtship terms require clarification. The word *novio* connotes several distinct sets of rights and obligations which change as the marriage date draws nearer. *Novio* in the most ordinary sense means "boyfriend" (*novia* is girlfriend) and it may be used jokingly to imply a casual romantic interest or more seriously, to suggest deeper feelings. Historically, informal alliances between *novios* were unheard of. Until the 1930s, parents arranged marriages well before the children were old enough to initiate their own romances. Even today in many *aldeas,* if parents witness a *novio* flirting with their daughter, they may confront his parents with the demand for commitment, or if they consider him unsuitable, force their daughter to dismiss him. Young *aldea* women behave in a shy and conservative manner with *novios* whom they are permitted to talk with only between six and seven at night, but town women have considerably more freedom and as such, a wider range of responses and behaviors.

Regardless of her location, when a girl encourages or does not actively resist a persistent suitor, he may be recognized as a *novio* of a higher status. It is then expected that he will visit her every night, meet her at the movies if she is a towngirl or arrange to encounter her at a fiesta or fair. They may exchange secret kisses, but their alliance is still publicly unrecognized by her family, so walking together in public or even acknowledging each other's presence on the street is not approved. At this stage of courtship, the *novio* is never invited into the house and the couple must meet in the street. Refusal to recognize the legitimacy of a *novio* often leads to the kind of secret meetings that permit illicit sex. Ironically, clandestine trysts during courtship may be the only moments a couple will ever have alone. Most *Sampedranos*—especially in the *aldeas*—are accustomed to living without privacy, and in fact, never sleep in a room by themselves throughout their marriage.

Only when a *novio* has spoken with a girl's father concerning his intention to marry may he be invited into the house on a regular basis. *Novio oficial* then achieves the status of betrothed and is a welcome family member. Before that level of courtship is reached, the girl's parents formally ignore the presence of her *novio* although his character and future may be a source of constant discussion and debate. Finally, the *novio* and *novia* mean bride and groom, the most serious courtship status when all restrictions on social and sexual intercourse may be relaxed as wedding plans are made and carried out.

This process of the socially defined selection of a mate has many inherent irregularities and mutations. Most of them are related to pre-marital sex as the following examples of courtship stories suggest.

Ana and Eduardo have been *novios* for two years. He is a 24-year-old *ladino* from San Marcos whose family owns a store. She is an Indian of 23, better educated and more achievement-oriented than he, going to college and working full-time. He drives a cab, a relatively low-status job, and is still in high school because of an adolescent illness. They are unique in San Pedro for the consistent and public nature of their romance, which, while it went on every night next to their bedroom, was formally ignored by her parents. The scene of their meetings was the small family-owned *tienda* which Ana ran by herself at night. Very little money changes hands in San Pedro in the evenings, and it was suspected that Ana kept the shop open only to have a relatively comfortable yet safely public place to meet Eduardo. The two would usually be accompanied by one of Ana's brothers or sisters, but since all were in sympathy with their courting, some long moments would pass when they were left alone. Still, the door to the street was open and the extent of their amorous interaction could only be an embrace or two, perhaps a quick embarrassed kiss. Mostly, they seemed to enjoy the tantalizing intimacy of the store simply as a place where they and their bodies could be close. This passionate "billing and cooing" went on practically every night, but since Ana was a firm believer in virginity, sexual propriety was maintained.

Juana's was an entirely different courtship. She was quite young when German "exploited" her, as she says, resulting in the birth of their son. As Juana tells it,

> I was fifteen when I got pregnant by him. No one told me to watch out, that I might end up that way. I was living at home with my mother and took to wearing a coat to hide myself. Finally, my mother asked me to take off the coat, and I had to confess what was in my heart and in my stomach. My mother went to speak with him right away, although I pleaded with her that I didn't want to live with him or marry him. Anyway, he was already married. He offered to take care of the child, but I refused, and continued to work. When Enrique was born, German didn't know. He went everywhere with me and we were content.

Three years later she came home one evening to find German asleep in her bed. Estranged from his first wife, he demanded his rights as the father of their baby and to her as his *amante* (lover). This time she acquiesced and that night their second child was conceived and their tumultuous life together began in earnest.

In another example, Katerina was a woman with a history of *novios*. By her own admission she had had twenty-five before she married Julio at age eighteen. They began to have sexual relations only because, she swears, she was "in his power" and could not refuse. What is more likely is that she was not a virgin when she began seeing him and her father, knowing this, confronted Julio at the first opportunity and forced the issue of marriage. Later events show that this plan might have had tragic results were it not for the intervention of *Dios* (God), as Katerina tells it. Julio became a rogue. He stole money from his new wife, gambled, and drank. He beat her, ignored the baby, and slept with other women. The new marriage seemed doomed until his friends took Julio to the first-level catechism course at the Catholic church where, with the help of the priests, a remarkable change came over him. Since then he has redirected his previously antisocial energy toward business and his family and is a very successful businessman and the father of five children.

Olga's story has a different ending. She is the 24-year-old owner of a vegetable stall in the *mercado* who was five months pregnant when she told this tale. The father of her baby was a 25-year-old unemployed construction worker who has been her *novio* for eight years. Like many women who are ashamed of their exploitability, she vowed that she had only succumbed once to his sexual demands and that a single mating resulted in her pregnancy. His parents wanted a wedding. Olga did not. She had opted instead to raise the child at home with her family. While her *novio* swore he would deny parentage if she refused to marry him, Olga was going ahead with her plans. Her family was dismayed at the visibility of her condition, but were supportive since the boyfriend was known to drink, was lazy, and had other women— sure signs that he would be a troublesome and unreliable husband. Olga was reconciled to her single parenthood and had already planned to deliver the child at home where she knew she would receive excellent care and attention. She hoped she might get married someday.

What emerges from analysis of these variations on the formal courtship theme is that sexual power plays an important role in undermining the standard rules. Because women are not socialized to want to enjoy sex and are taught instead to value their own innocence above all else, it is difficult to attribute to them strong erotic drives. Rather, given the emphasis on sexual conquest as the legitimation of the masculine role, the male partners are invariably the initiators of pre-marital sex. Women play an active role in these sexual activities not because they are too physically stimulated to resist, but because of the power men exercise over young women as authority figures and prospective husbands. Sex in courtship thus expresses male control over a relatively powerless teenage girl who is ignorant of the sex act and its immediate implications. The act itself portends future male dominance in a woman's life not only because of the loss of virginity but because of the pregnancy that so often results.

Where fathers and brothers are strong figures in the girl's life, they may intervene to salvage her reputation by forcing a marriage, and at the same time keep intact their own honor as "guardians of virtue." In many cases, however, when the woman is of relatively mature years, that is, eighteen to twenty-one, she may insist on making her own decision about marriage. Some *civilizada* women are able to reject an undesirable seducer because they are financially secure in their female family businesses, and prefer to raise their child at home without the problems and humiliation of a *macho* husband. A woman of character may reject attempts to control her further through monetary support, but she too may relinquish her claim to freedom when, as in Juana's case, the suitor is available as a legitimate mate, or when she has no family and is experiencing difficulties supporting herself and her child.

In any case, the pre-marital *patoja* period in a relationship may hold the key to the future conditions of the marriage because its consequences are so profound. The loss of virginity to a man who is not a potential marriage partner may stigmatize a girl and cause future difficulty in marrying unless she is very lucky. Pregnancy with or without a marriageable mate brings problems and a quick change of life-style. Settling down with someone chosen by the girl's father may have immediate negative results as it did with Katerina. But none of these consequences really touch males; women must personally bear all the social opprobrium and male callousness that comes from making a bad decision about whose company to keep. Only in rare cases, like Ana and Eduardo, does a woman manage to evade sexual intercourse and then only when she is clearly much stronger than he or of higher status, and more determined to manipulate the situation to her advantage.

Getting Married

During the average *Sampedrana* lifetime, a woman will marry at nineteen and have her first child at twenty. As discussed above, the birth of the first child often precedes marriage—indeed, many women with children never will formally marry. This is not to say that the town is overrun with unwed mothers. While a substantial number of children never live with their fathers, the variety of marriage types sometimes makes it difficult to say who is wed and who is not. As in other Indian communities in the highlands, there are four different types of marriage in San Pedro. These are *unidos* (consensual union), *unidos de hecho* (consensual union with papers), civil, and church. Of these, only the first is not recognized by law, and it is more common than the other three combined, due to its popularity among the more numerous *gente*. Local lawyers say that consensual unions are less common now than they were fifteen years ago largely because of the influence of the Catholic priests.

The power of the Catholic church in this area—however minimal—was demonstrated when fourteen middle-aged couples from one *aldea* all married on the same day in 1977. This peculiar mass marriage turned out to be a consequence of a policy of offering *unidos* the chance to get married in the church after years of living together. Another way *unidos* legalize their status is by verifying that they have been living together three years and have a family, but since becoming *unido de hecho* requires paperwork, a lawyer, and some expense, it is not popular. Single church marriages are also not prevalent among either the *civilizadas* or the *gente,* and civil ceremonies outnumber church weddings three to one. (One reason for this avoidance of church weddings may be the insistence of the priests that the couple attend a series of pre-nuptial talks on the problems of marriage, a commitment few couples are prepared to make.) A small percentage of church weddings are preceded by civil ceremonies, but since each involves a separate festivity, this expense of combining the two is taken on only by relatively few townfolk. Church weddings by themselves are a financial commitment for the families in that they usually mean buying or renting a dress, inviting several hundred friends and relatives to the mass and following party, paying the marimba band, and preparing food and drink for everyone. Nonetheless, in spite of the considerable financial burden, a fiesta can also be expected for the celebration of an *aldea* civil ceremony—even one that is of the variety we call "shotgun."

Odelio (19) and Tonita (17) are children of *gente* in the *aldea* of Chamac. During the town's Saint's Day celebrations, they were discovered by the police making love behind the church. No one was eager to discuss the event; family members shook their heads and chuckled at the foolishness of the *patojos*. The humiliation of being caught "in the act" coupled with intervention by the police in the matter forced the two into an early marriage, and the families were reconciled to the idea. They had been *novios* for quite some time, so neither family was as reticent as they might have been and the wedding date was quickly set. About one hundred friends and family were invited to Odelio's house for the party. Women wore their best *huipiles,* men sported suits and hats. The bride, whose family was in mourning, wore a dark dress and sweater. All the preparations were the responsibility of the groom's family and as is customary, they provided both lunch before the ceremony and dinner afterward. The bride's family paid for nothing.

The festivities were comparatively lavish. Chicken, rice, *tamalitos,* and coffee were served first to the bride's family in the main room of the house and then to the groom's family and friends in a side bedroom. Everyone drank many small glasses of rum passed around on trays. A few men got very drunk. After lunch about twenty-five people rode the local bus the few miles to the mayor's office in town where a quick ceremony took place. The bus waited and everyone gaily rode back.

Meanwhile aunts and female cousins of the groom were preparing dinner. They had been in the kitchen cooking and tending the fire all day, and would remain there throughout the night, cooking, feeding the children, and finally, eating the last bits of food themselves. The groom's mother and sisters-in-law mingled with the guests but mostly passed plates of food or poured more rum. When everyone had eaten and gotten properly intoxicated, it was time for the bride to be *entregada* or delivered to her new home with the groom's family. Tonita's father and uncles made many serious, if drunken speeches about what a sacrifice it was for her family, as indeed, it was, since her mother had died but a few months before, leaving her husband with Tonita and six younger sisters. There was much crying by aunts and by Tonita's father. Finally, his gift to the couple—a clothes closet—was brought in, signaling the end of the formalities, and guests began to leave.

In all, this wedding cost the groom's parents Q200.00. While they had some money saved from the mother's milk business, they had to borrow most of it from relatives. Many other *aldea* weddings are simpler than this one; they might not have chicken and rice, but only *chuchitos* (small *tamales* with tiny bits of pork inside), a volunteer marimba, and *cusha*—the locally made "white lightning"—instead of rum. Guests might bring some food if the family is exceptionally poor. But in every case where weddings are being celebrated, money is spent far beyond the means of the family, who must go into debt of one sort or another. The entry of the bride into the family productive unit rarely balances out this investment in a fiesta since the product of her work belongs not to the group but to her and her husband. As soon as they can, they will build a house of their own and be gone.

Why then, when the bride's work does not repay even the cost of the wedding, do families overextend themselves financially for a wedding celebration? There are several reasons. First, there is the obvious social status of hosting such a party. The occasions are rare enough that they are memorable. Second, as was noted earlier, the priests have been working to encourage legal marriages and to some degree are succeeding. Third, no wedding can be acceptably celebrated without some festivity, even as in this example, when a family is in mourning. Together, a legal marriage and a fiesta are a package that expresses upward mobility. Elaborate fiestas have historically expressed the family's social standing in a conspicuous manner. Today's legal marriages are different in that they are becoming popular in San Pedro as a symbol of the *modernity* of the bride and groom who are complying with national laws and expectations. As such, the cash expenditure that goes with the wedding celebrations is a further sign of their identification with the national consumer culture. Evidence of the growing trend to spend money on modern weddings can be seen in the number of white wedding gowns rented by *aldeanas* who want to be visibly *civilizada* but do not have sufficient capital or precedent for the purchase of a dress.

UNIDO MARRIAGES

While the number of wedding ceremonies in San Pedro has increased among the *gente* partly as an outgrowth of social and economic development, the favored marriage category remains *unido*. Sixty percent of baptized children are from *unido* relationships, a figure that has not significantly changed since marriage records began in 1925. Despite statistical evidence and testimony of lawyers that *unidos* far outnumber other marriage categories, almost no woman in San Pedro will easily admit to living with a man without benefit of a wedding ceremony. Nonetheless, marriage types are easily given away by the word men and women use to refer to their spouse. Married couples invariably use the words *esposo* and *esposa,* while *unido* couples call one another *marido* and *mujer,* words that connote a looser, more informal bond. In a few cases where women had been recently abandoned by their husbands, they would tearfully confess that they had never really married, although previously each had stated that they had had church weddings. It seems clear that women are being caught up in the public sentiment that values weddings over simply eloping or living together. But the variables at work in *unido* relationships are structured against women so as to make it quite difficult for them to force a legal marriage upon the male. Unless they are legally wed, the man has no legal obligation to the woman with whom he lives. Under Guatemalan law, he may abandon his woman and children without recompense.[5] Yet the law can incarcerate a runaway woman of any marriage type, charging her with desertion of the home, even if the children leave with her!

Unido relationships, more than legal weddings, invariably occur after the couple has had sexual intercourse. Usually, the girl involved is too traumatized or submissive to insist upon marriage of any sort and it is only when her father discovers her pregnancy or her sexual liaison that marriage will be discussed. Most rural teenage girls are totally ignorant about sex and assume a relatively passive role in these early sexual unions, feeling that they are "in his power" to be dominated physically and emotionally. Only when families take notice is pressure placed upon the boy for some commitment. Because the decision-making process is usually structurally removed from the couple, and especially because many *unidos* enter marriage unprepared and without much love for each other, they end up resenting each other for the changes and responsibilities newly demanded of them.

A further problem with the *unido* category is that once a woman has given birth, her chances of ever marrying someone other than the father with whom she is united are significantly diminished. She has proven to the community that she is no longer a virgin and thus too far from the ideal to again be popularly considered for a wife. Chances are, she will find someone later on, but public sentiment is quite discouraging on the odds. As a local lawyer explained, a man is never eager to help support a child who is not his own. Women know that a stepchild will be resented and sometimes mistreated, so that for her sake and the welfare of her child, she may enter into and remain in a union which she does not want simply because she has no other option.

Local women say that this was not always the case, that there "used to be more respect" so that a man would not take sexual advantage of a woman before they were married. This seems to be part of a nostalgic fantasy of the innocent past perhaps reflecting common female guilt. Indeed, baptismal records show a higher percentage of single mothers in 1910 than they do today (14% versus 7%). These records are significant in their measurement of the numbers of mothers who for one reason or another have borne children without benefit of spouse—*unido* or otherwise.[6] It is also implied evidence of sexual activity both before and outside of marriage, something *Sampedranos* like to deny as a female activity. In other words, local women agree that while men are entangled in sexual alliances outside of marriage, women rarely are. This is clearly an impossible situation; one that is refuted not only by logic and birth statistics, but by ethnographic evidence as well.

MARRIAGE AND THE POOR WOMAN

The pitfalls and predicaments of marriage in San Pedro may be further compounded for those women who lack sufficient resources or skills. With little preparation or ceremony, they enter into a life of conflict and difficulty further complicated by the arrival of babies. Early problems are exacerbated by the pattern of patrilocality since mothers-in-law are rarely sympathetic, especially when the girl's advanced pregnancy makes it hard for her to energetically help in household duties. The antipathy between the two centers on the son/husband whom mothers often see as victimized by their new wives. Mothers-in-law often repeat complaints that the girl got herself pregnant in order to coerce the boy into marrying her. Antagonism between these two women may continue throughout the marriage, especially when financial resources are scarce, sometimes boiling below the surface until it explodes as it did in the following example.

Doña Tomasina is a tired and toothless woman of thirty-eight whose emaciated state nonetheless gives her a certain beauty. She met her husband when she was fifteen, he twenty-one. Juan used to visit his aunt near where Doña Tomasina lived on the coast. Juan and Tomasina were each from poor landless families; like her father and his father, Juan worked in the fields for Qo.85 a day wages. After three months, they were *unido* and came to live in the *aldea* of Chamac with his parents, his brain-damaged brother and his mentally retarded sister. Subsistence had always been difficult for this family partly because of their obligation to the two non-productive members. Tomasina's presence only increased the burden as her marketable skills were minimal. But she took over the cooking, allowing her mother-in-law time to take in washing. For eighteen years she cooked for Juan's family and her own three sons—the only survivors of her ten homebirths. Then, seven years ago, she entered the hospital for treatment of one of her congenital maladies. Her father-in-law, then sixty-eight years old, visited her daily. Totally unfounded rumors flew around the neighborhood and the house that she and this man were sexually entangled. The result of these cruel suspicions was her immediate ouster from the house by her mother-in-law. They have not spoken since, but poverty and obligations to the feeble-minded brother and sister did not permit her to move completely away from her husband and sons as she would have liked. Since that time six of them have occupied one seven-by-seven-foot room in the house and have taken over a dark unchimneyed room as their kitchen. Juan and his sons get along with his mother, but Tomasina is an unwelcome outcast. Without daughters and completely isolated from her in-laws, Tomasina must do all the household tasks herself, a desperate situation for a poor *aldeana*.

Not all married women are such ready victims of their mothers-in-law's hostility. Many avoid conflict by moving into their own homes quickly. In fact, it is so clear a preference that in-laws usually donate the land for the house and a small field. But in the case of Tomasina this was never an available option. The absence of capital and a growing indebtedness to local money-lenders has firmly tied Tomasina to the wretched living situation in Chamac. Like so many poor women, her husband's laziness and drunkenness anchor the family to its low status. He works irregularly. Once he took advantage of church-sponsored food-for-work relief programs, but no longer. He, like all his family, is sick from life-long malnourishment, and drugs are expensive. He drinks. His beatings of Tomasina come so often that their dying 14-year-old son pleaded with them on his deathbed to stop fighting when he was gone. Juan has had a *querida* (sweetheart) for years. He visits her and their two children weekly. Tomasina's attempt to flee to her own family in Tejutla was foiled when he forced her back as he is legally entitled to do. Tomasina's own work is secondary to his. Two days a week she washes clothes and cooks in town for Q2.00 a day. Were she able to work six days, the money would be better, but her obligations to Juan preclude full-time employment since she must hand-carry his hot lunch to wherever he is working, cutting into the most important work time for domestics.

Tomasina has no expectations that life will ever improve for her. As long as her husband lives he will be an additional burden to her instead of providing sustenance and support for the home. Were he to leave her or die she would have all the responsibility for the home and the children and it is difficult to say if she could meet it with the minimal resources she has left. But as a widow, she could hold a full-time job, spending her earnings on food instead of handing them over to her husband for liquor or lovers.

Sex and the Parallel Marriage

Teresa and Gerónimo have been living together for eighteen years. They have never been married, but are recognized as a couple by townfolk. They have had five children together; one of them died in 1973 and Teresa has been unable to get pregnant ever since. It is difficult to tell if her infertility is real since she often alludes to the fact that Gerónimo no longer sleeps with her, or that when he tries to have sex with her, he is impotent. One of the factors contributing to their fragmented marital life is that Gerónimo has several other women with whom he cohabits. Twice a week he travels on business to Guatemala City where he has two lovers. Sometimes he stays with one for weeks at a time, then he will favor the other for a period. In San Pedro he maintains a *querida* around the corner from Teresa's house so that his comings and goings are commonly known. The problems associated with having other women are further exacerbated by his having had children with them, a situation that angers and annoys Teresa's children, who hardly see their father. Teresa constantly plans to leave Gerónimo, but never does. Although she runs the retail side of his business, she has no money of her own. Without Gerónimo, she would be unable to support her school-age children. She feels her victimization will never end.

Cases like this one are not rare in San Pedro. Although only the wealthiest men can afford to maintain separate homes for their various mistresses, more casual or temporary affairs seem an everyday occurrence.[7] Women's conversations are filled with tales of woe regarding philandering husbands. Few families have not been scarred by one or more lurid extramarital episodes which are regularly recounted as lessons to the uninitiated. Meanwhile, *mujeriegos,* or ladies' men, regularly boast of their many women as a long-standing masculine tradition. Rich and poor participate in wooing women. One toothless *campesino* who had been married for more than fifty years proudly recounted his strategies for conquering and maintaining women, and said that he had learned his technique from his own father, whose only mistake had been to give his women money rather than the other way around!

It is interesting to note that in spite of a fairly high incidence of marital infidelity, desertion and separation, the statistical evidence nonetheless suggests the norm to be one of family stability rather than of fragmentation. Specifically, Smith and Wilson's (n.d.) study shows only 11% of sampled households in San Pedro were headed exclusively by females, and of that number, more than half were widows.[8] My only research in San José Caben also shows remarkable familial continuity, with more than 90% of the sample of 52 women married and living with the father of their children. This situation is actually quite telling in terms of the solidity and flexibility of marriage in the town and its *aldeas.* It implies first that while some men permanently abandon their families, most husbands who leave their wives do so for short periods and usually return. In addition, men who have *casitas* (houses where lovers meet) are not likely to desert their families financially, as is common among *ladinos;* instead husbands continue to give money to their wives, however minimally.[9] Secondly, it suggests that if men are going to set up *casitas* with their lovers, few of them desert their wives in order to do so. Instead, they maintain both households, often for years. Third, *amantes* (lovers) tend to ignore the existence of the first wife to the extent of describing their own relationship as a marriage. Both women maintain the charade by shrugging off the indiscretions of their "husband" in an attempt to maintain family solidarity. Those few unforgiving women who do refuse re-entry to a straying male have been quietly applauded by others, but only infrequently do wives have the resources which might permit them that level of social and economic autonomy.

In short, while extramarital alliances are fairly common occurrences, they do little to disrupt the family or the male power base. Instead, they extend male dominance by providing support systems to several households. In the next section, I argue that the pattern of sexual trysting is in fact merely a replication of the primary family unit with its exchange of husband and wife services. Sex, passion, and lust, as we shall see, have little to do with it.

THE LATIN LOVER DEBUNKED

There are few *Sampedranas* who will admit to enjoying sexual contact. Sex is most frequently described as an obligation to masculine demands which is assumed as part of the role of a dutiful wife. The commonly held belief is that only men should enjoy the quick passion of the sex act; that it is the woman's part to lie still and tolerate the need her husband has for sexual release at her expense. This is his right as her husband, it is believed, and she must give in to his demands or risk losing him to someone else. Men share the belief that women should not enjoy sex and support institutionalized frigidity. A woman who might gain pleasure from sex is immediately suspect as a threat to her husband's dominance of her. It is an unanticipated switch in the balance of sexual power that suggests she might not be contained at home and might stray.

Even prostitutes share in the common assumption that women should not like sex. They do not feign pleasure during coitus with a customer. To the contrary, they behave in a cold, business-like manner, neither removing their blouses nor kissing. They see themselves as sexual repositories where men come to "do their deed."

With both prostitutes and women in general, the image that is conjured up is of half-clothed couples copulating quickly without affection or foreplay until the man ejaculates. Conversations with women suggest this is an accurate picture that tells us something about sexual behavior. The myth of female distaste for the sexual act is borne out in fact; women do not find pleasure in sexual intercourse because little if anything takes place during the act which is aimed at pleasing them. And sexual contact is, for women, not communication with a loved one or the imparting of mutual satisfaction, but a duty and the means to have children, who, unlike the husband, are a secure source of love and aid for her entire lifetime.

These points have implications for analysis of male-female interaction that go beyond sex and far beyond the married couple. In short, by and large women feel superior to men. They hold the adult male in disdain as sinful, lazy, and unreliable while they (women) are strong, hard working, caring mothers. Men tend to live up to their bad reputations without regret. Although marriages are characterized as stable, young single mothers or permanently abandoned women may be forced to fend for themselves, a difficult situation, especially for women without a supportive family nearby. Finally, women do not enjoy sex, partly because they are not supposed to and partly because men do nothing to encourage female pleasure.

Putting these factors together, one is led to wonder about the philandering behavior of men. Extramarital affairs are common in San Pedro and common sense implicates a great number of women. The question then is, if, as they claim, women have little use for men anyway, seeing them only as a source of conflict and heartache, and if they regard sex as a hidden and humiliating activity only to be passively tolerated, why then do women welcome the straying husband into an extramarital "liaison," particularly women who have already been seduced and abandoned once?

The answer to this puzzle lies in the explication of extramarital relationships as economic commitments rather than as sexual interludes. In this sense, women enter into illegitimate alliances with men for the same reason they marry initially: productive and reproductive security. In general, they may be seen then as "parallel" marriages where the couple cohabits periodically and has children together. The term "parallel marriage" is appropriate here because the exchange of wife-husband services is identical in both kinds of marriage: men provide material support, women provide domestic support, and together they produce children. Women who find themselves in this position rarely enter into a parallel marriage because they are promiscuous or in love. More often, they entertain the advances of a married man because they are seeking the essential ingredient of marriage in San Pedro— economic complementarity—and thus, a husband, not a lover.

Evidence from San Pedro suggests that within the context of a class society, it is through the exploitation of poor or isolated women that men commonly develop a *casita* alliance. But the exploitation implicit in the male choice of a lower status or economically vulnerable woman is reciprocated in her expectations of him. Essentially, he plays an important role in maintaining a mother-centered home that will endure even after he is gone. He does this first in creating the mother-centered home by fathering the children. Second, he provides financial support, however minimal. Some women may foolishly enter a sexual affair which has no monetary aspect, but the norm is that the man is received into the second home because he pays to get in. On the surface, this certainly looks like a variation on prostitution, but the exchange clearly goes beyond a simple sex for cash arrangement, as we see when we examine the motives of each of the partners.

Women enter into a "liaison" for economic and social security, namely children. Women in San Pedro love and desire children, and in a country without effective institutionalized social security it is easy to see why. The children provided women through sexual contact not only legitimate and enhance their status in the community, but can be a continued source of material support throughout their lives. In order to assure herself companionship and material comfort in her old age, a woman must concern herself with prolific childbearing. In a more immediate sense, from an early age children provide the necessary labor to maintain a domestic productive system that can succeed in supporting the family's needs independent of male intervention or assistance. But until her children are mature enough to be valuable laborers, a woman is glad to have the material support of their father to feed and clothe them.

What a man obtains from the maintenance of a parallel family is, of course, status, in the sense of being recognized as virile, *macho,* and powerful, but in a real sense what he sets up is a duplicate version of his first marriage: a woman with his children who tolerates his unpredictable behavior passively and who regularly and half-heartedly submits to his sexual demands. Having a *querida* means men ensure their freedom to act as they please, to debauch and drink with impunity, for they always have one woman or another who will accept them. When he quarrels with one wife or tires of her, he visits the other, sometimes to the extent that people speak of men whose clothes are washed in one place, dried in another, and ironed in a third. Therefore, while women may enhance their status with children and money, they are really on borrowed time where the man is concerned, for the objection of one woman to the arrangement means the man immediately quits her home for the solace of the parallel family.

A case illustrates the process. Don Manuel Velásquez is one of the town's leading professionals, a lawyer who is greatly respected and personally admired. It is no secret, however, that for more than fifteen years, he has had one household in San Marcos and one in San Pedro, each with a wife and the requisite number of children. Doña Susana, the lawyer's legitimate wife, is a 42-year-old *ladina* from Guatemala City who was training to be an accountant when she met her husband. Like many middle class wives, she gave up her work and her family connections to move to her husband's home town to look after his house and care for their seven children who range in age from two to twenty-one. The second wife is a 35-year-old secretary in San Marcos who has had a working relationship with Don Manuel for many years. They too, have children. In the beginning of his relationship with the secretary, the lawyer divided his time between the two households. Susana vigorously objected to this arrangement, especially when playmates taunted her children about the second family. But the lawyer had his career and his reputation to consider as well as his own security, and from the start, he denied the accusations, refused his wife a divorce, and yet continued to maintain two families. In recent years his habits have changed, and to Susana's relief, he only makes weekly visits to his San Marcos family. By this time, Susana has become somewhat inured to the existence of a parallel household and to the money the lawyer gives them, and now that some of her children are grown and her material support secure, she can afford to be *tranquila* (calm) about her husband's other life.

To sum up, men in San Pedro create a relatively stable pattern of parallel marriages where they, as providers and fathers, can be elusive in their loyalties and affection. While family stability seems to be the norm, there is always the painful expectation of desertion, or worse, the humiliating image of a man depriving his wife of the money he contributes to his lover. As such, women are forced to treat the most callous of men as valuable commodities who may disappear for good if mistreated or chastised. Furthermore, the generalized male need to constantly express themselves sexually is dubious. Although men are chided and disparaged for their voracious sexual appetites and philandering ways, they have lovers not primarily for sexual outlet, but to ensure their continued value as scarce resources. Women accept them in their beds not for their sexual prowess, nor for their erotic sensitivities, but for their crucial role in establishing and maintaining the family.

Marriage and Development

For many years parallel marriage has been a dependable survival strategy for isolated women who might otherwise be forced to migrate to an urban center for work. Changes in the character of female family production and in the nature of the labor force in general do not seem to have substantially affected the system yet, but may be expected to do so in the future. Right now there is no doubt that rising affluence has allowed greater numbers of men to establish "branches" of women, but no data are currently available to document the specific extent of this increase. While it seems too early in the modernization process to be sure, development appears to prefigure certain other trends as well. As female labor and autonomous female businesses lose ground in the developing economy, women are likely to become more dependent on the male breadwinner for financial support. The diminishing of domestic production in an expanding capitalist market means that the value of children as workers will be delayed until later in the life cycle, a factor which would further exacerbate female dependency. And since rising levels of education which are accompanying modernization in San Pedro can be correlated with lower fertility rates (Smith and Wilson n.d.), women will not only become male-dependent, but with fewer children, they will forfeit some of their status as mothers.

These predictions for the shifting gender relations within the family imply that both primary and parallel marriages will undergo some kind of structural transformation. While we may suggest that male social power will increase at the expense of female independence, it is difficult to say exactly what form these changes will take in terms of the strategies or options of primary and secondary wives. One form of domestic organization that immediately comes to mind is "matrifocality," an urban survival strategy based on serial monogamy and a supportive female kin group (Brown 1975; Stack 1974).

At first glance, it appears that the sexual antagonism and shifting economic emphasis in San Pedro might eventually result in the breakdown of the patriarchal family to the extent that women would rid themselves of the constricting bonds of matrimony—legitimate or otherwise—to assume complete responsibility for supporting their families. But it must be remembered that neither irresponsible male behavior nor socioeconomic development is in itself a sufficient precondition for the entrenchment of the matrifocal alternative. The essence of the matrifocal model is that it succeeds where the dire poverty of a hierarchal class system predisposes males to chronic unemployment and females to the lowest priority jobs or to public assistance. This is not the trend in San Pedro.

While it may be that in Guatemala City shantytowns or slum neighborhoods, poor women have abandoned marriage as a maladaptive economic practice (Bossen 1978), the expanding economy of San Pedro avails the population of a relatively high per capita income even among its poorest inhabitants. This means that while both systems are characterized by male social instability and female responsibility for offspring, *Sampedranas* have not been forced to extricate themselves from men who are unproductive. Rather, except for *Sampedranas* like Tomasina's husband whose lazy character and vices handicapped the family's productive potential, men continue to make themselves valuable as primary breadwinners by efficiently exploiting market and educational opportunities.

When faced with their own low-level, and in some cases diminishing, productive power, women are not about to disregard the material necessity of having a husband. Where women do have the option of discounting the importance of a spouse is among the middle class, i.e., those women whose educational level, family productive system, and entrepreneurial energy allow them to reject suitors and even become single parents. A case in point is Gloria Fuentes, who at the beginning of this book astonished her family by rejecting the marriage proposal of her unreliable and unsatisfactory lover. Gloria represents a small group of middle-class *civilizadas* for whom the model of increased male dependency does not work. At the same time that traditional *Sampedranas* are losing economic and personal autonomy to the developing economy, many middle-class women find their status enhanced. Education may deprive female family businesses of their daughters' labor, and thus turn independent businesswomen into proletarians, but women like Gloria benefit from schooling. Like the hundreds of educated young women from town and *aldeas* who are literate and worldly, Gloria has the skills and the confidence she needs to effectively exploit the local economy to her liking. She combined a high status teaching job with her own knitting business, and further secured her future by investing her Sunday labor in the family store. When Gloria described the victimization most women endure, she did not fully realize that her middle-class status, college education, and strong family productive system excused her from that fate.

I do not think Gloria is the exception to the rule she recounted. Other women, like Olga the vegetable dealer, are making similar decisions to stay home with their children rather than enter a potentially destructive marital arrangement. These alternative arrangements reflect the empowerment development offers to the women who can take advantage of local educational and commercial opportunities. Certainly some *civilizada* women will elect dependent, non-productive relationships reflective of the town's affluence. This is to be expected. But I also foresee that as the middle class expands and affords educated women new occupational opportunities, a restructuring of existing family patterns may occur that allows them the status of motherhood without the burden of marriage.

Unfortunately, most women in San Pedro cannot choose this option. Despite their inexhaustible energy for business, the majority of women are increasingly hampered by meager incomes from cottage industry, the insecurity of women's work, demanding domestic responsibilities, and the minimal educational levels they attain. Unlike Gloria, they do not have the power, either personal or financial, to scorn marriage partners. Unfortunately, the level of success of the Fuentes Velásquez family, as well as the marketable talents and self-esteem imparted to Gloria by her schooling, are largely class-specific. Poorer women constantly struggle and strategize in order to feed their families, and in the process, they seem to be losing ground as sexual stratification increases both in business and in the home. As this study has shown, it is not men, but poorer women, whose potential is shrinking with development, a situation which is making these women and their children increasingly dependent on the support of a male partner. It is ironic that in a town with a healthy and optimistic economic profile, so many women are losing their productive autonomy and becoming more dependent upon men than ever before. As one soft-spoken 76-year-old *aldea* woman said to me, "No matter what you do, the relationship between men and women is *muy jodido* (all screwed up!)."

Notes

1. There is an extensive social scientific literature on male-female relations in Latin America (See Elu de Lenero 1969, Bourque and Warren 1981, Nutini 1967, Rothstein 1983, 1986, Adams 1960, Maynard 1974, Pescatello 1973, Gissi Bustos 1976). As I mentioned in Chapter One, for a long time, female subordination and male dominance were treated as characteristics of social relations rather than behavior that required analysis and explanation. In spite of the tremendous variety of socioeconomic conditions and cultural relations, researchers assumed a permanence and universality in the balance of power between the sexes (e.g., Lewis 1959, Paz 1961, Stycos 1955, Stevens 1965). Until recently, ahistorical, static descriptions sufficed. But in the last few years, writers have been turning away from taking male dominance (and female subordination) for granted. As Bossen points out, ". . . increasingly, it is examined as a variable that can be magnified or diminished by socioeconomic change" (1983 : 39). Browner and Lewin (1982), for example, reject the common assumption that women—without any other means of self-expression—are only fulfilled through satisfying the needs of others. Instead, they argue that in some situations, "self-sacrifice, Marian purity and infinite patience are not ends in themselves, but rather means by which some women gain economic and social rewards" (63). Elsewhere, conditions call for a more assertive, self-centered strategy for females. The common thread in their argument is that women's survival strategies in Latin America, however varied, arise as a common response to economic scarcity, social marginalization, and deepening male dependence.

Similarly, male dominance or *machismo* is best understood not just as the exaggerated masculine stance stereotypically attributed to Latin men, but in part, as a response to insecure economic conditions. One analysis is that male dominance is commonly found in urban settings or in rural areas of scarce resources where the productive efforts of males are inadequate to ensure the survival of the family. Cross-cultural data on black families in the U.S. underclass (Stack 1974), Latinos in a New York slum (Sharff 1981), and poor families in Mexico City (Lewis 1959) show a remarkable commonality in the absence of job opportunities for men. Furthermore, this research suggests that urban cycles of poverty and unemployment create weak conjugal relations, and unreliable husbands and fathers. Women in these situations may have to be excepted from their home-based economic roles to enter into full or part-time participation in a money economy. The tensions arising from the clash of socially idealized sex roles and the economic realities of domestic life often result in male brutalization, desertion or culturally sanctioned humiliation of women. It may be then that *machismo* increases when expectations for the subordinate, submissive, dependent roles of women are no longer borne out in reality, that is, when women contribute enough to the family system to rival the male monopoly on production. As Martin and Voorhies point out, "Men [hold] onto their legacy of patriarchal authority all the more tenaciously in the face of shared provider roles" (1975:370). Michaelson and Goldschmidt (1971) support this contention in their cross-cultural analysis of sex roles among peasants which shows *machismo* limited to areas which idealize male dominance, but in which men lack clear cultural means to demonstrate their superior status. In other words, *macho* norms are the product of expectations for role behavior without adequate economic support for their realization.

Bossen (1984), in her consideration of machismo among Guatemalan Indians and *ladinos,* rejects the economic factors argument. She instead posits that economic forms, or modes of production, account for male dominance among commercialized *ladinos* as well as for the relatively equal gender relations among the indigenous peasantry. Among the rural Maya, she argues, the household is based upon male-female complementarity and mutual dependence. Because the sexes rely upon one another, men are less likely to abandon their wives, or out of fear of being abandoned themselves, behave irresponsibly. Thus, female economic security is achieved through the importance placed on a woman's labor and the labor of her children. As Indians become more integrated into the cash economy, however, their social relations come to resemble those of *ladinos.* Specifically, she suggests that as women's economic contribution is devalued, sharp discrepancies arise in gender-based income. This transforms working women into dependent, economic burdens who are less indispensable to their income-producing husbands. In short, families that are integrated into a capitalist market economy through access to individual incomes will place less importance on the husband/father role, and as such, discourage male emotional support or economic contributions.

2. Fran Rothstein has argued that among the poor, women are not alone in their economic circumstances; men are similarly restricted and constrained. Among the middle class, however, women are restrained and men are not (personal commun.). I would add that while this may be true among Latin American peasants, many middle class women in San Pedro seem to relish the personal and economic power they obtain by exploiting the diversity of economic opportunities available to them.

3. It is a curious note on development that in Lois Paul's work from the 1950s, women from San Pedro La Laguna seen alone at night were thought to be witches, while today in San Pedro Sacatepéquez women out late are assumed to be at best loose women, if not prostitutes (Paul 1974).

4. In gathering data I invariably ran all over town for interviews and chats with different women, thus obtaining the title of *paseadora* or "runaround" among the women of

my family who were both confused and bemused by my imperviousness to the restrictions accorded most women.

5. Local lawyers point out that Guatemalan law allows abandoned women who are legally married to put a stop on their husbands' salaries or property. Unfortunately, the cash awards are usually minimal (on the average Q3 per child each month), and the amount actually forthcoming far less than what is ordered by the court.

6. These figures are probably lower than the actual percentage of illegitimate children since women without husbands sometimes do not register their babies' births.

7. It has been difficult for me to accurately measure the amount of extramarital activity in San Pedro. Although I have hundreds of friends, acquaintances, and informants and have access to almost every house in the town, reliable evidence on the topic is problematic. Even my most trusted informants have kept this sort of personal or familial information secret for years, and I expect others do the same. Thus, I can only support my suppositions with the frequent reports I received about "other people." In his experience in San Pedro, John Hawkins reports that information on so-called "kept women" was often brought to his attention. He did not pursue it vigorously either, probably for the same reason I offer: it is an elusive variable that in this situation is almost impossible to quantify. Nonetheless, Hawkins estimated that between a third and a half of the town's wealthy men maintained subsidiary households. As for more casual unions, he could not even hazard a guess (1984:252).

8. This one statistic should not be overemphasized in isolation. It is but one bit of data from a long survey on fertility and socioeconomic status, and is actually being utilized here out of context. What this means is that there are many unanswered questions associated with the issue of head of household. For example, without more in depth interviewing, we do not know for sure that the wife of this household is the primary wife. We have no evidence on the husband's permanence in this residence. Nor do we know anything about the stability of their relationship. In short, this information on head of household is being used because it is an important indicator of what was already suspected about the longevity and stability of San Pedro households. But more extensive research is needed in this area in the future.

9. For amplification on this point, see Maynard's (1974) comparative analysis of *casitas* among *ladino* and indigenous families in Palin.

7

Women and Social Change

Compared to the endemic impoverishment of the surrounding highlands, San Pedro Sacatepéquez is remarkably affluent, and by any measure, an exciting and dynamic town. The level of commercial activity is so high that *Sampedranos* need neither migrate to coastal plantations nor seek urban employment in order to survive. A spirit of entrepreneurship and hard work are characteristic of local residents from low-level plaza traders to well capitalized *civilizadas*. As expected under conditions of commercial growth, a thriving urban middle class has emerged, and to some extent that status is spreading to rural people through education and economic gain. The influence of the *civilizadas* has been especially strong because, as Smith points out (1977), San Pedro has been uncommonly favored by educated elites who elect to remain in their home town to make their fortunes. Their preference for western clothes and consumer goods, along with the increased media access that *civilizadas* promote and support, symbolizes the transition away from traditional identification and behavior and toward a more cosmopolitan worldview.

However, at the same time that San Pedro's relative affluence, non-stop commercialism, and emphatic modernization are impressive achievements, the town's status as a highland oasis is uncertain. Indeed, although the rise of a sizeable indigenous middle class in only thirty-five years suggests economic progress, most people are poor and are obligated to labor long hours for very little money. The persistently high levels of malnutrition and a decline in quality of diets since the 1970s are evidence that the appearance of modernity does not inevitably lead to a better quality of life for everyone. In part, the town's growth has been limited by Guatemala's dependent status in the global economy, and since the early 1980s, by a depressed market for export crops that has had negative consequences for the entire country. Emphasis on military counterinsurgency has drained the national coffers, deflated the value of the *quetzal* internationally, and caused a serious inflationary crisis. The local repercussions of this situation have been to stall the growth of the *Sampedrano* middle class who, like the rural poor, currently find their previously soaring commercial options truncated. This rollercoaster situation, typical of many Third World economies, is likely temporary, and as it has done before, the town will probably rebound onto the economic track that was propelling it toward commercial prosperity.

While most people are holding on until the economy regains its momentum, traditional weavers, whose industry had already been in slow decline, find that their marketshare has evaporated practically overnight. New jobs and household production are taking the place of weaving, and although they alter women's relation to production, they evidence the vibrancy of the town's economy to fill in any gaps that occur with new economic alternatives.

What this study has shown is that a rising standard of living, though an obvious measure of socioeconomic development, does not necessarily disperse the benefits of development equally by sex or by class. Among women, access to opportunities provided by development varies considerably, to the extent that there are marked differences from one class to the next. Specifically, while development undermines economic control of female family businesses for a sector of largely rural productive women, it may accrue greater socioeconomic mobility to urban middle class women.

Social responses to economic change vary as well. Poor women continue to rely upon men for economic security because men amplify the family's income potential, while affluent females have responded to the question of dependence in several ways. Some women, accustomed to status derived from hard work, marry and continue to be active in the family business. Others become dependents of husbands who have adopted the *ladino* pattern of expressing their wealth through the non-working status of their wives. A third, and newer alternative is for unmarried *civilizada* women to reject inappropriate lovers, turning instead to utilizing their own resources to support themselves and their children. In short, although there are clear trends, there is no uniform response to development among all women in San Pedro. Class and sex play important roles in explaining how women have fared in the developing town.

In spite of uneven development, one thing that is clear is that through the introduction of modern consumer goods and manufacturing processes which change economic and social strategies, development has altered the traditional role women play in production and the control they have had over the labor of their daughters. In order to understand how development interfaces with women's status and their power in the home, the important variables are 1) the undermining of the market for home-made items with industrial products and modern goods, 2) the inability of women to replace obsolete artisan production with new work without loss of control over their businesses, and 3) the decrease in number of daughters wishing to maintain traditional cottage industry even where sales are stable.

Several development trends intersect at the female family business, specifically, as traditional female businesses are being devalued, the same complex factors responsible for their demise are also causing the dispersal of family labor. While a short time ago, a girl had been socialized to become a traditional woman at the loom, now the town pushes her toward school and modern employment. Whether or not her mother and grandmother had ever worked in her new chosen profession does not matter. What is important is that she identifies with a modern image of the Guatemalan woman, who through hard work and the right choices will have a better life than her parents did.

Like everyone else in town, independent women producers have been caught up in San Pedro's push toward modernization. What differentiates female strategies from male strategies in this bullish climate is that women's efforts to maximize their business opportunities have a specific ceiling. Two main factors limit them. Because they are undercapitalized, women must rely upon the labor of their daughters and daughters-in-law in order to run their businesses. Moreover, female producers work in the internal market and have little or no access to the external market where men are investing in transport and large-scale trade. One consequence of these structural limitations to the expansion of female capital investments is that women's efforts to improve their status are redirected to education for their children, especially their daughters. Women believe that to modernize is to progress, and mothers encourage their daughters in that direction. Educated children are a status symbol and a source of future cash remittances that women look forward to with great anticipation. Ironically, this emphasis on educating daughters ushers girls away from old-fashioned mother-centered production, thus bringing to a quicker end the traditional female family business. As girls are schooled, many lose interest in their mothers' entrepreneurial styles, turning instead toward more solitary forms of employment.

Since the returns from traditional cottage industry are consistently low and because with development household producers (especially weavers) are losing whatever economic ground they had previously, opting for more modern work is in some ways a sensible choice. In the long run, schooling certainly increases a woman's potential. Yet at the same time that new avenues are opening for women, they are persistently problematic. First, rather than developing and controlling autonomous money-making cottage industries involving family labor, many women are instead becoming dependent laborers working at piecework rates for powerful male contractors. Secondly, when lack of family labor or competition over an increasingly smaller marketshare forces women out of their old family business, many move into market trade which is rapidly becoming saturated and unprofitable. Last, a teaching position, the job of choice for female high school graduates, is an elusive goal. Every year, several dozen women are certified as teachers, one of the most prestigious statuses a *Sampedrana* can achieve. However, by all accounts there are too many teachers. Most female high school graduates wait for years before the proper combination of pull, bribes, and luck results in a job. Even then, the position is usually at a school in a remote area of the highlands or on the coast some distance away. Many women eventually turn down jobs that require them to relocate away from their families. In contrast, male teachers can accept these jobs, even if it means leaving wives and children alone in San Pedro during the week. With relatively less mobility, female teachers stay home, filling the ranks of contract laborers and traders.

The expansion of a female proletarian labor force in San Pedro, while certainly affording incomes to more women than ever before, seems to be an aspect of development that is transitional and as such, temporary. Like the textile mills of the Industrial Revolution in the United States and England, women have played an important role in the beginning stages of the factories, but if the industrial model is consistent, they will probably be replaced by sophisticated machinery or unskilled and uneducated male laborers. In fact, this trend has already begun in San Pedro. Thus, piecework, which has both positive and negative impacts on women's work, may eventually disappear entirely, leaving women in a more vulnerable economic position.

Female traders appear to be holding onto a large portion of the internal market, but prospects are poor for expansion into the more lucrative external market which is controlled by men. Within the trading arena, women have quickly filled in niches which come with expansion and capitalization of plaza trade, so that, for example, women with small stalls have credit relations with suppliers allowing for a certain flexibility. In spite of obvious commercial advantages of stall *mercado* exchange compared to the penny capitalism of plaza trade, the possibilities are extremely limited for capital investment on a larger scale.

Among the stores and warehouses of the town, women play important managerial roles, but not all are owners. Often they are excluded from control of these profitable retail-wholesale enterprises which are owned by their husbands or male relatives. While female shopkeepers may have a higher level of consumption than either stall owners or *canasta* traders, they have the least control over production of the three. Stall owners and plaza traders have more physical mobility and maintain their businesses as autonomous female enterprises. Control of their profits is directly connected with business success and thus remains inviolable to male interference. Dependent shopkeepers rarely take part in fiscal management decisions, being little more than clerks. Like the town's middle class women in general, their household budgets have increasingly fallen under the control of their husbands, who dole out allowances in households where women once held the purse strings.

In terms of male-female interaction, this study reveals a strong economic bias for marriage emanating from persistent difficulties in maintaining a stable and satisfactory level of subsistence. Men and women both rely upon the productivity of a spouse in order to fulfill household budgetary demands. Romance and courtship are preludes to the reality of coping with the problems of supporting a family, but this pre-nuptial wooing simply sets the stage for expectations of life-long conflict. Male-initiated sexual intercourse is a common precursor to marriage, and the repercussions of sexual contact usually mean pregnancy, separation of the woman from her natal home, and the institutionalized male control of the new bride. In general, women tend to endure the sex act as a duty and in order to have children, thus ensuring themselves future material aid and emotional stability. Some men, meanwhile, set up polygynous relationships which essentially replicate husband-wife services. These "parallel marriages" reinforce male callousness toward women because they make men into valuable, scarce resources who may live where they please, giving money and emotional support to one family at the expense of the other.

Diminishing female control in the productive arena correlates with increased dependence on men as the primary breadwinner. One clear indication of this trend is the growing emphasis on female seclusion, particularly among upwardly mobile families. Another notable change which might harken a diminishing female status is the availability of consumer goods and services which means men can dispense with wives for some important services and instead purchase restaurant food, factory clothes, and other domestic goods and services. Little by little, women are becoming important not so much for their valuable productive efforts which in the past had effected a kind of economic complementarity, but as symbols of affluence whose consumption activities and productive seclusion visibly express the conspicuous and independent success of their husbands.

One of the study's arguments was that the stereotype of the submissive, pure, long-suffering Latin American woman was in part a cultural strategy by women to have access to the productive and reproductive services of men. Men seduce vulnerable teenagers or single mothers who permit sexual access and thereby legitimize their status as mothers, establish male financial support, and assure the labor and love of children. At the systemic level of analysis, this behavior is partially conscious and partially unconscious on the part of women. *Marianismo,* however, is not a characteristic of all Latin American women; it is a result of specific economic and cultural conditions. Other researchers have examined the relation between female subordination and material conditions, and found that as conditions vary, women utilize different social strategies in order to survive.

In their comparison of Caleñas from Cali, Colombia, and Latinas from San Francisco, California, Browner and Lewin (1982) note that female passivity works in some situations to obtain economic and social rewards, but that elsewhere women have to be assertive and self-centered. Both groups view marriage as a lottery that women have little chance of winning due to the unreliability of men. Nonetheless, Caleñas and Latinas marry because they know they may get something positive out of the arrangement. They differ in just what those rewards might be. Latinas in San Francisco minimize the conjugal relationship, emphasizing the motherhood that results instead. Since children are primarily valuable to Latinas for the care they provide when the mother ages, mothers adopt a stance of sacrificial martyrdom to ensure future loyalty of their offspring. Although the authors do not stress the more immediate importance of welfare payments that accompany the birth of a child, this seems an additional motive for an abandoned woman to carefully cultivate the mother-child bond.

Meanwhile, in Cali, Colombia, women cannot rely upon financial support from their children as workers, as a basis for welfare payments, or in the form of remittances when they are grown. Moreover, children undermine Caleñas' labor force participation. As such they downplay the cultivation of loyal sons and daughters, and do not devote themselves to motherhood as do the Latinas. But since employment options are limited, Caleñas feel they cannot manage on their own, and must rely upon the contributions of a husband. The authors point out that ". . . without the possibility of public support, Caneñas find themselves in competition with one another for economic support from men . . ." (71). In a city with more females than males, conflict over potential husbands is exacerbated by emphatic *machismo* which discourages marital permanency. In order to find a man to marry them and then hold onto him, Caleñas have adopted an aggressively romantic and sexual demeanor that contrasts with the passive maternal Latinas.

Like many *Sampedranas,* the women in these two settings have limited economic potential, and must rely upon support systems external to their own resources. Women in each group manipulate their linkages to men, some more effectively than others.

In another case of Latin American women acting to protect their own interests, LeVine et al. show that educated women in Los Robles, a Cuernavaca neighborhood, are demanding more equality in marriage through the use of birth control. Because they understand the cost to their own mothers who had "as many children as God sent" (1986 : 200), these women attempt to control their futures by taking advantage of modern contraceptives. While they value the maternal role, the young women of Los Robles understand the rising costs of having children, and want more from the marital relationship than motherhood. They want their husbands to respect and trust them, and to forego extramarital affairs and other forms of abuse. One way of protecting their own interests is to delay motherhood while they go to school. Those who are educated seem to be more successful in controlling their husbands' irresponsible behavior and hold more decision-making power within the marriage. Moreover, young women believe that education will provide them an escape hatch should their marriage turn sour. LeVine et al. support these strategies because they seem to be leading to a higher status for women in the family. Although the authors agree with Rothstein (1985) that education in Mexico does not necessarily result in employment, they argue for the importance of schooling based upon a positive correlation between women's educational goals, increased marital communication, and female decision making in the family.

These studies of female domestic and extradomestic strategies show that women's behaviors are to some extent determined by their socioeconomic environment. Furthermore, in the process of explaining female status, they suggest that researchers need to go beyond sexism to analysis of the circumstances that produce stereotypes such as *marianismo.*

One of the purposes of this study has been to contribute new research to the relative dearth of material on Guatemalan women. By chronicling the contingencies and possibilities *Sampedranas* face in confronting a changing world, I hoped to combine an intimate ethnographic approach with an analysis of the impact of development on the status of women. One common assumption in the development literature has been that socioeconomic growth resulted in improvements in women's lives. In the last twenty years, scholars have begun to understand that without documenting development's effect on women in particular, analysis of the general influence of change is partly skewed. In works that address this problem, writers have concluded that modernization, through industrialization or the spread of agribusiness, leads to a deterioration in female economic and social status and an increase in sexual stratification (e.g., Bossen 1975, Chaney and Schminck 1976, Chinchilla 1977). This study of women in a highland Guatemalan town departs from this analysis by concluding that within a context of uneven development, some women benefit from socioeconomic change and others do not. Moreover, development can have both positive and negative effects on individual women who may be losing economic control, but gaining a better standard of living.

Understanding how women fare under changing social and economic conditions is no simple matter, especially when dealing with a large and complex community like San Pedro Sacatepéquez. Although they are concentrated in labor intensive work with low-level profitability and limited potential, *Sampedranas* are not a homogeneous group. There is a sizeable and influential middle class, and a growing sector of educated women among the rural poor. The town is surrounded by rural hamlets quite distinct from the town and each other. And there is a large group of household producers, traders, entrepreneurs, and workers who are affected by socioeconomic change in a variety of ways.

Overall, in accordance with the town's reputation for business acumen and flexibility, women have shown their ability to adapt to new conditions of production. They have readjusted their short term productive goals and abandoned outmoded and impractical means for making a living. In the long run, however, malleability alone will not sustain them when the potentials that development offers benefit so few. It is hoped that in the future women from all socioeconomic sectors will be incorporated into the development process on a more equal footing with men. If they can expand their economic alternatives by gaining access to productive enterprises, especially the profitable external markets and transport systems that sustain the town's growth, *Sampedranas* would enhance both their own economic potential and that of the town.

References

Adams, Richard N. 1960. An Inquiry into the Nature of the Family. In *Essays in the Science of Culture: In Honor of Leslie A. While.* Gertrude Dole and R. Carneiro, eds., pp. 30–49. New York: Crowell.

Americas Watch Committee. 1982. *Human Rights in Guatemala: No Neutral Allowed.* New York.

———. 1984. *Guatemala: A Nation of Prisoners.* New York.

———. 1986. *Human Rights in Guatemala During President Cerezo's First Year.* New York.

Anderson, Marilyn. 1978. *Guatemalan Textiles Today.* New York: Watson-Guptill Publications.

Annis, Sheldon. 1988. Story from a Peaceful Town: San Antonio Aguas Calientes. In *Harvest of Violence: The Maya Indians and the Guatemalan Crisis.* Robert M. Carmack, ed., pp. 155–173. Norman: University of Oklahoma Press.

———. 1987. *God and Production in a Guatemalan Town.* Austin: University of Texas Press.

Beals, Ralph L. 1946. *Cherán: A Sierra Tarascan Village.* Smithsonian Institution. Institute of Social Anthropology, Publication No. 2, Washington, D.C.

Benería, Lourdes, ed. 1982. *Women and Development: The Sexual Division of Labor in Rural Societies.* New York: Praeger.

Bigsten, Arne, and Rick Wicks. 1996. Used-Clothes Exports to the Third World: Economic Considerations. *Development Policy Review* 14: 379–390.

Boserup, Ester. 1970. *Woman's Role in Economic Development.* New York: St. Martin's Press.

Bossen, Laurel H. 1984. *The Redivision of Labor: Women and Economic Choice in Four Guatemalan Communities.* Albany: State University of New York.

———. 1983. Sexual Stratification in Mesoamerica. In *Heritage of Conquest: Thirty Years Later.* Carl Kendall, John Hawkins, and Laurel Bossen, eds., pp. 35–71. Albuquerque: University of New Mexico Press.

————. 1975. Women in Modernizing Societies. *American Ethnologist* 2 : 587–601.

Bourque, Susan C., and Kay Barbara Warren. 1981. *Women of the Andes: Patriarchy and Social Change in Two Peruvian Towns.* Ann Arbor: University of Michigan Press.

Brintnall, Douglas E. 1983. The Guatemalan Indian Civil Rights Movement. *Cultural Survival* 7 : 14–16.

————. 1979. *Revolt against the Dead: The Modernization of a Mayan Community in the Highlands of Guatemala.* New York: Gordon and Breach.

Brown, Susan E. 1975. Love Unites Them and Hunger Separates Them: Poor Women in the Dominican Republic. In *Towards an Anthropology of Women.* Rayna Reiter, ed., pp. 322–332. New York: Monthly Review Press.

Browner, Carole, and Ellen Lewin. 1982. Female Altruism Reconsidered: The Virgin Mary as Economic Woman. *American Ethnologist* 9 : 61–75.

Bruce, Judith. 1989. Homes Divided. *World Development* 17(7) : 979–991.

Bujra, Janet. 1975. Women and Fieldwork. In *Women, Cross Culturally: Change and Challenge.* R. Rohrlich-Leavitt, ed., pp. 551–557. The Hague: Mouton.

Bunch, Roland, and Roger Bunch. 1977. *The Highland Maya: Patterns of Life and Clothing in Indian Guatemala.* Visalia, California: Indigenous Pubs.

Bunzel, Ruth L. 1952. *Chichicastenango, A Guatemalan Village.* Locust Valley, New York: JJ Augustin Publisher.

Burgos-Debray, Elisabeth, ed. 1984. *I, Rigoberta Menchú: An Indian Woman in Guatemala.* London: Verso Editions.

Buvinic, Mayra. 1976. *Women and World Development: An Annotated Bibliography.* Washington, D.C.: Overseas Development Council.

Carlsen, Robert S. 1997. *The War for the Heart and Soul of a Highland Maya Town.* Austin: University of Texas Press.

————. 1993. Discontinuous Warps: Textile Production and Ethnicity in Contemporary Highland Guatemala. In *Crafts in the World Market: The Impact of Global Exchange on Middle American Artisans.* June Nash, ed., pp. 199–222. Albany: SUNY Albany Press.

Carlsen, Robert S., and David A. Wenger. 1996. The Dyes Used in Guatemalan Textiles: A Diachronic Approach. In *Textile Traditions of Mesoamerica and the Andes: An Anthology.* M. Schevill, J. Berlo, and N. Dwyer, eds., pp. 359–378. Austin: University of Texas Press.

Carmack, Robert M., ed. 1988. *Harvest of Violence: The Maya Indians and the Guatemalan Crisis.* Norman: University of Oklahoma Press.

Centro de Salud, San Pedro Sacatepéquez, San Marcos. 1986. *Diagnostico de Salud.* Mimeo.

Chaney, Elsa M., and Marianne Schminck. 1976. Women and Modernation: Access to Tools. In *Sex and Class in Latin America.* June Nash and Helen Icken Safa, eds., pp. 160–182. New York: Praeger.

Charlton, Sue Ellen M. 1984. *Women in Third World Development.* Boulder, Colorado: Westview Press.

Chiñas, Beverly L. 1976. Zapotec Viajeras. In *Markets in Oaxaca.* Scott Cook and Martin Diskin, eds., pp. 169–189. Austin: University of Texas Press.

Chinchilla, Norma S. 1977. Industrialization, Monopoly Capitalism, and Women's Work in Guatemala. *Signs* 3 : 38–56.

Colby, Benjamin N., and Pierre Van Den Berghe. 1969. *Ixil County: A Plural Society in Highland Guatemala*. Berkeley: University of California Press.

Collier, Jane. 1986. From Mary to Modern Woman: The Material Basis of Marianismo and its Transformation in a Spanish Village. *American Ethnologist* 13:100–107.

Conte, Christine. 1984. *Maya Culture and Costume*. Colorado Springs: The Taylor Museum.

Davis, Shelton. 1988. Introduction: Sowing the Seeds of Violence. In *Harvest of Violence: The Maya Indians and the Guatemalan Crisis*. Robert M. Carmack, ed., pp. 3–36. Norman: University of Oklahoma Press.

———. 1983. State Violence and Agrarian Crisis in Guatemala: The Roots of the Indian-Peasant Rebellion. In *Trouble in Our Backyard: Central America and the United States in the Eighties*. Martin Diskin, ed., pp. 155–171. New York: Pantheon Books.

de León Carpio, Ramiro. 1997. Comentario. *La Prensa Libre* (Guatemala City, Guatemala), July 10.

Davis, Shelton, and Julie Hodson. 1982. *Witness to Political Violence in Guatemala: The Suppression of a Rural Development Movement*. Boston: Oxfam America.

Dwyer, Daisy, and Judith Bruce. 1988. *A Home Divided: Women and Income in the Third World*. Stanford; Stanford University Press.

Earle, Duncan. 1988. Mayas Aiding Mayas: Guatemalan Refugees in Chiapas. In *Harvest of Violence: The Maya Indians and the Guatemalan Crisis*. Robert M. Carmack, ed., pp. 256–273. Norman: University of Oklahoma Press.

Ehlers, Tracy Bachrach. 1998. Women and the False Promise of Microenterprise. *Gender & Society* 12(4):424–440.

———. 1993. Belts, Beads and Business: An Alternative Model for Guatemalan Artisan Development. In *Crafts in the World Market: The Impact of Global Exchange on Middle American Artisans*. June Nash, ed., pp. 181–196. Albany: SUNY Albany Press.

———. 1991. Debunking Marianismo: Economic Vulnerability and Survival Strategies among Guatemalan Wives. *Ethnology* 30(1):1–16.

———. 1987. A Guatemalan Town Ten Years Later. *Cultural Survival* 11:25–29.

———. 1982. The Decline of Female Family Business: A Guatemalan Case Study. *Women and Politics* 2:7–21.

———. 1980. *La Sampedrana: Women and Development in a Guatemalan Town*. Ph.D. dissertation, University of Colorado.

Elu de Lenero, Maria del Carmen. 1969. *Hacia Donde Va La Mujer Mexicana? Proyecciones a partir de los Datos de Una Encuesta Nacional*. Mexico, D.F.: Inst. Mexicano de Estudios Sociales.

Gillen, John P. 1951. *The Culture of Security in San Carlos: A Study of a Guatemalan Community of Indians and Ladinos*. New Orleans: Tulane University of Louisiana.

Gissi Bustos, Jorge. 1976. Mythology about Women, with Special Reference to Chile. In *Sex and Class in Latin America,* June Nash and Helen Icken Safa, eds., pp. 30–45. New York: Praeger.

Goldin, Liliana. 1986. *Organizing the World through the Market: A Symbolic Analysis of Markets and Exchange in the Western Highlands of Guatemala*. Ph.D. dissertation, SUNY Albany.

Haggblade, Steven. 1990. The Flip Side of Fashion: Used Clothing Exports to the Third World. *Journal of Development Studies* 26(3): 505−521.

Harris, Marvin. 1971. *Culture, Man and Nature.* New York: Thomas Y. Crowell and Company.

Hawkins, John. 1984. *Inverse Images: The Meaning of Culture, Ethnicity and Family in Post-colonial Guatemala.* Albuquerque: University of New Mexico Press.

Hill, Robert M., and John Monaghan. 1987. *Continuities in Highland Maya Social Organization: Ethnohistory in Sacapulas, Guatemala.* Philadelphia: University of Pennsylvania Press.

Hinshaw, Robert. 1975. *Panajachel: A Guatemalan Town in Thirty-year Perspective.* Pittsburgh: University of Pittsburgh Press.

Inter-American Commission on Human Rights. 1985. *Report on the Situation of Human Rights in the Republic of Guatemala.* Washington, D.C.

———. 1983. *Report on the Situation of Human Rights in the Republic of Guatemala.* Washington, D.C.

———. 1981. *Report on the Situation of Human Rights in the Republic of Guatemala.* Washington, D.C.

Irías de Rivera, M. A., and I. V. Alfaro de Carpio. 1977. Guatemalan Working Women in the Labor Movement. *Latin American Perspectives* 4: 194−202.

Jiggins, Janice. 1989. How Poor Women Earn Income in Sub-Saharan Africa and What Works against Them. *World Development* 17(7): 953−963.

Jonas, Susanne, and David Tobis, eds. 1974. *Guatemala.* Berkeley: North American Congress on Latin America.

Kinzer, Nora Scott. 1973. Priests, Machos and Babies: Or, Latin American Women and the Manichean Heresy. *Journal of Marriage and the Family* 35: 300−312.

Krueger, Chris, and Kjell Enge. 1985. *Security and Development Conditions in the Guatemalan Highlands.* Washington D.C.: Washington Office on Latin America.

LaFarge, Oliver. 1947. *Santa Eulalia: The Religion of a Cuchumatan Indian Town.* New York: University of Chicago Press.

LeVine, Sarah Ethel, Clara Sunderland Correa, and F. Medardo Tapia Oribe. 1986. The Marital Mortality of Mexican Women: An Urban Study. *Journal of Anthropological Research* 42: 183−202.

Lewis, Oscar. 1964. *Pedro Martínez: A Mexican Peasant and His Family.* New York: Vintage Books.

———. 1963. *Life in a Mexican Village: Tepoztlán Restudied.* Urbana: University of Illinois.

———. 1959. Family Dynamics in a Mexican Village. *Journal of Marriage and the Family* 21: 218−226.

Manz, Beatriz. 1988. *Refugees of a Hidden War: The Aftermath of Counterinsurgency in Guatemala.* Albany: State University of New York Press.

Margolies, Barbara Luise. 1975. *Princes of the Earth: Subcultural Diversity in a Mexican Municipality.* American Anthropological Association. Special Publication of the AAA, No. 2.

Martin, M. Kay, and Voorhies, Barbara. 1975. *Female of the Species.* New York: Columbia University Press.

Maynard, Eileen Anne. 1974. Guatemalan Women: Life under Two Types of Patriarchy. In *Many Sisters.* Carolyn Matthiasson, ed., pp. 77−98. New York: Free Press.

————. 1963. *The Women of Palin: A Comparative Study of Indian and Ladina Women in a Guatemalan Village.* Ph.D. dissertation, Cornell University.

McBryde, F. W. 1947. *Cultural and Historical Geography of Southwest Guatemala.* Institute of Social Anthropology Publication No. 4. Washington, D.C.: Smithsonian Institution Press.

————. 1933. *Solólá: A Guatemalan Town and Cakchiquel Market Center.* Middle American Research Institute. New Orleans: Tulane University.

McClintock, Michael. 1985. *The American Connection, Volume Two: State Terror and Popular Resistance in Guatemala.* London: Zed Books.

McDowell, Paul. 1976. Guatemalan Stratification and Peasant Marketing Arrangements: A Different View. *Man* 2 : 273–281.

Michaelson, Evalyn Jacobsen, and Walter Golschmidt. 1971. Female Roles and Male Dominance Among Peasants. *Southwestern Journal of Anthropology* 27 : 330–352.

Mintz, Sidney. 1971. Men, Women, and Trade. *Comparative Studies in Society and History* 13 : 247–269.

Nash, June. 1976. A Critique of Social Science Roles in Latin America. In *Sex and Class in Latin America.* June Nash and Helen Safa, eds., pp. 1–24. New York: Praeger.

Nash, June, and Maria Patricia Fernández-Kelly, eds. 1983. *Women, Men and the International Division of Labor.* Albany: SUNY Press.

Nash, June, and Helen Icken Safa, eds. 1976. *Sex and Class in Latin America.* New York: Praeger.

Nash, Manning. 1958. *Machine Age Maya.* Chicago: University of Chicago Press.

Nutini, Hugo G. 1967. A Synoptic Comparison of Mesoamerican Marriage and Family Structure. *Southwestern Journal of Anthropology* 23 : 383–404.

O'Neale, Lila M. 1945. *Textiles of Highland Guatemala.* Washington, D.C.: Carnegie Institute of Washington.

Oakes, Maud. 1951. *The Two Crosses of Todos Santos.* New York: Pantheon Books.

Orozco Fuentes, Otto Rubén. 1985. *Estadistica Sobre Atencion Prestada en el Departamento de Gineco-Obstetricia del Hospital de San Marcos durante los Meses de Julio a Diciembre de 1984.* Mimeo.

Osborne, Lilly deJongh. 1935. *Guatemala Textiles.* New Orleans: Tulane University.

————. 1965. *Indian Crafts of Guatemala and El Salvador.* Norman, Oklahoma: University of Oklahoma Press.

Ottenberg, Phoebe. 1959. The Changing Economic Position of Women among the Afikpo Ibo. In *Continuity and Change in African Cultures.* W. Bascom and M. Herskovits, eds., pp. 205–223. Chicago: University of Chicago Press.

Oxfam America. 1984. *Project Report on Guatemala.* Boston.

Painter, James. 1987. *Guatemala: False Hope, False Freedom.* London: Catholic Institute for International Relations.

Paul, Benjamin. 1986. *The Operation of a Death Squad in a Lake Atitlán Community.* Unpublished manuscript.

Paul, Benjamin, and Lois Paul. 1975. The Maya Midwife as Sacred Specialist: A Guatemalan Case. *American Ethnologist* 2 : 707–726.

————, 1963. Changing Marriage Patterns in a Highland Guatemala Community. *Southwestern Journal of Anthropology* 19 : 131–148.

Paul, Lois. 1974. The Mastery of Work and the Mystery of Sex in a Guatemala Village.

In *Women, Culture and Society*. Michele Z. Rosaldo and Louise Lamphere, eds., pp. 281–299. Stanford: Stanford University Press.

Paz, Octavio. 1961. *The Labyrinth of Solitude: Life and Thought in Mexico*. New York: Grove Press.

Pescatello, Ann. 1973. *Female and Male in Latin America: Essays*. Pittsburgh: University of Pittsburgh Press.

Petersen, Carmen L. 1976. *The Maya of Guatemala: Their Life and Dress*. Guatemala City: Ixchel Museum.

Reina, Reuben E. 1966. *The Law of the Saints*. New York: The Bobbs-Merrill Company Inc.

Rivera B., Sandra Haydee, and Carlos Yoc Pérez. 1987. *Ejercicio Profesional Supervisado: San Pedro Sacatepéquez, San Marcos*. Facultad de Arquitectura, Universidad Nacional de San Carlos, Guatemala, Guatemala.

Rothstein, Frances. 1986. The New Proletarians: Third World Reality and First World Categories. *Comparative Studies of Society and History* 28 : 217–238.

———. 1985. Capitalist Industrialization and the Increasing Cost of Children. In *Women and Change in Latin America*, June Nash and Helen Icken Safa, eds., pp. 37–52. South Hadley, Massachusetts: Bergin and Garvey, Pubs.

———. 1983. Women and Men in the Family Economy: An Analysis of the Relations Between the Sexes in Three Peasant Communities. *Anthropological Quarterly* 5 : 10–23.

Rowe, Ann Pollard. 1981. *A Century of Change in Guatemalan Textiles*. New York: The Center for International Relations.

Safa, Helen. 1977. The Changing Class Composition of the Female Labor Force in Latin America. *Latin American Perspectives* 4 : 26–136.

———. 1976. Class Consciousness Among Working Class Women in Latin America: A Case Study in Puerto Rico. In *Sex and Class in Latin America*. June Nash and Helen Safa, eds., pp. 69–85. New York: Praeger.

Saffioti, Heleith. 1977. Women, Mode of Production, and Social Formations. *Latin American Perspectives* 4 : 27–37.

Schoultz, Lars. 1983. Guatemala: Social Change and Personal Conflict. In *Trouble in Our Backyard: Central America and the United States in the Eighties*. Martin Diskin, ed., pp. 173–202. New York: Pantheon Books.

Sennett, Richard. 1970. *Families Against the City: Middle Class Homes of Industrial Chicago, 1872–1890*. Cambridge, Mass.: Harvard University Press.

Sharff, Jagna Wojcicka. 1981. Free Enterprise and the Ghetto Family. *Psychology Today* 15 : 40–48.

Slade, Doren. 1975. Marital Status and Sexual Identity: The Position of Women in a Mexican Peasant Society. In *Women Cross-Culturally*. Ruby Rohrlich-Leavitt, ed., 129–148. The Hague: Mouton.

Smith, Carol A. 1988. Destruction of the Material Bases for Indian Culture: Economic Changes in Totonicapán. In *Harvest of Violence: The Maya Indians and the Guatemalan Crisis*. Robert M. Carmack, ed., pp. 206–231. Norman: University of Oklahoma Press.

———. 1984. *Indian Class and Class Consciousness in Prerevolutionary Guatemala*. Working Paper 162. Latin American Program. Washington, D.C.: Wilson Center.

———. 1983. Does a Commodity Economy Enrich the Few While Ruining the Masses? Differentiation among Petty Commodity Producers in Guatemala. *Journal of Peasant Studies* 11:60–95.

———. 1978. Beyond Dependency Theory: National and Regional Patterns of Underdevelopment. *American Ethnologist* 5:574–617.

———. 1977a. How Marketing Systems Affect Economic Opportunity in Agrarian Societies. In *Peasant Livelihood: Studies in Economic Anthropological and Cultural Ecology.* Rhoda Halperin and James Dow, eds., pp. 117–146. New York: St. Martin's Press.

———. 1972. *The Domestic Marketing System in Western Guatemala.* Ph.D. dissertation, Stanford University.

Smith, Waldemar R. 1977. *The Fiesta System and Economic Change.* New York: Columbia University Press.

———. 1975. Beyond the Plural Society: Economics and Ethnicity in Middle American Towns. *Ethnology* 14:225–244.

Smith, Waldemar R., and Kathleen Moody Wilson. n.d. *Women and Fertility in a Developing Guatemala Community.* Boulder, Colorado: Department of Anthropology, University of Colorado.

Stack, Carol. 1974. Sex Roles and Survival Strategies in an Urban Black Community. In *Women, Culture and Society.* Michele Z. Rosaldo and Louise Lamphere, eds., pp. 113–128. Stanford: Stanford University Press.

Staudt, Kathleen, and Jane Jaquette. 1983. *Women in Developing Countries: A Policy Focus.* New York: Haworth Press.

Stevens, Evelyn P. 1973a. Machismo and Marianismo. *Society* 10:57–63.

———. 1973b. Marianismo: The Other Face of Machismo in Latin America. In *Female and Male in Latin America.* Ann Pescatello, ed., pp. 89–102. Pittsburgh: University of Pittsburgh Press.

———. 1965. Mexican Machismo: Politics and Value Orientation. *Western Political Quarterly* 18:848–857.

Stoll, David. 1988. Evangelicals, Guerrillas, and the Army: The Ixil Triangle Under Ríos Montt. In *Harvest of Violence: The Maya Indians and the Guatemalan Crisis.* Robert M. Carmack, ed., pp. 90–116. Norman: University of Oklahoma Press.

———. 1983. Guatemala: The New Jerusalem of the Americas. *Cultural Survival* 7:28–31.

Stycos, J. Mayone. 1955. *Family and Fertility in Puerto Rico: A Study of the Lower Income Group.* New York: Columbia University Press.

Sudarkasa, Niara. 1973. *Where Women Work: A Study of Yoruba Women in the Marketplace and the Home.* Ann Arbor: University of Michigan Press.

Swetnam, John T. 1973. Oligopolistic Prices in a Free Market—Antigua, Guatemala. *American Anthropologist* 75:1504–1510.

Tax, Sol. 1953. *Penny Capitalism: A Guatemalan Indian Economy.* Smithsonian Institution Institute of Social Anthropology Publication No. 16. Washington, D.C.

———. 1937. The *Municipios* of the Midwestern Highlands of Guatemala. *American Anthropologist* 39:432–444.

Tax, Sol, ed. 1952. *Heritage of Conquest: The Ethnology of Middle America.* Glencoe, Ill.: The Free Press.

Torres-Rivas, Edelberto. 1985. *Report on the Conditions of the Central American Refugees and Migrants.* Washington, D.C.: Center for Immigration Policy and Refugee Assistance, Georgetown University.

Tumin, Melvin. 1952. *Caste in a Peasant Society.* Princeton: Princeton University Press.

Wagley, Charles. 1949. *The Social and Religious Life of a Guatemalan Village.* Menosha, Wisconsin: American Anthropological Association.

Warren, Kay. 1978. *The Symbolism of Subordination: Indian Identity in a Guatemalan Town.* Austin: University of Texas Press.

Whetten, Nathan L. 1961. *Guatemala: The Land and the People.* New Haven: Yale University Press.

Wilson, Janet. 1997. Making Donated Rags into Riches. *Los Angeles Times,* July 28, pp. 1, 16.

Wisdom, Charles. 1940. *The Chorti Indians of Guatemala.* Chicago: University of Chicago Press.

Wood, Joséphine, and Lilly deJongh Osborne. 1966. *Indian Costumes of Guatemala.* Akademische Druckund Verlagsanstalt, Graz.

World Bank. 1987. *World Development Report.* Washington, D.C.

Index